D1258467

DISTORTING SCRIPTURE?

The Challenge of Bible Translation & Gender Accuracy

MARK L. STRAUSS

InterVarsity Press
Downers Grove, Illinois

InterVarsity Press
P.O. Box 1400, Downers Grove, IL 60515
World Wide Web: www.ivpress.com
E-mail: mail@ivpress.com

InterVarsity Press® is the book-publishing division of InterVarsity Christian Fellowship/USA®, a student movement active on campus at hundreds of universities, colleges and schools of nursing in the United States of America, and a member movement of the International Fellowship of Evangelical Students. For information about local and regional activities, write Public Relations Dept., InterVarsity Christian Fellowship/USA, 6400 Schroeder Rd., P.O. Box 7895, Madison, WI 53707-7895.

Cover photography: Michael Goss

ISBN 0-8308-1940-1

Printed in the United States of America ♾

Library of Congress Cataloging-in-Publication Data

Strauss, Mark L.
Distorting Scripture?: the challenge of Bible translation and gender accuracy/Mark L. Strauss.
p. cm.
Includes bibliographical references.
ISBN 0-8308-1940-1 (pbk.: alk. paper)
1. Bible—Translating. 2. Nonsexist language—Religious aspects—Christianity. 3. Bible. English—Versions. I. Title.
BS449.S75 1998
220.5'2—DC21 *98-19815*
CIP

---

20 19 18 17 16 15 14 13 12 11 10 9 8 7 6 5 4 3 2 1
14 13 12 11 10 09 08 07 06 05 04 03 02 01 00 99 98

Abbreviations

"Traditional" Bible Versions

ASV	American Standard Version (1901)
KJV	King James Version (1611)
LB	Living Bible (1971)
NASB	New American Standard Bible (1970)
NIV	New International Version (1978)
NKJV	New King James Version (1982)
RSV	Revised Standard Version (1952)
RV	Revised Version (1885)

"Gender-Inclusive" (or "Gender-Accurate") Bible Versions

CEV	Contemporary English Version (1995)
GNB	Good News Bible (revised 1992)
GW	God's Word (1995)
ICB	International Children's Bible (1986)
NAB	New American Bible (revised 1988, 1990)
NCV	New Century Version (1987)
NIrV	New International Reader's Version (1996)
NIVI	New International Version, Inclusive Language Edition (1996)
NJB	New Jerusalem Bible (1985)
NLT	New Living Translation (1996)
NRSV	New Revised Standard Version (1990)
REB	Revised English Bible (1989)
TEV	Today's English Version (same as GNB)

"Feminist" Versions

ILL	An Inclusive Language Lectionary (1983)
NTPI	New Testament and Psalms: An Inclusive Version (1995)
INT	The Inclusive New Testament (1994)

Other Abbreviations

CBMW	Council on Biblical Manhood and Womanhood
CBE	Christians for Biblical Equality
CBT	Committee on Bible Translation (for the NIV)
IBS	International Bible Society (holds copyright for the NIV)
LXX	Septuagint (the Greek Old Testament)
MT	Massoretic Text (the Hebrew Old Testament)
NT	New Testament
OT	Old Testament
v., vv.	verse, verses

A Note on the Hebrew and Greek Used in This Book

For those unfamiliar with Hebrew and Greek, I have transliterated all Hebrew and Greek terms.[1] Since certain of these Hebrew and Greek terms are used very frequently throughout the book, it may be helpful for the reader to become familiar with them.

Hebrew

'ādām	"man," "Adam," "humanity" or "human being"
'îsh	"man," usually referring to males, but sometimes to human beings in general
bēn	"son," "child," "descendant" (also used in many other idioms to indicate a relationship of some kind)
bānîm	the plural of *bēn,* "sons," "children" (also used in many other idioms)
'āb	"father," "forefather," "ancestor"
'ābôt	"fathers," "ancestors," "parents"

Greek

anthrōpos	"man," "human being," "person," "humanity"
anthrōpoi	the plural of *anthrōpos,* "men," "human beings," "people," "persons"
anēr (root, *andr-)*	"man," "husband," sometimes "person"
andres	the plural of *aner*
adelphos	"brother," "fellow believer," "brother or sister"
adelphoi	the plural of *adelphos* (can refer to men and women)
huios	"son," "child," "descendant" (also used in many other idioms to indicate a relationship of some kind)
huioi	the plural of *huios,* "sons," "children" (also used in many other idioms)
patēr	"father," "ancestor," "predecessor"
pateres	the plural of *patēr,* "fathers," "ancestors," "parents"

For Greek students I should also point out that when a term is identified in a translation, it appears in its nominative form, either singular or plural. I do this to avoid confusing non-Greek students with the variety of forms that words can take in their various case forms. When two or more words occur in a phrase, I retain the necessary cases to make the phrase understandable. For example, "the Word of God" would be written *ho logos tou theou. Theou* retains its genitive case. Hebrew words are given in their standard lexical forms.

One
INTRODUCTION

WHEN THE PROPOSAL FOR A NEW BIBLE VERSION FIRST REACHED THE translator's desk, he was excited about the project. The language of the translation to be replaced was archaic, and in some places its rendering of the original Hebrew and Greek texts was inaccurate. For the translator, this would be a chance to bring a more accurate and relevant Bible translation to the Christian public. As he reflected on the project, however, he became increasingly concerned about the negative reaction his work might provoke.

Finally he sat down to write a letter expressing his doubts to his financial sponsor: "My concern is that some readers, whether they are educated or not, will realize that this translation does not agree with what they are accustomed to and will react against me with abusive language, calling me an evil person and a forger for having the audacity to add anything to the ancient text, as though I were trying to make changes or corrections to it."

The Perils and Pitfalls of Bible Translation

While these words could well have come from a modern translator, in fact they are from the early church father Jerome, writing in the fourth century A.D. Jerome had been commissioned by Pope Damasus to provide a revision of the Old Latin translation of the Bible. Jerome's concerns turned out to be justified, and criticism of his work followed him throughout his life.[1] Yet one generation's innovation becomes the next generation's tradition, and the version Jerome produced—the Latin Vulgate—became the standard Bible of the Western church for a thousand years.

Jerome's letter demonstrates that controversies about Bible translations are nothing new. Indeed, it is probably fair to say that every new translation that has appeared in the history of the church has been greeted with some level of suspicion, from mild criticism to violent outrage.

The Bible in English

The history of the translation of the Bible into English is full of such stories of rejection and outrage. It is somewhat ironic, considering Jerome's concerns, that fourteenth-century attempts to translate the Bible into English came at a time when Jerome's own Vulgate was viewed as the "real" Bible, and any translation was considered a dangerous innovation. The first English translation of the entire Bible was completed in 1382 under the direction of Oxford theologian John Wycliffe. Though Wycliffe's influence and position protected him from harm during his lifetime, he was denounced and his translation was condemned. His followers were harassed and imprisoned; some were burned at the stake. As a result of Wycliffe's work, in 1408 a synod of the clergy at Oxford forbade anyone to translate or even read a vernacular version of the Bible without approval from the church. Sir Thomas More later referred to Wycliffe as the "great arch-heretic" who undertook "of a malicious purpose" to translate the Bible into English and "purposely corrupted the holy text."[2]

William Tyndale has the distinction of being the first to produce a printed version of the New Testament in English. His translation, which was also the first English version translated directly from the Greek, is recognized today as a great improvement in accuracy and style over Wycliffe's version. Yet the rules against translation established at the Oxford synod still applied in Tyndale's day, so he was forced to flee

England for the Continent. His work was published in 1526 and copies were smuggled back into England. Tyndale's opponents followed him relentlessly, however, and in 1535 he was kidnapped, imprisoned and, a year later, executed and his body burned.[3] Though viewed as heretical by the official church, Tyndale's idiomatic translation captured the hearts of the people. Its widespread use was a key factor in the growing acceptance of English translations by the reading public, and its language and style had a major impact on all subsequent versions.[4]

The King James Version

Though the work of Tyndale and others brought a growing acceptance of common-language translations, new versions continued to be viewed with suspicion and concern. The King James Version (KJV) itself arose out of controversy over competing versions. The official Bible of the Church of England at the time was the Bishop's Bible (1568), a revision of the Great Bible (1539), which itself drew strongly on Tyndale's translation. The Puritans, however, favored the Geneva Bible (1560), a version that also had its roots in Tyndale's work. Though the Geneva Bible was a superior translation, its pro-Calvinist and anti-Catholic marginal notes offended many readers, including King James I of England. When a nonsectarian revision was proposed, James enthusiastically endorsed the idea.[5] Commissioned in 1604, the translation work was accomplished in seven years by forty-seven of the leading biblical scholars in Britain. It was first published in 1611.

Though the King James Version would prove to be the most significant and enduring English translation of all time, it was not above criticism. The Pilgrims, for example, refused to allow the new version on the *Mayflower*, preferring the Geneva Bible.[6] Hugh Broughton, one of the leading biblical scholars of his day, wrote with reference to the KJV:

> Tell His Majesty that I had rather be rent in pieces with wild horses, than any such translation by my consent should be urged upon poor churches. . . . The new edition crosseth me. I require it to be burnt.[7]

The KJV translators expected such criticisms and in their own preface they praise earlier translations, admit that their own work is far from perfect and defend the need for continual revision and updating. "Truly, good Christian Reader," they write, "we never thought from the beginning that we should need to make a new translation, nor yet to make of a bad one a good one; . . . but to make a good one better."[8] They further note that "no cause therefore why the word translated should be denied to be the word, or forbidden to be current, notwithstanding that some imperfections and blemishes may be noted in the setting forth of it." Though all translations contain "blemishes," even the "meanest translation of the Bible in English set forth by men of our profession . . . containeth the word of God, nay, is the word of God."[9] Considering this humble perspective of the KJV translators—that they were merely one link in the long chain of necessary revisions—it is again ironic that for many readers today any version since the KJV is an illegitimate corruption of the "real" Bible.

Revising the King James Version

The KJV has had a profound influence on our language and culture. Rightly has it been called "the noblest monument of English prose."[10] No translation in history has received so much admiration and loyalty. It is a testimony to the KJV's enduring significance that no major revision was attempted for over 250 years. In the course of time, however, changes in the English language, advances in biblical scholarship and the discovery of older manuscripts resulted in calls for a revision. This task was begun under the authority of the Church of England in 1870 and ended with the publication of the Revised Version (RV) between 1881 and 1885. A separate American version, reflecting preferences of the American scholars involved in the project, was published in 1901 as the American Standard Version (ASV).

Considering that by this time the KJV had been the English-speaking world's standard Bible for over two centuries, it is not surprising that these new versions were viewed with suspicion by many in the church. One of the chief critics of the Revised Version was John Burgon, Dean of Chichester in England. He called the RV "the most astonishing, as well as the most calamitous literary blunder of the Age." Condemning the use of older Greek manuscripts, he wrote that the translators' work was "nothing else but poisoning of the River of Life at its sacred source.

Our Revisers stand convicted of having deliberately rejected the words of Inspiration in every page."[11]

Neither the RV nor the ASV significantly challenged the dominance of the KJV among English readers. Both were overly literal and failed to match the majesty of language and the style of the KJV. Though the translators utilized better manuscripts and drew on recent advances in biblical studies, the improvements they made were of little consequence to the general reading public. Their most significant contribution was to begin a process of revision that has accelerated throughout the twentieth century. Since the publication of the Revised Standard Version (RSV) in 1952, an extraordinary number of new versions have appeared on the market.[12] All this activity has resulted in an acceptance of a diversity of versions. Translations such as the New American Standard Bible (1970), the New International Version (1978) and the New King James Version (1982) are widely used among evangelical Christians. "Freer" versions such as the Living Bible (1971) and the Good News Bible (1976) have also gained a wide readership.

This is not to say that these versions are universally accepted. When the Revised Standard Version first appeared, some ministers publicly burned copies of it.[13] Even today a small but vocal minority continues to consider the KJV the only authentic Bible.[14] Books with titles such as *God Wrote Only One Bible, The Paraphrased Perversion of the Bible, The Corruption of the Word, New Age Bible Versions* and *The Bible "Babel"*[15] reveal the extreme side of this movement. Yet the majority of evangelical scholars, pastors and thoughtful laypersons recognize that by updating the archaic language of the KJV, by utilizing older and more reliable manuscripts and by drawing on modern methods of linguistics, contemporary versions are able to produce translations of God's Word that are more accurate and reliable. Even most of the people who still favor the KJV admit that contemporary translations have a role to play in the life of the church.

A New Controversy: The "Gender-Inclusive" Language Debate

In the last decade or so a new controversy has emerged in the field of Bible translation. This issue concerns what are being called "gender-inclusive" Bible versions. If the early stages of this debate are any indication, it promises to be more complex, more confusing and more divisive than any translation controversy in history. The primary reason for this, no doubt, is that these new versions have been linked closely to the current debate over the role of women in the church and in the home. This controversy pits egalitarians, who believe that men and women should share equal leadership roles in the church and the home, against complementarians, who argue for distinct and complementing roles for men and women. Egalitarians claim that their position reflects the biblical perspective of full equality of both sexes before God. Complementarians point to biblical texts affirming male leadership and view the issue as a culture war between those who respect the roles that God has ordained and radical feminists pushing a social agenda. With issues of leadership, authority and power at stake, the debate has divided the evangelical church, polarizing many churches, denominations and theological schools.

The link between this volatile issue and the inclusive language debate has resulted in similar polarization and division. One of the most disturbing features of the debate has been the lack of clear definition. Labels such as "feminist," "unisex" and "gender neutral" have been applied to these translations. What, then, is a gender-inclusive version? A simple definition would be *a translation that seeks to avoid masculine terminology when the original author was referring to members of both sexes.*

Proponents of these versions point out that the goal must be to capture the author's intended meaning. For example, when the apostle Paul writes in Romans 3:28, "For we maintain that a man *[anthrōpos]* is justified by faith," he does not intend to say that only males are justified by faith but that all people are justified by faith. In this context the Greek term *anthrōpos* clearly carries the generic sense "people." In other contexts, where only males are intended, the exclusive term "man" is retained. For example, in Matthew 9:9 the NRSV reads, "As Jesus was walking along, he saw a *man* called Matthew sitting at the tax booth." Here *anthrōpos* clearly means "a male human being." Other masculine generic terms are treated similarly. When Paul addresses the church in Philippi with the statement, "Finally, my brothers *[adelphoi]*, rejoice in the Lord!" (Phil 3:1 NIV), he uses the Greek term *adelphoi* to address both men and women. A gender-inclusive version might reflect this inclusive sense by translating "brothers and sisters." This translation is intended to capture the author's intended meaning, that is, what Paul meant his readers to understand when they read or heard *adelphoi*. Gender-inclusive versions are those that intentionally use an inclusive term *when this inclusive sense is intended by the author.*

The careful reader might note already that when "gender inclusive" is defined in this way, the label itself becomes unnecessary, especially if it would tend to bias a reader against that translation. The only difference between "gender-inclusive" and "traditional" versions is that the former are intentionally sensitive to readers who might misunderstand masculine generic terms such as "man" or "brothers" as referring to males only or to readers who might feel excluded by their use. Proponents argue that since the generic use of terms such as "man" and "he" are in serious decline in contemporary English, more inclusive terms better convey the sense of the original Greek.[16] They are now more precise and thus more accurate.

Because their goal is precision and accuracy, these versions are sometimes called "gender-accurate" translations. This is an appropriate description, since the goal of these versions—at least in their stated claims—is not to promote a feminist agenda but to convey accurately the sense of the original in contemporary English. The term "gender inclusive," on the other hand, has sometimes been misconstrued to mean that the translation renders passages as inclusive regardless of the author's intent.[17] Despite this imprecision, I employ the term "gender inclusive" throughout this book because it is the most widely accepted designation. It should be kept in mind, however, that the term is here defined as "a translation that explicitly seeks to include women when the original author so intended." Almost all Bible translations produced in recent years may be called gender inclusive (or gender accurate) in this sense.

The Historical Background of the Debate

The debate over gender-inclusive language has its roots in the women's rights movement. As women gained a greater voice in society, they called for language that reflected their position of equality beside men. In this context the generic use of "man" and "he" was sometimes viewed as inaccurate and offensive. The result over the years has been a significant shift in English usage. It is impossible to deny that the public at large uses masculine generic terms with much less frequency than was true even a decade ago. This is especially the case for young people who have grown up in a context where such terms are rarely used. Most English speakers, including Christians, are much more sensitive about using terms such as "he" and "man" when referring to both men and women. When I preach a sermon before a mixed congregation, I do not address them as "brothers" but as "brothers and sisters." When I am teaching on the doctrine of salvation, I normally say that "*people* are justified by faith" instead of "*men* are justified by faith." While there is nothing inherently evil or wrong with masculine generic terms (both Hebrew and Greek use them), neither is there anything evil or wrong with more inclusive language.

But some Christians consider the use of gender-inclusive language an inappropriate capitulation to the feminist agenda. By adopting such language, they argue, we are caving in to the world's standards and are thus compromising biblical truth. While such a perspective expresses legitimate concerns, it is surely an overreaction. The real issue is not whether gender-inclusive language is related to the women's movement (it certainly is) but whether such language accurately conveys the intention of the original author. *Is the use of gender-inclusive language in Bible translation inherently inaccurate?* This is the question we will be dealing with throughout this book.

From the beginning, however, we may point out that even the most vehement critics admit that there is nothing inherently wrong with such language. Wayne Grudem, professor of theology at Trinity Evangelical Divinity School and president of the Council on Biblical Manhood and Womanhood (CBMW)—the leading complementarian organization today—has written several articles opposing gender-inclusive language in Bible translation. Even as he attacks individual instances of such language, he repeatedly admits its legitimacy when used appropriately. For example, in Galatians 3:11, the Revised Standard Version (RSV) reads, "Now it is evident that *no man* is justified before God by the law." But the New Revised Standard Version (NRSV; a gender-inclusive version) has "*no one* is justified before God." Similarly, in John 12:32 the RSV has "and I, when I am lifted up from the earth, will draw *all men* to myself." The NRSV reads "all *people*." Concerning these revisions Grudem writes, "These are helpful changes because they use gender inclusive language without sacrificing accuracy in translation."[18] In a discussion of the use of the generic "he" in contemporary English, he similarly notes that "everyone seems to agree that gender-neutral terms are preferable to 'he, him, his' when they can be used without awkwardness and without loss of clarity or precision (and I too would agree)."[19]

Grudem's parenthetic comment ("and I too would agree") indicates that he is not attacking gender-inclusive translations per se but rather the inaccurate use of such language. He admits that gender-inclusive language can actually improve the accuracy of a traditional translation.[20] If this is the case, then this is not a "good versus evil" debate. Each example of inclusive language must be examined individually for accuracy and faithfulness to the original Greek or Hebrew text.

The "Gender-Inclusive" Versions

It is impossible to identify a precise starting point for the use of inclusive language in Bible translation, since every English translation since Wycliffe has utilized some inclusive terms for masculine generics in Hebrew and Greek. The King James Version, for example, frequently uses the gender-neutral "children" for masculine plural terms usually translated "sons" (*bānîm* in Hebrew; *huioi* in Greek). The recent increase in such language, however, can be attributed to two key factors. First is the subtle English language change noted above. It is beyond dispute that masculine generic terms such as "man" and "he" are used less today than they were in the past. As the English language has changed, Bible translations have occasionally and incidentally introduced more inclusive terms.

The second and equally important factor is related to advances in linguistics and modern methods of Bible translation. Recent translations that focus more on the meaning of the text and less on its form have tended to introduce inclusive terms more frequently than their more "literal" counterparts (see chap. four for a detailed discussion of these terms). In the very literal New American Standard Bible (NASB), for example, Romans 2:6 reads that God "will render to every *man* according to his deeds." The more idiomatic New International Version (NIV) has "God will give to each *person* according to what he has done." Without any agenda or mandate to introduce inclusive language, the NIV translators recognized that in this context *anthrōpos* meant "person," not "man."[21] Although in most cases the NIV retains the masculine generic "man," in dozens of others it uses a more inclusive term.[22]

Whereas these kinds of gender-inclusive renderings arose more or less incidentally in the normal process of Bible translation, by the mid-1980s translators of English Bibles were taking conscious steps to introduce such language in a more consistent and systematic manner. Almost every major version that has been prepared or revised over the last decade has adopted the extensive use of such language. The rationale has always been the need to keep up with the changing state of the English language.

Translations or major revisions using moderately inclusive language that have appeared since 1985 include the New Jerusalem Bible (1985), the New Century Version (1987), the New American Bible (revised 1988, 1990),[23] the Revised English Bible (1989), the New Revised Standard Version (1990), the Good News Bible (revised 1992), The Message (1993), the Contemporary English Version (1995), God's Word (1995) and the New Living Translation (1996). In addition, various children's versions have adopted inclusive language, including the International Children's Bible (1986; an edition of the New Century Version) and the New International Reader's Version (1994, 1996). In 1995 an "Inclusive Language Edition" of the popular New International Version was published in Great Britain. These versions are surveyed in chapter two.

Of the early gender-inclusive versions, the New Revised Standard Version (NRSV) was the most widely publicized and celebrated. Because it was a major revision of the widely used Revised Standard Version (RSV), its appearance was eagerly anticipated. When publicity went out that the NRSV would introduce the systematic use of gender-inclusive language, its 1989 release generated even more attention. Reviews of the new version were generally favorable, with one commentator calling the NRSV "the finest American translation yet."[24] Among evangelicals reaction was mixed. On the positive side D. A. Carson, research professor of New Testament at Trinity Evangelical Divinity School, noted that "on the whole, their efforts [at inclusive language] are judicious, thorough and effective. . . . Most of the changes introduced by these commitments are happy ones." He concludes with a statement on the importance of relevance in Bible translation: "What is clear is that for use in any context where virtually all the people are sensitized to inclusivist language (not least the university environment), the NRSV sounds incomparably more modern than its closest rivals."[25] John Stek, former professor at Calvin Theological Seminary, similarly writes, "Readers will find that by and large this [attempt at inclusive language] has been thoroughly and judiciously achieved." He criticizes the NRSV committee, however, for going beyond their basic mandate in their "zeal to achieve sex-neutral language."[26]

A less positive assessment came from Robert Thomas, professor of New Testament at The Master's Seminary. In a review of the new version, he expressed concern both for its theologically liberal bias and for some inaccuracies in its use of inclusive language.[27] The most negative critique came from Wayne Grudem. In a paper read at the 1996 national convention of the Evangelical Theological Society in Jackson, Mississippi, Grudem severely criticized the NRSV's use of inclusive language, arguing that it resulted in serious distortion of the meaning of Scripture. His conclusion was that the NRSV was wholly unsuitable for use by evangelicals:

> With much regret, I must conclude that the NRSV has disqualified itself for use by the majority of the evangelical world. . . . By making the goal of "eliminating masculine-oriented language" more impor-

> tant than the goal of accuracy in translation, the NRSV has made thousands of intentional changes in the sense of the text, and in so doing it has become a translation that cannot be trusted. And if it cannot be trusted, then it will not be widely used.[28]

Grudem's highly critical paper turned out to be a preview of things to come. Up to this time, the sweeping trend toward gender-inclusive language in Bible translation had gone mostly unnoticed by the evangelical public. Events in March 1997 were about to change that, thrusting the inclusive-language issue into the arena of public debate.

The NIV "Inclusive Language Edition" Controversy

"The Stealth Bible: The Popular *New International Version* Bible Is Quietly Going 'Gender-neutral.'" So trumpeted the March 29, 1997, cover of *World* magazine, a Christian news magazine based in Asheville, North Carolina. The article, written by assistant editor Susan Olasky, claimed that by the year 2000 or 2001 the New International Version's Committee on Bible Translation (CBT) planned to substitute a gender-neutral version for the present one. "Say goodbye to the generic *he, man, brothers,* or *mankind,*" Olasky wrote. "Make way for *people, person, brother and sister,* and *humankind.*" She pointed out that the NIV Inclusive Language Edition (NIVI) had already been published in 1995 in Great Britain and would soon be introduced into the North American market.

Olasky's characterization of the NIVI as the "Stealth" Bible, together with her claim that the translators were "quietly going 'gender neutral,'" gave the *World* article an air of intrigue and scandal. The article's repeated use of the explosive term "unisex" to describe the translation, together with its link to creeping feminism in the church, provided all the ingredients for controversy (the actual title of the article was "The Feminist Seduction of the Evangelical Church, Femme Fatale"). Indeed, most of the article was devoted to a critique of the egalitarian movement in the church.

Despite *World*'s modest circulation, the article created a sensation. Complaints began to pour in at the International Bible Society (IBS), which holds the NIV copyright, and Zondervan Publishing House, the

NIV publisher. One man even drilled holes through several NIVs and sent them to the IBS.[29] Zondervan and the IBS moved rapidly for damage control, releasing press statements explaining the reason for the revisions. This was not an issue of a radical feminist agenda, they argued, but about keeping the NIV both accurate and contemporary. Gender-inclusive language was being introduced only when changes in the English language warranted it. Since the generic term "man" no longer meant "men and women" for many readers, more inclusive terms such as "person" were being used.

These explanations did little to reassure critics. Public opposition grew as influential voices entered the fray. In a second article in *World*, Olasky called the debate "The Battle for the Bible"[30] and cited evangelical senior statesman J. I. Packer as weighing in against the inclusive version. Packer is quoted as saying that "adjustments made by what I call the feminist edition are not made in the interests of legitimate translation procedure. These changes have been made to pander to a cultural prejudice that I hope will be short-lived."[31] In another *World* article, Wayne Grudem compares the two NIVs and warns that "once evangelical translators give in to the principle of changing what the Bible says in order to make it acceptable to our culture, the demands for changes will never end."[32]

Other criticisms were not so intellectually focused. In one blistering attack published in Jerry Falwell's *National Liberty Journal*, Paige Patterson, president of Southeastern Baptist Theological Seminary, warned the NIV translators that "monkeying with the Word of the Lord may get a slippery banana peel in the NIV cage, but it will get no banana!" He went on to challenge the NIV translators: "I call on you to be entirely forthcoming and label your translation as the 'NIV-Unisex translation.'"

Influential organizations also expressed alarm. When the family advocacy organization Focus on the Family learned that its own Odyssey Bible (which uses the text of the International Children's Bible) contained gender-inclusive language, it pulled it from the market and announced that parents who asked for a refund would be reimbursed. Cook Communications Ministries similarly announced it would delete quotations from the New International Reader's Version (NIrV) from its Bible-in-Life curriculum.[33]

The straw that broke the camel's back, however, came when the nation's largest denomination, the Southern Baptist Convention, considered dropping the NIV from its Sunday-school curriculum. In the face of impending catastrophe, the IBS executive committee met in an emergency session. On May 23, 1997, the committee approved a statement abandoning "all plans for gender-related changes in future editions of the New International Version (NIV)." They also pledged to continue publishing the present (1984) NIV, to begin revising the gender-inclusive New International Reader's Version, and to enter into negotiations with Hodder and Stoughton, the British publisher of the NIV, on the matter of ceasing publication of the NIVI.

The surprise decision by the IBS actually came a few days before another scheduled meeting arranged by James Dobson of Focus on the Family. In a move toward resolution, Dobson had invited individuals from the IBS, the CBT, Zondervan, the CBMW and *World* magazine to Focus on the Family headquarters in Colorado Springs, Colorado, on May 27. In what was later called the Conference on Gender-Related Language in Scripture, the participants affirmed the IBS decision and drafted a series of guidelines on gender-related language in Bible translation. A text of the original guidelines, together with later revisions, is found in appendix one.

Why So Much Controversy?

Why, if there were already at least eleven major gender-inclusive versions on the market, did so much public outrage accompany the publicity surrounding the NIVI? For one thing, moderate inclusive-language changes had gone mostly unnoticed by the Christian public, probably because most of these changes were in line with contemporary English usage. A case in point is the fact that Focus on the Family had for some time been using the International Children's Bible in its Odyssey Bible without recognizing or perhaps without caring that it was gender inclusive. Most readers hardly noticed the changes introduced in these versions.

Another reason for the furor must be the present popularity of the NIV among evangelicals. It seems to have been, at least partly, a victim of its own success. No translation since 1611 has come as close to usurping the dominance of the KJV in the English-speaking world as the NIV. Among many evangelicals (as well as among many other Christians), the NIV has become the Bible of choice.[34] Evangelicals who keep up with new Bible versions may have looked askance at Roman Catholic versions such as the New Jerusalem Bible and the New American Bible, which adopted moderate gender-inclusive language, and at "ecumenical" versions such as the New Revised Standard Version that did the same. This was of little consequence since, for most evangelicals, these were somebody else's Bible. But when one of "our" Bibles—indeed the most popular and widely read of evangelical Bibles—was accused of caving in to feminist demands for political correctness, the translators had a scandal on their hands. The title of an article in *Christianity Today* sums up the evangelical response: "Hands Off My NIV!"[35]

A third reason the NIVI created so much controversy was the manner in which it was published and marketed. While many other versions had introduced gender-inclusive language, none had continued to produce two separate versions, one inclusive and one noninclusive. For example, when the New American Bible and the Good News Bible were revised using gender-inclusive language, previous versions were no longer published. These versions did not identify themselves in their titles as "gender-inclusive versions" but merely as "revisions" (though the prefaces did describe the inclusive revisions). By publishing two different NIVs in Great Britain and explicitly labeling one an "inclusive language version," the publishers invited accusations that they were being "politically correct" and catering to feminist demands. If inclusive language revisions were just part of the normal revision process, as they claimed, why should the publishers continue to publish the un-updated (and seemingly less accurate) version? This apparent contradiction between stated purpose and publishing practice opened the NIVI up to accusations of being an agenda-driven translation.

The Issue Resolved?

Though the IBS and Zondervan had decided not to publish the NIVI in North America, all parties recognized that the issue of gender-inclusive language was far from resolved. In the June 14/21, 1997, edition of *World,* Susan Olasky complained that while the IBS and Zondervan were "bailing out of the Stealth Bible," they were "all the while maintaining the gender-neutral translation would have been more accurate." IBS board chairman Victor Oliver is quoted as saying, "It has become very clear that many people in North America don't want the NIV changed, even if many Bible scholars feel a revision could more clearly reflect shifts in English language usage and more precisely render the meaning of the original texts."[36] In an editorial in the same edition, *World* publisher Joel Belz similarly warns that "spokesmen for the NIV continued to argue that what they had planned was entirely proper—but that their evangelical audience simply wasn't ready for it."[37]

It is almost certainly true that the scholars of the IBS and the CBT reversed their decision to publish the NIVI not because of a significant change in conviction concerning the legitimacy of such a translation but because the public outrage and media hype made it impossible to conduct a serious debate. When the issue became one of either losing credibility for the NIV among the Christian public or dropping plans for the revision, the decision was an easy one. The potential loss (spiritually *and* financially—both must have played a role in the decision) was much greater than the gain.

For their part, the opponents of the NIVI viewed the battle as just beginning. The communiqué from the Conference on Gender-Related Language in Scripture took note of the many inclusive translations on the market and called on other Bible publishers and copyright holders to issue public statements similarly rejecting inclusive language. While the skirmish over the NIVI was over, the real battle was just beginning.

The Present Book

This book is an attempt to provide a balanced and reasoned evaluation of the legitimacy of gender-inclusive language in Bible translation. One of the credentials I bring to this task is having one foot in both camps. In terms of the role of women in the church and home, I am a (moderate) complementarian rather than an egalitarian. I believe Scripture sets out distinct roles for men and women in the church and the home. It disturbs me when I see egalitarians lining up in support of inclusive Bible versions and complementarians lining up against them. This suggests to me that our individual social agendas are coloring our search for truth. The inclusive language debate concerns issues such as translation philosophy, linguistics and Bible interpretation (hermeneutics). The issue of the role of women in ministry concerns hermeneutics but also focuses on the theology of man and woman, the interpretation of certain biblical texts, and the historical role of women in the church.

All this to say that though I am a complementarian, from a linguistic and hermeneutical perspective I see validity in the introduction of inclusive language—when that language demonstrably represents the biblical author's intended meaning. This perspective is not based on a social or political feminist agenda (I oppose such an agenda) but on the nature of language and translation.

It must be admitted from the start that it is impossible for any of us to approach Scripture free from bias, since we all bring to the table our own backgrounds and experiences. Yet if we can establish some common linguistic and hermeneutical ground rules, perhaps we can produce Bible translations that are faithful to the original text and also speak clearly and accurately to the hearts of people today.

Moving the Discussion Forward

One of the most unsettling aspects of the NIVI controversy has been the heated tone that has dominated the discussion. Inflammatory accusations and name calling can only obscure the real issues. I would like to make several suggestions with a view toward moving the discussion forward in a reasonable and charitable manner.

Use clear definitions. It is first of all necessary to determine the nature of these translations. In her original *World* magazine article, Susan Olasky repeatedly used the term "unisex" to describe the NIVI. My dictionary defines the noun "unisex" as the "elimination or absence of sexual distinctions, especially in dress," and the adjective as "not distinguished or distinguishable on the basis of sex; androgynous in appearance."[38] The term commonly conjures up images of cross-dressing or a radical feminist approach that abolishes any distinction between men and women.[39] A quick glance at the NIVI, however, reveals that it does *not* eliminate gender distinctions and so cannot accurately be called a "unisex" translation. Compare the NIVI with the original NIV on four biblical passages concerning the role of women:

1 Timothy 2:11-12
NIV: A woman should learn in quietness and full submission. I do not permit a woman to teach or to have authority over a man; she must be silent.
NIVI: A woman should learn in quietness and full submission. I do not permit a woman to teach or to have authority over a man; she must be silent.

1 Corinthians 14:33-34
NIV: As in all the congregations of the saints, women should remain silent in the churches. They are not allowed to speak, but must be in submission, as the Law says.
NIVI: As in all the congregations of the saints, women should remain silent in the churches. They are not allowed to speak, but must be in submission, as the Law says.

Ephesians 5:22-23
NIV: Wives, submit to your husbands as to the Lord. For the husband is the head of the wife as Christ is the head of the church, his body, of which he is the Savior.
NIVI: Wives, submit to your husbands as to the Lord. For the husband is the head of the wife as Christ is the head of the church, his body, of which he is the Savior.

Titus 2:4-5
NIV: Then they [the older women] can train the younger women to love their husbands and children, to be self-controlled and pure, to be busy at home, to be kind, and to be subject to their husbands, so that no one will malign the word of God.
NIVI: Then they [the older women] can train the younger women to love their husbands and children, to be self-controlled and pure, to be busy at home, to be kind, and to be subject to their husbands, so that no one will malign the word of God.

Not a single word has been altered in the NIVI. It should be clear to even the most casual reader that the NIVI is not a "unisex" translation. Yet even after being informed by others that her use of the term was inaccurate, Olasky continued to use it in subsequent articles.[40] Olasky's unhelpful and provocative language did nothing to move the debate forward.

If the debate over inclusive language is to be conducted in a productive manner, it is essential that all parties (1) carefully examine these versions themselves so as to recognize their true nature and (2) seek to use clear and accurate designations and descriptions. As their treatment of passages concerning the role of women in the church and the home shows, neither the NIVI nor the NRSV can accurately be termed either "feminist" or "unisex." There are indeed two New Testament versions published in the United States that could appropriately be called "feminist" (discussed in chap. three). These translations differ dramatically from the "gender-inclusive" versions described here.

Clarify the nature of Bible translation. Much of the confusion generated by the NIVI controversy has resulted from a misunderstanding of the nature of Bible translation. The most obvious example of this is the tendency to confuse *fallible human translations* with the *infallible Word of God*. Claims have been made that while traditional translations represent the authentic Word of God, inclusive translations are distortions of that Word. For *World* publisher Joel Belz, for example, the "ultimate journalistic sin" is to misquote a source, and that is what the inclusive versions are doing: "This story about the NIV revision is about people who, for supposedly good reasons, are willing to misquote God."[41] Belz naively assumes that the original NIV (or the KJV, RSV, NASB, NKJV, or any other English translation for that matter) consists of direct quotes from God and that the NIVI is changing these quotes. Wayne Grudem, too, falls into this error when he says, "Such [inclusive] revisions are not the words God originally caused to be written, and thus they are not the words of God. They are human words that men have substituted for the words of God, and they have no place in the Bible."[42] But since every English translation uses different English words, which of them gets God's quotes right? Which of them contain the actual words of God? The only way to directly "quote" God (to use Belz's strange terminology), or to reproduce "the words God originally caused to be written" (to quote Grudem), would be to publish only Hebrew and Greek texts.[43] Or, of course, one could claim a "direct quote" English translation by taking a "King James only" perspective. But no credible scholar would hold such a position.

The inclusive language debate is not about altering the original texts of Scripture (the Hebrew or Greek texts) but about *how best to translate those texts into clear, accurate and contemporary English*. Any linguist or translator will confirm that every translation is an interpretation, and decisions must constantly be made concerning the most accurate way to translate a particular word or phrase. While we certainly have the Word of God (God's message to us) in all translations that are faithful to the original texts, in none of them do we have "the words God originally caused to be written," since these words were given in a different language. It is the skilled translator's task to find the best English equivalents to convey the sense of the original Hebrew, Greek and Aramaic.

To prove that the so-called inclusive versions are distorting God's word, critics have tended to find a few examples of poor translation in a particular version and then draw sweeping conclusions about the inaccuracy of inclusive language. The simple fact is that *all* translations are the work of human beings who make interpretive decisions concerning the meaning of the original text. Any Bible scholar who examines any Bible version can point to dozens of examples of inaccurate translations. There is no such a thing as a perfect translation. This is why competent linguists and Bible scholars must continue the process of examination and revision.

The question that must be asked, then, is not whether the NIVI or any other "inclusive version" contains some inaccurate renderings (all translations do) but whether the use of inclusive terms is inherently evil or wrong. As noted above, even the most severe critics of these versions admit that it is not.

Another important issue concerning the nature of Bible translation is the goal or philosophy behind that translation. Should a Bible translation seek to reproduce as closely as possible the *form* of the original Greek or Hebrew, or should it seek to capture instead the *meaning* of the original? Should translations always be done in a word-for-word (or "literal") manner, or should idiomatic renderings be introduced? These are complex questions that require detailed answers. In chapter four we will examine the nature of Bible translation, relating these issues to the inclusive language debate.

Set aside our agendas. Perhaps most important, for the present discussion to move forward evangelicals must set aside (or at least place on hold) their egalitarian and complementarian agendas and establish some common ground on the issue of Bible translation. If the debate gets bogged down over the role of women in the church, crucial issues of hermeneutics and Bible translation will not be resolved.

Much of the furor over the NIVI, for example, arose from the claim that this translation was driven by the agenda of radical feminism and was thus an attack on the very foundations of biblical Christianity. This claim was promoted by *World* magazine when it referred to the "Stealth Bible" and accused the NIV of "quietly" going gender neutral. This gave readers the impression that the IBS, Zondervan and the CBT were seeking to introduce an inclusive edition surreptitiously and foist a feminist agenda on their unsuspecting readers.[44]

Considering the evangelical credentials of the CBT and the fact that a majority of the committee are complementarians,[45] such an accusation would seem unjustified. The goal of the translators was rather to keep the translation in line with contemporary English usage.[46] (Whether or not contemporary English actually demands such inclusive language is another issue and will be addressed later.) That there were no insidious motives behind the translation should be clear from the fact that other conservative Bible translations, such as the New Living Translation (NLT), use inclusive language and clearly explain their translation procedures in prefatory remarks. When the NIVI edition appeared in Great Britain, the preface clearly stated its preference for inclusive language. It is virtually certain that the North American version of the NIVI would have included a similar statement.

Further evidence that there was no deep conspiracy was the fact that before the controversy erupted, CBT members spoke freely with *World* magazine about the inclusive revisions taking place. As far as they were concerned, these changes were just part of the normal revision process. Scholars from the CBT and the IBS appeared genuinely surprised when the controversy surrounding the NIVI erupted. One must indeed ask who has the stronger social agenda: the CBT, many of whom are complementarians and whose goal is to produce the clearest and most accurate translation of Scripture, or the CBMW, whose whole purpose is to promote complementarianism in the church?

While admitting that the CBT has no feminist agenda, other critics have claimed that these scholars are the unwitting and ignorant pawns of feminist forces in the church. Such a claim, however, demeans scholars who are among the best evangelical minds in the English-speaking world. These scholars made inclusive changes not because they were "duped" but because they believed such changes were faithful to the original intent of the biblical writers.

Evidence that the debate has been agenda driven comes out loud and clear in the original "Stealth Bible" article in *World*, where Susan Olasky severely criticizes Willow Creek Community Church in South Barrington, Illinois, for excluding complementarians from its church staff. She quotes Wayne Grudem, who says that "the way an egalitarian view triumphs is by a suppression of information and discussion." Olasky then turns around on the following pages and *praises* R. Albert Mohler, president of Southern Baptist Seminary in Louisville, Kentucky, for "sticking to his guns" and refusing to hire faculty who support an egalitarian perspective.[47] "Where is Grudem when you need him?" asks Doug Koop of *Christian Week*, ironically pointing out the inconsistency in Olasky's position.[48] There is something wrong when both sides call for the other to be tolerant and then exclude opposing views from the discussion.

The agreement and guidelines established at the so-called Confer ence on Gender-Related Language were hailed later in *CBMW News* as a consensus. But conspicuously absent from the meeting were representatives from any egalitarian organization (such as Christians for Biblical Equality, CBE) or, for that matter, any women at all. Excluding opponents from the table is no way to work out a consensus.

The question is, Are we able to set aside our social and cultural agendas, establish common ground hermeneutically, and get back to the hard work of translating God's Word? If evangelicals fail to do this and begin producing multiple versions (inclusive and noninclusive, egalitarian and complementarian), we risk doing what the cults have done: changing the Bible from the authoritative Word of God into a handbook supporting each of our own personal agendas. This is the greatest danger of all.

The guidelines set out in the communiqué from the Focus on the Family meeting represent a positive step forward in that they attempt to distinguish accurate inclusive language from inaccurate. Although these guidelines are seriously flawed both hermeneutically and linguistically, they provide a helpful introduction to a discussion on what constitutes the legitimate use of inclusive language in Bible translation.

Evangelicals have been accused of discarding their minds when confronted with difficult theological and textual issues. To the contrary, let us approach the issues using all the resources—textual, historical and linguistic—that we can muster, while maintaining the highest possible reverence for the authoritative and inspired Word of God. Then and only then will we be able to answer the question of whether or not these so-called gender-inclusive versions are legitimate.

Part 1

SURVEY OF BIBLE VERSIONS

Two

THE GENDER-INCLUSIVE VERSIONS

THE USE OF INCLUSIVE LANGUAGE IS NOTHING NEW, SINCE ALMOST ALL translations have introduced some inclusive language for masculine generic terms in Hebrew and Greek. In the King James Version (KJV), for example, the generic masculine Hebrew terms *bēn* (usually translated "son") and *bānîm* (usually translated "sons") are frequently rendered as "child" and "children."[1] Genesis 3:16 KJV reads, "In sorrow thou shalt bring forth children *[bānîm]*." The translation "children" is especially common in the phrase "children of Israel." Exodus 1:7 KJV reads, "And the children *[bānîm]* of Israel were fruitful, and increased abundantly."

Later revisions of the KJV, such as the Revised Standard Version (1952), the New American Standard Bible (1970) and the New King James Version (1982) frequently use "children" for *bānîm* and, occasionally, "child" for *bēn*. Proverbs 17:6 in the NKJV reads, "Children's children [literally "sons of sons"] are the crown of old men." In the New Testament too the KJV often rendered the Greek plural *huioi* (usually translated "sons") as "children": "Blessed are the peacemakers: for they shall be called the children of God" (Mt 5:9 KJV).[2] Occasionally the singular *huios* is rendered "child" instead of "son" (Mt 23:15; Acts 13:10 KJV).[3]

Gender-Inclusive Language in Traditional English Versions

While generally retaining generic "man" for the Hebrew terms *'ādām* and *'îsh,* the KJV occasionally introduces more inclusive language. Ezekiel 44:25 KJV reads, "And they shall come at no dead person [*'ādām*] to defile themselves," and Jonah 3:5 reads, "So the people [*'anᵉshê,* plural construct of *'îsh*] of Nineveh believed God, and proclaimed a fast."

Most literal translations since the KJV have continued to use masculine generic terms. Occasionally, however, more inclusive language is introduced. Romans 2:9 in the RSV reads, "There will be tribulation and distress for every human being [*psychē anthrōpou,* literally, 'soul of man'] who does evil," and Romans 7:1 is translated, "Do you not know, brethren . . . that the law is binding on a person [*anthrōpos*] only during his life?" Note that in this case, while the inclusive term "person" is used for *anthrōpos,* the resumptive masculine pronoun "his" follows and gives the subject of the sentence a masculine sense.[4]

The NASB occasionally uses inclusive terms such as "person" and "human being." Numbers 19:18 NASB reads, "And a clean person [*'îsh*] shall take hyssop and dip it in the water." The context here is ceremonial defilement, which could affect either men or women. Isaiah 13:14 NASB is translated, "They will each [*'îsh*] turn to his own people; And each one [*'îsh*] flee to his own land." In Ecclesiastes 12:13 the context makes it clear that the Hebrew *'ādām* is inclusive: "The conclusion, when all has been heard, is: fear God and keep His commandments, because this applies to every person [*'ādām*]."[5] In the New Testament too the masculine generic term *anthrōpos* is sometimes rendered as "people." Mark 8:27 NASB reads, "And on the way He questioned His disciples, saying to them, 'Who do people [*anthrōpoi*] say that I am?'" (compare Mt 16:13 NASB). In Luke 6:31 NASB Jesus says, "And just as you want people [*anthrōpoi*] to treat you, treat them in the same way." Like the RSV, the NASB renders *anthrōpos* in Romans 7:1 as "person" (compare 2 Pet 1:21).

The NKJV, another very literal translation, also occasionally renders Hebrew and Greek terms for "man" with more inclusive terms. In the laws related to leprosy in Leviticus 13, the NKJV reads, "When the leprous sore is on a person *['ādām]* then he shall be brought to the priest" (Lev 13:9; compare Ezek 44:25). Psalm 62:12 NKJV reads, "For You render to each one *['îsh]* according to his work," and Judges 17:6 NKJV is rendered "everyone *['îsh]* did what was right in his own eyes." Deuteronomy 24:16 reads, "Fathers shall not be put to death for their children *[bānîm]* . . . a person [*'îsh,* NASB 'everyone'] shall be put to death for his own sin."[6] In Jonah 4:11 NKJV, the translators recognized that *'ādām* probably referred to all the inhabitants of Nineveh: "And should I not pity Nineveh, that great city, in which are more than one hundred and twenty thousand persons *['ādām]?*"[7]

In the New Testament too the NKJV occasionally translates *anthrōpos* using inclusive language. In Luke 1:25 NKJV Elizabeth rejoices that "thus the Lord has dealt with me . . . to take away my reproach among people *[anthrōpoi],*" and in 1 Peter 3:4 NKJV we read, "Rather let it be the hidden person *[anthrōpos]* of the heart with the incorruptible beauty of a gentle and quiet spirit." The translators evidently recognized that since the reference here was to women, "the hidden *man* of the heart" was not quite appropriate!

The versions mentioned above (KJV, RSV, NASB, NKJV) are among the most "literal" presently available.[8] More idiomatic or "dynamic" translations (versions more concerned with the sense of the original than its form) have always used inclusive language to a greater extent than their literal counterparts. A good example of this is the New International Version. In dozens of cases in the Old Testament, inclusive terms such as "people" or "person(s)," "one," "each," "anyone" or "someone" are used to capture the sense intended by the Hebrew terms *'îsh* and *'ādām.*[9] Proverbs 24:12 reads in the NIV, "Will he not repay each person *['ādām]* according to what he has done?" (compare Ps 62:12), and Leviticus 24:17 is rendered, "If anyone *['îsh]* takes the life of a human being, he must be put to death."[10]

The Greek term *anthrōpos* is also frequently translated with inclusive language in the NIV. In Matthew 16:13 NIV Jesus asks his disciples,

"Who do people *[anthrōpoi]* say the Son of Man is?" and in Mark 8:24 the blind man says, "I see people *[anthrōpoi]*; they look like trees walking around." In 2 Corinthians 3:2 Paul says to the Corinthian believers, "You yourselves are our letter, written on our hearts, known and read by everybody [*hypo pantōn anthrōpon,* literally, 'by all men']." James says in James 2:24 NIV, "You see that a person *[anthrōpos]* is justified by what he does and not by faith alone."

The Greek words for "son(s)," *huios* and *huioi,* are occasionally translated as "child" or "children." When questioned by the Sadducees about the state of marriage in the resurrection, Jesus responds that believers "are God's children *[huioi],* since they are children *[huioi]* of the resurrection" (Lk 20:36 NIV). Similarly, in Galatians 3:7 NIV, for Paul, "those who believe are children *[huioi]* of Abraham." In Acts 13:10 NIV the apostle accuses the magician Elymas of being "a child *[huios]* of the devil and an enemy of everything that is right!"

There are many such inclusive renderings in the NIV.[11] Comparing the translation of *anthrōpos* and *anēr* in the NIV and the NIVI, Andreas Köstenberger found that ninety-five of the 550 appearances of *anthrōpos* and thirty of the 216 appearances of *anēr* were translated inclusively in the original NIV.[12] It must be kept in mind that these translations were made in the absence of any mandate or agenda to use inclusive language. The translators were simply trying to capture the sense intended by the original author when the masculine generic was used.

In these examples, the translators of these "traditional" versions clearly chose terms such as "person," "people" and "human being" over masculine terms because the meaning of the original Hebrew or Greek appeared inclusive, that is, the original author intended to refer to men and women. What is surprising is that these kinds of inclusive renderings became the source of controversy with the publication of the NIVI. Why is it that objections to such renderings were not raised in the past?

It is also interesting to note that while inclusive terms were used in these few cases, in many hundreds of others generic "man" was retained. This indicates that the English language is in a state of flux, with both masculine generics and inclusive terms in common use. This raises further questions concerning how to maintain consistency in translation. How often should translators introduce inclusive language in order to reflect contemporary English usage? Occasionally? Frequently? Always? Never? This issue is complicated by the fact that (1) most of these translations reflect a very conservative translation philosophy ("literal," or "formal equivalence"—see chap. four) and (2) the translators themselves were almost all men, and men in their senior years. Do these versions in fact reflect the state of contemporary English usage? These are complex issues that are covered in greater detail in subsequent chapters.[13]

New Revised Standard Version (NRSV, 1990)

We may now turn to a survey of the various gender-inclusive versions currently on the market. As noted in chapter one, though the NRSV was not the first of the gender-inclusive versions, it was certainly the most celebrated. We will therefore consider the NRSV in detail, using it as a standard against which to compare other inclusive versions.

Like its predecessor, the Revised Standard Version (RSV), the NRSV was not intended to be an entirely new translation but to stand in a line of revision that began with the King James Version of 1611.[14] After the RSV was published in 1952, its translation committee continued to meet every few years to consider future changes and to make minor corrections to the text. In 1974 the National Council of Churches, which held the copyright to the RSV, authorized work to begin on a new revision. The complete Bible of the NRSV was copyrighted in 1989 and was published September 30, 1990.

The gender-inclusive policy of the NRSV. The basic rationale for the NRSV, as with its predecessors, was to update the language of previous versions and to keep up with advances in biblical, textual and linguistic studies. The committee did not begin with a mandate to make the language inclusive. It was a decision taken along the way, and in stages, as the work progressed.[15] The process began with a letter to the translation committee by the late George MacRae, S.J., containing guidelines for avoiding masculine language when it was clear that men and women were intended. These general guidelines eventually resulted in an official policy to "remove all masculine language referring to human beings apart from texts that clearly referred to men."[16] The preface to the NRSV reads:

> During the almost half a century since the publication of the RSV, many in the churches have become sensitive to the danger of linguistic sexism arising from the inherent bias of the English language towards the masculine gender, a bias that in the case of the Bible has often restricted or obscured the meaning of the original text. The mandates from the Division[17] specified that, in references to men and women, masculine-oriented language should be eliminated as far as this can be done without altering passages that reflect the historical situation of ancient patriarchal culture.[18]

The committee adopted a number of conventions to achieve gender inclusion, chief among them the use of the plural instead of the singular. Other techniques include using generic terms such as "human," "humankind" and "person," adopting indefinite pronouns for masculine ones, using the adjective "human" for "man," altering third person constructions to first or second person, and replacing active verbs with passive. Examples of each of these are provided below, comparing the RSV with the NRSV.

Plural pronouns for singular:
RSV: He who walks in uprightness fears the LORD. (Prov 14:2)
NRSV: Those who walk uprightly fear the LORD. (Prov 14:2)

Generic terms such as "humankind," "human," "human being" and "person" for "man":
RSV: "The sabbath was made for man, not man for the sabbath." (Mk 2:27)
NRSV: "The sabbath was made for humankind, and not humankind for the sabbath." (Mk 2:27)

RSV: So the LORD said, "I will blot out man whom I have created." (Gen 6:7)
NRSV: So the LORD said, "I will blot out from the earth the human beings I have created." (Gen 6:7)

RSV: Whoever sheds the blood of man, by man shall his blood be shed; for God made man in his own image. (Gen 9:6)
NRSV: Whoever sheds the blood of a human, by a human shall that person's

blood be shed; for in his own image God made humankind. (Gen 9:6)

RSV: Why, one will hardly die for a righteous man. (Rom 5:7)
NRSV: Indeed, rarely will anyone die for a righteous person. (Rom 5:7)

RSV: But Peter lifted him up, saying, "Stand up; I too am a man." (Acts 10:26)
NRSV: But Peter made him get up, saying, "Stand up; I am only a mortal." (Acts 10:26)

Indefinite pronouns for "man" and for third-person masculine pronouns:
RSV: Do you see a man who is hasty in his words? There is more hope for a fool than for him. (Prov 29:20)
NRSV: Do you see someone who is hasty in speech? There is more hope for a fool than for anyone like that. (Prov 29:20)

RSV: He who kills a man shall be put to death. (Lev 24:17)
NRSV: Anyone who kills a human being shall be put to death. (Lev 24:17)

RSV: He who walks with wise men becomes wise. (Prov 13:20)
NRSV: Whoever walks with the wise becomes wise (Prov 13:20). (Note also the substantival adjective "the wise" for "wise men.")

RSV: A man who flatters his neighbor spreads a net for his feet. (Prov 29:5)
NRSV: Whoever flatters a neighbor is spreading a net for the neighbor's feet (Prov 29:5). (Note also the repetition of "neighbor" for "his.")

The adjective "human" for the noun "man":
RSV: We must obey God rather than men. (Acts 5:29)
NRSV: We must obey God rather than any human authority. (Acts 5:29)

RSV: For the foolishness of God is wiser than men. (1 Cor 1:25)
NRSV: For God's foolishness is wiser than human wisdom. (1 Cor 1:25)

RSV: For from within, out of the heart of man, come evil thoughts. (Mk 7:21)
NRSV: For it is from within, from the human heart, that evil intentions come. (Mk 7:21)

First-person or second-person pronouns for third person:
RSV: A man's steps are ordered by the LORD; how then can man understand his way? (Prov 20:24)

NRSV: All our steps are ordered by the LORD; how then can we understand our own ways? (Prov 20:24; compare Ps 41:5)

RSV: What does it profit, my brethren, if a man says he has faith but has not works? Can his faith save him? (Jas 2:14)
NRSV: What good is it, my brothers and sisters, if you say you have faith but do not have works? Can faith save you? (Jas 2:14)

Passive verbs for active:
RSV: Can a man carry fire in his bosom and his clothes not be burned? (Prov 6:27)
NRSV: Can fire be carried in the bosom without burning one's clothes? (Prov 6:27)

RSV: If the work which any man has built on the foundation survives, he will receive a reward. (1 Cor 3:14)
NRSV: If what has been built on the foundation survives, the builder will receive a reward. (1 Cor 3:14)

Hebrew and Greek terms traditionally rendered "fathers" are often translated "parents" or "ancestors":
RSV: Then the LORD said to Jacob, "Return to the land of your fathers." (Gen 31:3).
NRSV: Then the LORD said to Jacob, "Return to the land of your ancestors." (Gen 31:3)

RSV: A fool despises his father's instruction, but he who heeds admonition is prudent. (Prov 15:5)
NRSV: A fool despises a parent's instruction, but the one who heeds admonition is prudent. (Prov 15:5)

The Greek and Hebrew terms for "sons" are often rendered as "children," "descendants," or with other inclusive terms:
RSV: I have become . . . an alien to my mother's sons. (Ps 69:8)
NRSV: I have become . . . an alien to my mother's children. (Ps 69:8)

RSV: Blessed are the peacemakers, for they shall be called sons of God. (Mt 5:9)
NRSV: Blessed are the peacemakers, for they will be called children of God. (Mt 5:9)

RSV: The sons of Japheth: Gomer, Magog. (Gen 10:2)

NRSV: The descendants of Japheth: Gomer, Magog. (Gen 10:2)

RSV: Then Joseph took an oath of the sons of Israel. (Gen 50:25)
NRSV: So Joseph made the Israelites swear. (Gen 50:25)

The Greek terms adelphos *and* adelphoi, *when used of believers in general, are usually rendered in the NRSV as "brother or sister" and "brothers and sisters" respectively:*[19]
RSV: Why do you pass judgment on your brother? (Rom 14:10)
NRSV: Why do you pass judgment on your brother or sister? (Rom 14:10)

RSV: Finally, my brethren, rejoice in the Lord. (Phil 3:1)
NRSV: Finally, my brothers and sisters, rejoice in the Lord. (Phil 3:1)

Exceptions to gender-inclusive language. There are some notable exceptions to the general rule of gender inclusion in the NRSV, the most important of which concern certain legal texts in Leviticus and Deuteronomy. It was decided that putting the passage in the plural or introducing additional nouns would have "obscured the historic structure and literary character of the original."[20] Legal language "is conven tional, stereotyped language, well understood by the community to apply to all, but necessarily put in fixed, conventional terms."[21] Leviticus 14:2, for example, reads in the NRSV, "This shall be the ritual for the leprous person at the time of *his* cleansing: *He* shall be brought to the priest."

A number of Jesus' parables constitute another exception. Masculine references are retained even though the reference may be general: "The kingdom of heaven is like a mustard seed that someone took and sowed in *his* field" (Mt 13:31 NRSV; compare Mt 18:12).

Other exceptions occur when the translators found that eliminating masculine singular pronouns made the language too confusing and cumbersome. In Psalm 109, for instance, language related to the psalmist and his enemies became confusing when the generic plural "they" was introduced, so the masculine "he" was retained.[22]

Inclusive language where men are intended. According to Walter Harrelson, vice chair of the translation committee, the NRSV translators chose to adopt inclusive language "even in some instances in which the committee believed that only males were involved."[23] This would seem to exceed the original inclusive goal, which according to Robert Denton, another vice chair of the translation committee, was to ensure "that no words *intended by the original writer to refer to all human beings* were translated by English words that might be understood to refer only to members of a single sex"[24] (italics mine). One would expect the flip side of this policy to be true also, that in passages intended by the author *to refer to men,* the masculine would be retained. Yet this is not always the case.

In certain texts in Proverbs, for example, young men are warned against the temptations of a seductress. While the RSV refers to "my son" and "my sons," the NRSV adopts the term "my child":

> *My child* [RSV "my son"], be attentive to my wisdom; incline your ear to my understanding. . . . For the lips of a loose woman drip honey, and her speech is smoother than oil. . . . And now, *my child* [RSV "my sons"], listen to me, and do not depart from the words of my mouth. (Prov 5:1-7 NRSV)

Since in its historical context this text is clearly about young men (not young children[25]), the NRSV here seems to go beyond its mandate by adopting the generic "child," especially considering the feminine references to the seductress in the context and the call several verses later to "rejoice in the wife of your youth" (v. 18). Though the sexual purity prescribed in the passage could certainly be applied, by analogy, to women today, the original author was obviously referring to men.

It seems that here and in other places the NRSV committee chose these inclusive renderings in order to allow for the contemporary application to women without explicitly stating that women are included in the original context. This kind of explanation is provided by Walter Harrelson in the context of inclusive language for the cities of refuge in Joshua 20. He writes that "even if it was the case that women did not use the institution of cities of refuge, the [use of inclusive] language does not falsify that fact."[26]

Language related to God and Jesus Christ. The committee was in agreement that masculine terminology related to God should be retained. There is no attempt, for example, to render "Father" as "Father-Mother" or to eliminate masculine pronouns for God. At times, however, such pronouns were dropped when they seemed unnecessary.[27] For example, where the RSV reads, "Behold, the eye of the LORD is on those who fear him . . . *that he may deliver* their soul from death" (Ps 33:18-19 RSV), the NRSV has "truly the eye of the LORD is on those who fear him . . . *to deliver* their soul from death" (Ps 33:18-19). While there is little if any loss of meaning here, and masculine references are retained in the previous phrase, one still wonders why the change was necessary.

Masculine references to Jesus Christ as a man are retained. Occasionally, when the translators felt that Christ's humanity, not his maleness, was being stressed, more generic terms replace "man." First Corinthians 15:21, for example, reads, "For since death came through *a human being* [RSV 'a man'], the resurrection of the dead has also come through *a human being* [RSV 'a man']. Similarly, 1 Timothy 2:5 reads, "For there is . . . one mediator between God and humankind, Christ Jesus, *himself human*" (RSV "the man Christ Jesus"; compare Phil 2:7-8). References to Jesus as "Son of God" and "Son of Man" in the New Testament are retained, though Old Testament passages in which the Hebrew phrase "son of man" are used are rendered with more inclusive language.[28]

The role of women and men. In passages related to the role of women and men, the NRSV remains quite conservative. If the NRSV has a feminist agenda, it is not evident here:

> Let a woman learn in silence with full submission. I permit no woman to teach or to have authority over a man; she is to keep silent. (1 Tim 2:11-12 NRSV)

> Women should be silent in the churches. For they are not permitted to speak, but should be subordinate, as the law also says. (1 Cor 14:34 NRSV)

> Wives, be subject to your husbands as you are to the Lord. For the husband is the head of the wife. (Eph 5:22-23 NRSV)

A mild agenda may perhaps be evident in the qualifications for elders in Titus 1:5-6, where there is no explicit reference in the NRSV to *male* elders:

> RSV: I left you in Crete, that you might . . . appoint elders in every town as I directed you, if any man is blameless, the husband of one wife, and his children are believers. (Tit 1:6)

> NRSV: I left you behind in Crete . . . [to] appoint elders . . . someone who is blameless, married only once, whose children are believers. (Tit 1:6)

The word "man" in the RSV phrase "if any man is blameless" does not occur in the Greek (the Greek word is the indefinite relative pronoun *tis,* "someone," "anyone"), so the NRSV text is accurate here. Yet the following phrase (literally "a one-woman [or 'wife'] man"), together with the masculine pronouns, indicates that Paul has male elders in view. This does not necessarily mean, however, that the NRSV represents a mistranslation. The enigmatic phrase *mias gynaikos anēr* (literally, "a one-woman [or wife] man") is much disputed by commentators. It could mean "only one wife" (NIV, TEV), "faithful to his wife" (NLT), "married only once" (NRSV) or simply "married" (not single). The original RSV (1952) had "married only once," but this was changed to "husband of one wife" in its 1971 revision. The NRSV returns to the original RSV interpretation, which eliminates any specific references to male elders. Is this part of an egalitarian agenda? Perhaps. But it should be noted that the requirements for bishops (overseers) which follow retain masculine pronouns (cf. 1 Tim 3:1-7, where masculine pronouns are also retained).

Assessment. The response to the NRSV among biblical scholars—both evangelical and others—has already been noted in chapter one. In general the NRSV appears to stay faithful to its goal of rendering the original text accurately in contemporary English. Inclusive language is introduced when the author is referring to both men and women. In some cases, however, inclusive language occurs in passages that were intended to refer to men (as in "seductress" passages in Proverbs) or where the author is clearly speaking *as a man.* At times the inclusive language of the NRSV becomes awkward. The term "humankind," for example, is overused as a replacement for "man."

Another criticism that has been leveled against the NRSV is that although it is characterized as "essentially a literal translation" in the preface, this policy of literalness is abandoned in the case of gender-inclusive language. The preface candidly notes this difficulty, pointing out that "more than once the Committee found that the several mandates stood in tension and even conflict." The question that must be asked in this regard is whether the movement away from a "literal" or "formal equivalent" translation results in less accuracy or precision. This issue is addressed in detail in chapter four.

All of the moderate "gender-inclusive" versions examined below use the same basic techniques that are found in the NRSV. Furthermore, all of them retain masculine pronouns for God and retain traditional titles such as "Son of God" (rather than "Child of God") and "Son of Man" for Jesus Christ. The discussion that follows briefly describes each version and notes a few of its distinctives. Details concerning use of inclusive language in these versions are found in appendix two.

New Jerusalem Bible (NJB, 1985)

The New Jerusalem Bible[29] (NJB) introduced an extensive use of inclusive language into a contemporary Bible version before the publication of the NRSV. A Roman Catholic translation, the NJB was a revision of the Jerusalem Bible (JB), which itself was an English edition of the widely acclaimed French Bible de Jérusalem (BJ, 1956). When a new edition of the Bible de Jérusalem was published in 1973, the decision was made to update the JB. The NJB is a somewhat freer translation than the more literal New American Bible (NAB), another Roman Catholic version.

The preface to the NJB says that "considerable efforts have . . . been made, though not at all costs, to soften or avoid the inbuilt preference of the English language, a preference now found so offensive by some people, for the masculine; the word of the Lord concerns women and men equally." The phrase "though not at all costs" suggests that the inclusive agenda of the NJB is less comprehensive or consistent than that of the NRSV, and this is certainly the case. While generally eliminating generic "man," the NJB often retains masculine pronouns. At Leviticus 25:29, for example, the NJB reads, "If *anyone ['îsh]* sells a dwelling house . . . *he* will have the right of redemption." Though translating *'îsh* as "anyone" instead of "man," the NJB retains the resumptive pronoun "he." There are many other examples of this more moderate approach. The name "Man" is retained for the human race in Genesis 5:2: "He blessed them and gave them the name *Man*" (NRSV "humankind"). Throughout the New Testament "brother" and "brothers" are retained for Christian believers.

In a number of cases, the NJB retains the generic use of "man." It is sometimes difficult to determine whether these were merely slips or whether the translators felt that only males were intended. In Psalm 119:9, the NJB reads, "How can a young *man* [NRSV 'young people'] keep his way spotless?" Genesis 9:6 NJB reads, "He who sheds the blood of man" (NRSV "a human"). In Matthew 12:12 Jesus says, "Now a *man* [NRSV 'a human being'] is far more important than a sheep."[30]

In some cases the NJB demonstrates a greater sensitivity than the NRSV to the historical context. Where men are clearly in view, no attempt is made to eliminate masculine references. In 1 Samuel 4:10, for example, it is "every man" who flees to his tent (NRSV "everyone"), since male warriors are obviously in view.

In a review of the NJB, Bruce Metzger, then professor of New Testament at Princeton Theological Seminary (and chair of the NRSV translation committee), commends the translation because "efforts to eliminate masculine-oriented language are not carried to such limits as would result in contrived English, and all expressions imbedded in historical situations of antiquity are retained."[31]

New Century Version (NCV, 1987) and International Children's Bible (ICB, 1986)

The New Century Version is a new translation (not a revision) that according to its preface was guided by two basic premises. While seeking to be "faithful to the manuscripts in the original language," the translators also sought to "make the language clear enough for anyone to read the Bible and understand it for himself."[32] The former goal is achieved by utilizing a team of fifty "highly qualified and experienced Bible scholars and translators," many of whom had worked on versions such as the NIV, the NASB and the NKJV. Clarity of expression is achieved especially through vocabulary selection based on the *Living Word Vocabulary,* the standard used by the editors of the *World Book Encyclopedia.* Difficult words are replaced with more easily understood terms: "justify" becomes "make right," "genealogy" becomes "family history," "scribes" are "teachers of the law." Figures of speech are simplified ("the Virgin Daughter of Zion" is simply translated "the people of Jerusalem") and idiomatic expressions are clarified ("he rested with his fathers" becomes "he died").[33]

The simplified language of the NCV makes it especially appropriate for children, and a simplified edition known as the International Children's Bible (ICB, 1986) was published a year prior to the NCV itself. It was this edition, used in Focus on the Family's Odyssey Bible, that came under attack in the NIVI controversy.

While the preface to the International Children's Bible does not specifically mention the use of gender-inclusive language, the preface to other editions of the *New Century Version* include such a statement:

> *Gender language* has also been translated with a concern for clarity. To avoid the misconception that "man" and "mankind" and "he" are exclusively masculine when they are being used in a generic sense, this translation has chosen to use less ambiguous language, such as "people" and "humans" and "human beings," and has prayerfully attempted throughout to choose gender language that would accurately convey the intent of the original writers. Specifically and exclusively masculine and feminine references in the text have been retained.[34]

Like all of the gender-inclusive versions examined in this chapter, the NCV stresses that its inclusive language intends to clarify the meaning of the original authors by introducing less ambiguous language.

New American Bible (NAB; Revised New Testament, 1988; Revised Psalms, 1991)[35]

The New American Bible was originally published in 1970 as a new version (not a revision). In 1986 a revised edition of the NAB New Testament appeared that introduced, among other changes, the moderate use of inclusive language. In 1991 a revised edition of the book of Psalms appeared, also incorporating inclusive changes. Though it was a Roman Catholic version, five of the fifteen members of the revision committee were Protestants.[36]

In a section concerning discrimination in language, the preface to the revised NAB reads:

> Above all . . . the question of discrimination against women affects the largest number of people and arouses the greatest degree of interest and concern. At present there is little agreement about these problems or about the best way to deal with them. In all these areas the present translation attempts to display a sensitivity appropriate to the present state of the questions under discussion, which are not yet resolved and in regard to which it is impossible to please everyone, since intelligent and sincere participants in the debate hold mutually contradictory views.

It is significant that the translators here note that their goal is to reflect the present state of gender sensitivity, not to eliminate all generic masculine references (as the NRSV committee mandated). Faithfulness to the original text and to good English style is stressed:

> When the meaning of the Greek is inclusive of both sexes, the translation seeks to reproduce such inclusivity insofar as this is possible in normal English usage, without resort to inelegant circumlocutions or neologisms that would offend against the dignity of the language.[37]

Though generic "man" is generally eliminated, the NAB, like the NJB, "continues to use the masculine resumptive pronoun after *everyone* or *anyone,* in the traditional way, where this cannot be avoided without infidelity to the meaning."[38] Luke 8:18 NAB reads, "To *anyone* who has, more will be given, and from the one who has not, even what *he* seems to have will be taken away." Nor is the generic "man" always eliminated. Matthew 10:41 NAB reads, "Whoever receives a righteous *man* because he is righteous will receive a righteous *man's* reward" (NJB and NRSV "a righteous person").[39] Like the NJB, the NAB retains the masculine term "brothers," explaining that "there has never been any doubt that this designation includes *all* the members of the Christian community, both male and female."[40]

In short, the revised NAB (New Testament and Psalms) adopts a moderate inclusive strategy similar to the NJB. Inclusive language is introduced systematically but not comprehensively.

Revised English Bible (REB, 1989)[41]

The Revised English Bible (REB), a major revision of the New English Bible (NEB, 1961), was published in late 1989, shortly before the NRSV appeared. The NEB was a dynamic rather than a literal translation, and it had already introduced a measure of inclusive language into contexts where both men and women were intended. "Person" or "anyone" sometimes takes the place of generic "man." The REB carries this on in a more systematic manner. The preface reads:

> The use of male-oriented language, in passages of traditional versions of the Bible which evidently apply to both genders, has become a sensitive issue in recent years; the revisers have preferred more inclusive gender reference where that has been possible without compromising scholarly integrity or English style.

Like the NJB and the NAB, the REB uses less inclusive language than the NRSV, especially when it comes to masculine pronouns. In Psalm 1, for example, the resumptive masculine pronouns are retained after the initial inclusive phrase: "Happy is *the one* who does not take the counsel of the wicked . . . *he* is like a tree . . . *he* too prospers in all *he* does" (Ps 1:1-3). Notice the move back and forth between masculine pronouns and inclusive terms in Proverbs 28: "If *anyone* [NEB 'a man'] turns a deaf ear to God's law, even *his* prayer is an abomination. . . . *The person* who is rich [NEB 'the rich man'] may think *himself* wise, but the discerning poor will see through *him*" (Prov 28:9-11 REB).

The inclusive policy of the REB is the least consistent and comprehensive of the versions discussed in this chapter, and it retains the generic "man" in many contexts. For example, Job 7:17 REB reads, "What is *man,* that you make much of him?" and Matthew 4:4 REB reads, "*Man* is not to live on bread alone."[42] While commonly translating *adelphoi* as "my friends" (as the NEB already did), other familial terms such as "father(s)" and "son(s)" usually remain masculine.

In a review, Robert Bratcher criticizes the REB's inconsistent use of inclusive language, especially with regard to resumptive masculine pronouns. He writes, "I can only conclude that the elimination of exclusive language did not have a very high rating with REB revisors. Certainly the NRSV has done a more thorough job of it."[43]

Good News Bible/Today's English Version (GNB/TEV; Revised 1992)

In 1966 the American Bible Society produced The New Testament in Today's English Version (TEV). This was followed in 1976 by the publication of the Good News Bible (GNB), which included both Old and New Testaments. Partly as a result of requests from readers, a revised edition of the GNB was introduced in 1992. Among the key issues addressed were "passages in which the English style was unnecessarily masculine-oriented." In the preface to the revised GNB it is pointed out that since the first edition of the GNB,

> the built-in masculine linguistic biases of both the ancient languages and the English language caused some Bible readers to feel excluded from being addressed by the scriptural Word. . . . In practical terms it means that, where references in particular passages are to both men and women, the revision aims at language that is not exclusively male-oriented. At the same time, however, great care was taken not to distort the historical situation of the male-dominated culture of Bible times.[44]

As in the versions already discussed, the focus here is on updating the language while retaining the historical distance with the Biblical culture. While quite systematic and consistent in its use of inclusive language, the GNB (TEV) retains masculine terms when reflecting the patriarchal culture of biblical times or when the translators felt only males were intended. Reviewing the revised GNB in *The Expository Times,* editor C. S. Rodd writes,

> First let me say as forcefully as I can: the changes have been made, so far as I can discover from some judicious sampling, with great sensitivity and care. Caution appears to have controlled the work of the revisers at every point. They seem to have followed their guideline that changes are to be made only where references are clearly to both men and women.[45]

Rodd then goes on to note occasional slips in this policy. In a few places masculine terms are used when the Greek is inclusive, as in Matthew 5:15 GNB: "No one lights a lamp and puts it under a bowl; instead *he* puts it on a lampstand." In a few other cases, inclusive language is inappropriately introduced, as in Exodus 21:22-25, where the Hebrew surely envisions two *men* fighting, but the GNB introduces inclusive language. Significantly, since Rodd's review, both of these examples have been corrected in the GNB. The present edition now reads at Matthew 5:15, "Instead *it is put* on the lampstand," and Exodus 21:22 now refers to "men" who are fighting. The editors of the GNB are clearly sensitive to needed corrections and revisions (and they read their reviews).

The Message (1993)

The popular and idiomatic The Message, a New Testament translated by Eugene Peterson,[46] has appealed to many people in the 1990s as the Living Bible did in the 1970s. Its striking and evocative language strikes a chord with many pastors and teachers. Though no explicit inclusive agenda is set forth in the introduction, Peterson's paraphrastic style means that inclusive language is frequently introduced. Peterson writes,

> This version of the New Testament in a contemporary idiom keeps the language of the Message current and fresh and understandable in the same language in which we do our shopping, talk with our friends, worry about world affairs, and teach our children table manners. The goal is not to render a word-for-word conversion of Greek into English, but rather to convert the tone, the rhythm, the events, the ideas, into the way we actually think and speak.[47]

This goal of contemporary idiom translates into many inclusive renderings. For example, "Blessed is the *man* whose sin the Lord will never count against him" (Rom 4:8 NIV) is translated in The Message as "Fortunate the *person* against whom the Lord does not keep score." The Greek *adelphoi* is usually translated "friends" or "dear friends" (Phil 1:12; 4:1); "fathers" often becomes "parents" (Luke 1:17) or "ancestors" (Acts 5:30). In many passages, masculine generics are avoided by complete rewording. "*Man* does not live on bread alone" (Mt 4:4 NIV) becomes "It takes more than bread to stay alive."

Contemporary English Version (CEV, 1995)

The American Bible Society's Contemporary English Version (CEV) is another idiomatic version that has adopted a moderate use of gender-inclusive language. The introduction to the CEV begins by praising the King James Version as "the most important document in the history of the English language." While translations of the past have often sought to retain the form of the King James Version, the CEV claims instead to capture its spirit. This is accomplished by following certain principles set forth by the KJV translators, including accuracy of translation, beauty and dignity for the oral reading of Scripture, and clarity and simplicity so that the ordinary person can understand God's Word.

This focus on easily understandable language results in the adoption of gender-inclusive language:

> In everyday speech, "gender generic" or "inclusive" language is used because it sounds most natural to people today. This means that where the biblical languages require masculine nouns or pronouns when both men or women are intended, this intention must be reflected in translation, though the English *form* may be very different from that of the original.[48]

This distinction between "form" and "meaning" is a significant one. Can a translation alter the form of the Greek or Hebrew original and still be accurate? Or is form inextricably linked to meaning? This issue is discussed in chapter four.

Though not as free a translation as The Message, the CEV is more idiomatic than most other versions. This allowed the translators more freedom to reword texts in an inclusive manner. For example, where the NIV at Exodus 21:12 reads, "Anyone who strikes a man *['îsh]* and kills him shall surely be put to death," the CEV reads simply, "Death is the punishment for murder."

The CEV is probably the most inclusive of the versions examined in this chapter. While maintaining a general sensitivity to the original context, the CEV has a tendency to introduce inclusive terms when males seem to be the primary referents. For example, while the NRSV usually retains masculine references in Jesus' parables, the CEV sometimes eliminates them. In the parable of the sower (Mt 13:3-9), masculine pronouns referring to the sower disappear from the CEV, and in Matthew 7:24 CEV it is a "wise person" rather than a "wise man" (NRSV) who builds a house on a rock.

The CEV also seems to have a more egalitarian perspective than other versions. In Ephesians 5:22, for example, the CEV reads, "A wife should put her husband first, as she does the Lord," instead of the traditional rendering, "Wives, submit to your husbands" (NIV). In the qualifications for church leaders in 1 Timothy 3:1-7 and Titus 1:5-9, masculine references are removed, perhaps to allow the interpretation that women can fill these church offices.

It should be noted in this context that the CEV explicitly identifies itself as an attempt to cross cultural boundaries that other versions do not. The preface states, "In this regard, the *Contemporary English Version* should be considered a companion—the *mission* arm—of traditional translations, because it takes seriously the words of the apostle Paul that 'faith comes by *hearing*.'" Of course the essential goal of crossing cultural boundaries must always be balanced with the need for fidelity to the meaning of the original text. Whether the CEV attains this balance must be judged on a case-by-case basis.

God's Word (GW, 1995)

God's Word (GW),[49] a version produced by God's Word to the Nations Bible Society and published by World Publishing in 1995, is heralded on its cover as "today's Bible translation that says what it means." Identified as "a brand new translation of the Bible from the original languages of Hebrew, Aramaic, and Greek,"[50] the editors claim to be using neither "form-equivalent" nor "function-equivalent" translation methods; instead, they are using what they call "closest natural equivalent." This method is meant to avoid the "awkwardnesss and inaccuracy" associated with formal equivalent translations as well as "the loss of meaning and oversimplification" associated with functional equivalent translations.[51] Despite this attempt to distinguish God's Word as unique in its translation strategy, it clearly fits into the genre of "meaning-driven" rather than "form-driven" translations (for example, NIV, TEV, NJB, REB, NLT, CEV).[52] (In chap. four these two main types of Bible translation are examined in depth.)

In the preface to God's Word, a moderate gender-inclusive policy is set out. Since the Scriptures "contain many passages that apply to all people . . . *God's Word* strives to use gender-neutral language . . . so that all readers will apply these passages to themselves." For example, Psalm 1:1 is translated, "Blessed is the *person* who does not follow the advice of the wicked," not "blessed is the *man*." When the passage refers to an individual, however, the GW (like the REB) does not seek to modify masculine generic pronouns. Psalm 1 continues in verses 2 and 3: "*He* delights in the teachings of the LORD. . . . *He* is like a tree planted beside streams." While most inclusive versions introduce plural or other constructions in these cases, GW retains resumptive masculine pronouns.

In most cases GW stays consistent in its gender-inclusive policy, retaining masculine terms when the context is gender specific while introducing inclusive language when both males and females are in view. Mark 2:27 GW reads, "'The day of worship was made for *people* [NIV 'man'], not *people* for the day of worship." While serious doubts may be expressed concerning GW's consistent use of "day of worship" for "Sabbath," Jesus was certainly referring to *people* here rather than males.

An example of GW's sensitivity to context may be seen in Proverbs, where proverbial material that appears to refer to men only is kept masculine, whereas more general proverbs are made inclusive. Reflecting the fact that only men would have gone to battle, it is "a wise *man*" who "attacks a city of warriors," (Prov 21:22 GW), but it is "an arrogant, conceited *person*" who "is called a mocker" (Prov 21:24 GW).

New International Version, Inclusive Language Edition (NIVI, 1995)

As already noted in chapter one, the controversial NIVI is an inclusive version of the New International Version published in Great Britain in 1995. The rationale for the translation is described in its introduction. After pointing out that no living language ever stands still, the preface continues:

> A major challenge facing the Committee [on Bible translation, CBT] is how to respond to significant changes that are taking place within the English language with regard to gender issues. The word "man,"

> for example, is now widely understood to refer only to males, even though that is often not the intention of the corresponding Greek or Hebrew words.[53]

Citing the potential for confusion in statements like 1 Corinthians 11:28 ("A *man* ought to examine himself") and Psalm 1:1 ("Blessed is the *man*"), the preface notes that "in these and many other passages, it has become increasingly necessary to have a translation that makes it clear that women and men are both included."[54]

Although the NIVI is generally very conservative in its use of inclusive language, one statement in the preface became a lightning rod in the NIVI controversy:

> It was recognised that it was often appropriate to mute the patriarchalism of the culture of the biblical writers through gender-inclusive language when this could be done without compromising the message of the Spirit.

This statement, taken as it was to mean that the NIVI intentionally altered the original author's cultural perspective in order to be politically correct, was criticized as "regrettable and sadly misleading" in the communiqué issued following the Conference on Gender-Related Language in Scripture.[55] The last phrase, "without compromising the message of the Spirit," together with the following statement, may render the controversial sentence more innocent than it first appears:

> This involved distinguishing between those passages in which an activity was normally carried out by either males or females, and other cases where the gender of the people concerned was less precisely identified. While in cases of the former the text could be left unaltered, in cases of the latter words like "workmen" could be changed to "worker" or "craftsman" to "skilled worker."

By "muting" the patriarchalism of the biblical culture, the CBT seems to mean muting the patriarchal *sound* of the language to modern ears when the original author may have been referring to both men and women. If the "workman" in the original Greek or Hebrew context could have been a woman, then terms like "worker" are introduced. If this is what the CBT meant, the phrase "to mute the patriarchalism of the culture of the biblical writers" was indeed an unfortunate choice of words.

Though more systematic and comprehensive in its use of inclusive language than some other versions (NJB, NAB, REB), the NIVI at the same time represents a cautious and judicious use of such language. Occasional slips notwithstanding,[56] when contexts refer only to males, masculine terms are retained; when the referents would likely include women, inclusive terms are utilized.

New Living Translation (NLT, 1996)

The New Living Translation (NLT) is the long-awaited revision of the now thirty-year-old Living Bible (LB). In many respects the NLT is a completely new translation. While the LB was the work of a single translator (Kenneth Taylor), the NLT was the work of some ninety evangelical scholars from various theological backgrounds. Though many individual phrases of the LB are retained, many passages are entirely rewritten, and few verses remain untouched. While the original LB was called a paraphrase, the NLT identifies itself as a dynamic equivalent version—a "thought-for-thought" translation that seeks the closest natural equivalent in the receptor language. The goal is to have "the same impact on the modern readers as the original had on its own audience." The intentional shift from paraphrase to dynamic equivalence is evident in a verse like John 1:1. Whereas the LB reads, "Before anything else existed, there was Christ," the NLT retains both the allusion to Genesis 1:1 and the christological title "the Word": "In the beginning, the Word already existed."

The NLT gives a detailed defense of its inclusive agenda. Sensitivity both to contemporary English usage and to the biblical cultural context is stressed:

> The English language changes constantly. An obvious recent change is in the area of gender-inclusive language. This creates problems for modern translators of the ancient biblical text, which was originally written in a male-oriented culture. The translator must respect the nature of the ancient context while also accounting for the concerns of the modern audience.[57]

Like the NIVI, the NLT is generally both consistent and judicious in its use of inclusive language. When generic language is meant to refer to men and women, inclusive terms are introduced. When males are intended, exclusive terms are retained.

New International Reader's Version (NIrV, 1996)

The New International Reader's Version is a basic English version based on the New International Version. It is designed for children as well as for "older people who are learning how to read or for those who are reading the Bible for the first time."[58] While simplicity and ease of understanding are emphasized, no specific mention of gender-inclusive language is made in the preface. This would seem to be because the NIrV preface is written in very basic English for beginning readers themselves, not for parents or for those with stronger reading skills. Presumably, a complex issue such as gender-inclusive language was not deemed appropriate for such an introduction.

Conclusion

This chapter included a brief survey of various translations that use gender-inclusive language in place of masculine generic terms in Hebrew and Greek. All of these versions have certain features in common. (1) They identify their goals as staying current with contemporary English usage and seeking to retain as accurately as possible the original author's intended meaning. (2) All use a variety of techniques to achieve gender inclusion, including generic terms such as "persons" and "human beings," introducing plurals for singulars, using indefinite pronouns and switching third-, first- and second-person constructions. (3) All retain masculine references for God and traditional titles ("Son of God," "Son of Man") for Jesus Christ. Chapter three examines three of the more radical "feminist versions," all of which go well beyond this moderate approach to gender-inclusive language.

Three

THE FEMINIST VERSIONS

IN CHAPTER ONE A "GENDER-INCLUSIVE" VERSION IS DEFINED AS ONE THAT seeks to capture the inclusive sense intended by the original author. For some feminists, however, a truly inclusive version goes beyond the author's meaning, which is bound to his culture and worldview, and reinterprets the text in order to draw out its contemporary significance. Some argue that the problem is *not* that the terms "man" and "brothers" were generic in Greek but are no longer generic in English. The problem is that the very presence of masculine generic terms in Greek reflects a sexist culture of male domination. Language reflects culture, it is argued, and the fact that the Greeks used *anthrōpos* for both "man" and "person" but did not use "woman" in the same generic manner demonstrates the inferior status of women.

For proponents of what I will call the "feminist versions," it is necessary not only to reproduce in contemporary idiom the meaning of the original text but also to remove the cultural bias in order to capture the text's significance for today. For example, the NRSV (a moderate "gender-inclusive" version) translates Ephesians 5:22 in a traditional manner: "Wives, be subject to your husbands as you are to the Lord." There is little doubt that Paul's original intent here is for wives to submit or defer to the authority of their husbands. The NRSV adequately captures this sense. The Inclusive New Testament (INT), a feminist version, "translates" this passage, "You who are in committed relationships, be submissive to each other." All reference to the role of wives is eliminated, and only mutual submission is enjoined. Indeed, the traditional husband-wife relationship is omitted, with reference only to those in "committed relationships."

Although the translators of the INT would almost certainly agree that Paul's original intent was to enjoin wives to submission, they have departed from this interpretation, presumably because they considered Paul's meaning to be tied to his own cultural bias and worldview. The text, they would say, has a deeper meaning that transcends Paul's perspective, and this meaning should be brought out in translation.

Such an approach deviates from both traditional and gender-inclusive versions. While the goal of gender-inclusive, or gender-accurate, versions is to reproduce the author's intended meaning as accurately as possible, this feminist version intentionally "transculturates" (as opposed to merely "translates") the meaning in a way that makes it relevant to the feminist perception of contemporary cultural reality. Recognizing that the labels I have chosen, "gender-inclusive" and "feminist," are not wholly adequate,[1] I nevertheless use them throughout this book to distinguish between these two very different kinds of translations.

This chapter surveys three feminist versions of the Bible. There are several key differences between feminist versions and gender-inclusive versions. First, feminist versions have a much broader inclusive agenda, encompassing not only gender issues but also other kinds of exclusion. Second, feminist versions alter masculine terms and pronouns in relation to language about God and Jesus Christ. All of the versions surveyed in chapter two retain them. Third, feminist versions have less concern for the historical and cultural context of the original author and pay more attention to the need to correct the societal effects of the historical oppression of women.

An Inclusive Language Lectionary (ILL, 1983)

The first major attempt at inclusive translation was published six years before the the NRSV appeared. It was not a Bible version per se but a "lectionary"—a fixed selection of readings intended to be used in church worship services. This project began in the late 1970s when the Division of Education and Ministry (DEM) of the National Council of the Churches of Christ (NCCC) appointed a task force on biblical translation. The task force was directed to investigate how the language of the Bible presented the characteristics of God and of people. After three years of study, the task force recommended the preparation of an inclusive language lectionary, and in 1980 the twelve-member Inclusive Language Lectionary Committee was appointed. The first results of this effort were published in 1983 as *An Inclusive Language Lectionary: Readings for Year A* (ILL).[2] The lectionary's subtitle emphasizes its preliminary nature: *Prepared for Experimental and Voluntary Use in Churches*. This is "a first attempt to rethink the language of scripture as inclusive of both men and women, and as such it is provisional and experimental."[3]

The preface to the ILL begins with the statement that "all persons are equally loved, judged and accepted by God" and then notes that

> basic to a sense of equality and inclusiveness is the recognition that God by nature transcends all categories. God is more than male or female, and is more than can be described in historically and culturally limiting terms. . . . Seeking to express the truth about God and about God's inclusive love for all persons, the Division of Education and Ministry of the National Council of the Churches of Christ authorized the preparation of *An Inclusive Language Lectionary*.[4]

With this justification the committee produced a lectionary based on the RSV, but with the text revised in "those places where male-biased or otherwise inappropriately exclusive language could be modified to reflect an inclusiveness of all persons."[5] This is necessary, it is argued, because "women have been denied full humanity by a pattern of exclusion in English usage."[6] The introduction to the ILL is careful to distinguish a lectionary from a Bible version. Although reading a passage in context is crucial when studying the Bible, a lectionary intentionally lifts a passage out of its context and gives it a new place in the worship service of the church. A lectionary thus plays a special role distinct from a Bible.

Like gender-inclusive translations, the ILL uses inclusive language when the original author intended the passage to apply both to men and women, changing "man" to "persons," "brethren" to "sisters and brothers," and avoiding masculine pronouns. The ILL goes significantly farther, however, by intentionally muting the patriarchal culture of the biblical text. It introduces inclusive language even in passages where the original text depicts only males. The "watchman" in Ezekiel 33:2 becomes a "watcher" and terms like "kingdom" and "king" are replaced with "realm" and "ruler."

Other types of exclusion are also addressed in the ILL. For example, the ILL avoids the term "slave" with reference to service to God because of its implications of oppression. It even avoids the biblical symbols of light and darkness to contrast good and evil because such language "has unfortunately led some persons and groups to condemn and reject anything that is black or any dark-hued person as evil or somehow condemned by God."[7]

Most controversial is language about God and Jesus Christ. While the maleness of Jesus is taken for granted in the lectionary, it is deemphasized "so that in hearing the gospel, the church may be reminded of the inclusiveness of all humanity in the incarnation." The pronoun "he" with reference to Jesus is often replaced by the noun "Jesus." The lectionary intentionally seeks to "overcome the implication that in the incarnation Jesus' *maleness* is decisive—or even relevant—for the salvation of women and men who believe." The phrases "Son of Man," "Son" and "Son of God," are replaced, respectively, with "the Human One," "Child" and "Child of God."[8]

Since "the God worshiped by the biblical authors, and worshiped in the church, is beyond sex, as God is also beyond race or any other limiting attribute," masculine imagery related to God is downplayed. Noting various feminine biblical images for God, the lectionary adds "*and Mother*" in places where God is referred to as "Father."

Additions to the text are italicized and are enclosed in brackets. For example, Isaiah 2:3 (Advent 1, lesson 1) includes the phrase "the God of Jacob, *[Rachel, and Leah]*." Romans 15:6 (Advent 2, lesson 2) has "with one voice glorify God the Father *[and Mother]*." These brackets are intended to allow the voluntary use of such phrases without requiring it. An appendix at the end of the volume provides the justification for various types of alterations to the RSV text.

The ILL did not create a major stir among evangelicals partly because it was produced by the NCCC, which is viewed by many as a liberal organization, and partly because few evangelical churches use lectionaries in their services. While many feminists applauded the ILL, other moderate and mainstream voices responded negatively. Elizabeth Achtemeier, Old Testament scholar and professor at Union Theological Seminary, wrote: "In short, the canon of the Christian faith has been turned into a propaganda document for a special-interest group. Faith has become subservient to ideology, scholarly honesty to current notions. The authority operative here is no longer the canon, but the views of radical women's groups."[9]

John Meyendorff, professor of church history at St. Vladimir's Orthodox Seminary in Crestwood, New York, noted similarly that "any translation is always an interpretation, but this translation departs from the intention of the writers. It's a deception."[10] Bruce Metzger of Princeton Theological Seminary, who chaired the translation committee for the NRSV, adds, "The changes introduced in language relating to Deity are tantamount to rewriting the Bible. As a Christian, and as a scholar, I find this altogether unacceptable. It will divide the church, rather than work for ecumenical understanding."[11]

The New Testament and Psalms: An Inclusive Version (NTPI, 1995)[12]

The New Testament and Psalms: An Inclusive Version (NTPI) is closely related to the Inclusive Language Lectionary in that all six editors served on the committee that produced the ILL.[13] While the ILL was based on the RSV and was officially authorized by the National Council of

Churches of Christ in the U.S.A., the NTPI is an independent work that uses the NRSV as its starting point. The NTPI appears to have been produced because of discontent among feminists, many of whom felt that the NRSV had not gone far enough in its inclusive language (although this is not explicitly stated in its introduction).

In the introduction the editors justify their work on the basis of the changing state of the English language. As English uses greater specificity with regard to gender, translations must reflect that change. The inclusive agenda is clearly set out:

> This version has undertaken the effort to *replace or rephrase all gender-specific language not referring to particular historical individuals, all pejorative references to race, color, or religion, and all identifications of persons by their physical disability alone, by means of paraphrase, alternative renderings, and other acceptable means of conforming the language of the work to an inclusive idea.*[14]

The authority for this inclusive agenda is said to come from the equality of all persons before God:

> Human beings are created in the image of God—both male and female. This means that every human being, a woman or a man, a boy or a girl, is equally precious to God and should be treated accordingly by every other person. Thus, the equal value of all people, both genders, every race, religion and physical condition, is premised by these central biblical concerns.[15]

Thus the goal of the NTPI goes beyond gender inclusion to other kinds of inclusion. For example, in regard to people with disabilities, the editors argue that traditional translations that use terms like "the blind" and "the deaf" define the identity of these individuals by their infirmity. The NTPI refers to them as individuals distinct from their infirmities. Matthew 11:5, for example, speaks of "those who are blind" and "those who are deaf." Similarly, since slavery is a condition of a human being rather than a person's true identity, "his slaves" in a text like Matthew 21:34 NRSV becomes "those enslaved to him" in the NTPI. Concerned with issues of anti-Semitism, the editors also alter the term "the Jews" when it appears to carry a pejorative sense. They point out that in John's Gospel, the term is used in two ways, either neutrally of the ethnic people or negatively of those who are hostile to Jesus. Whereas in the former case the term is retained, in the latter it is replaced with terms like "the religious authorities" or simply "leaders" or "authorities."

Like the ILL, the NTPI avoids darkness as a symbol of ignorance or evil in order to avoid offending dark-skinned peoples. In place of the NRSV's "some sat in *darkness* and in gloom," the NTPI renders Psalm 107:10 as "some sat in *captivity* and in gloom." The editors justify this rendering by pointing to contextual indicators that the metaphor refers to captives emerging from the darkness of prison.[16]

While the NTPI's inclusive agenda encompasses more than gender inclusion, most alterations are in fact gender related. In many areas these alterations go well beyond the NRSV and other versions. The goal is not just to reflect accurately the author's inclusive intention but "to rephrase all gender-specific language not referring to particular historical individuals."[17] This would seem to suggest that even passages relating specifically to males or females would be rendered in a gender-inclusive manner. Only particular historical individuals (such as Abraham, Sarah, David) would retain their gender.

When the origin or generation of people is under discussion, wives' names are included with their husbands'. For example, the genealogy in Matthew lists the names of Sarah, Rebekah and Leah together with Abraham, Isaac and Jacob: "*Abraham and Sarah* were the parents of Isaac" (Mt 1:2 NTPI). Instructions for wives to be "subject" or "submissive" to their husbands become in the NTPI "be committed to" husbands (Eph 5:22; Col 3:18; Tit 2:5; 1 Pet 3:1). The editors justify this translation by pointing to 1 Corinthians 16:16, where the same verb *(hypotassō)* is translated in the NRSV as "put themselves at the service of."[18]

Masculine pronouns for the devil, Satan and angels are also eliminated in the NTPI. Matthew 12:26, which appears in the NRSV as "If Satan casts out Satan, *he* is divided against *himself;* how then will *his* kingdom stand?" becomes in the NTPI, "If Satan casts out Satan, *Satan* is divided; how then will *Satan's* dominion stand?" Evidently the awkward English was viewed as less of a problem than the masculine references.

The most significant gender-related changes are those for God and

Jesus Christ. As we have seen, the NRSV, together with all of the more moderate inclusive versions, retains masculine references for God. The NTPI, like the ILL, eliminates them. Noting the difference between grammatical gender (which all nouns have in Greek) and biological gender, the editors point out that although the words for God in Greek and Hebrew are grammatically masculine, God is not a male: "Because the church does not assume that God is a male being, or indeed, that God has a sex, in this version God is never referred to by a masculine pronoun, or by any pronoun at all."[19] This is accomplished by repeating the word "God," by using another expression for God or by changing the syntax of a sentence so as to avoid using a pronoun. The term "Father," it is argued, is a metaphor connoting family intimacy, authority, care and protection. Since the term may inappropriately convey the sense of a male being and since God is sometimes described in the Bible with imagery associated with mothers, the term "Father-Mother" is used. Male imagery related to the metaphor of God as "King" is also considered offensive, so terms like "Ruler" or "Sovereign" are adopted. In Psalm 24:7, the NRSV's "lift up your heads, O gates! . . . that the *King* of glory may come in" becomes in the NTPI "that the *Ruler* of glory may come in." For human kings, however, the title "king" is retained (for example, Ps 45:1 NTPI). Similarly the term "dominion of God" is used for the traditional "kingdom of God" (compare Mt 6:33 NTPI). Justification provided for this is not only the "androcentric and patriarchal character" of "kingdom" but also the ambiguity of the Greek *basileia,* which can mean either "reign" or "realm." While "kingdom" captures only the latter sense, "dominion" is able to express both.[20]

The translators note that some people view the title "Lord" as a male-oriented term, whereas others consider it to be gender neutral. They therefore retain it in some situations and replace it in others. When "Lord" clearly refers either to God or to Jesus, "God" and "Jesus" are often used as substitutes. The title is retained in the presence of ambiguous antecedents and in expressions like "the Lord Jesus" or "the Lord Jesus Christ."[21]

While "son" is retained with reference to Jesus' sonship to his earthly parents, in titles like "Son of God" or "Son of the Blessed One" the term

"Child" is used and masculine pronouns are avoided (Lk 1:35 NTPI). In this way, "readers are enabled to identify themselves with Jesus' *humanity*."

> If the fact that Jesus was a man, and not a woman, has no christological significance in the New Testament, then neither does the fact that Jesus was a *son* and not a *daughter*. If Jesus is identified as "Son," believers of both sexes become "sons" of God, but if Jesus is called "Child," believers of both sexes can understand themselves as "children of God."[22]

The title "Son of Man" is replaced with the designation "the Human One," since the former term "may easily be misunderstood . . . as referring to a male offspring" (see Mk 8:31 NTPI). The editors argue that it is Jesus' humanity, not his maleness, that the term is meant to convey.

While masculine pronouns are frequently retained for the historical Jesus, they are avoided with reference to either the preexistent or postcrucifixion Jesus. Justification provided for this is that "if God the 'Father' does not have a sex, then neither does the 'Son.'"[23]

Significantly, the NTPI introduction states that the editors "were committed to accelerating changes in English usage toward inclusiveness in a holistic sense."[24] Their goal, in other words, was not just to stay current with the present state of the English language but to encourage more comprehensive use of inclusive language. The more moderate inclusive versions, in contrast, attempt to reflect the way people commonly speak and understand.

The Inclusive New Testament (INT, 1994)

The Inclusive New Testament (INT) is published by Priests for Equality (PFE), an organization that describes itself as "a movement of women and men—lay, religious and clergy—that works for the full participation of women and men in the church and society."[25] The project began in 1988 when PFE received permission to use inclusive language texts developed by an organization called Dignity, San Francisco. After preparing a two-volume set of daily lectionary readings and a three-year Sunday lectionary, PFE undertook a translation of the whole New

Testament. It was published in 1994.

Without mentioning the NRSV by name, the INT indirectly criticizes its moderate use of inclusive language: "One of the biggest misconceptions about inclusive language is that it involves a mere 'spot cleaning' for male pronouns . . . tossing in a few 'sisters' wherever brothers are mentioned, or taking out all the 'hes' and 'hims.'" In fact, "the intent of inclusive language is to make the Bible accessible to everyone, particularly to those who have felt that sexist language creates an uncomfortable (and, at times, insurmountable) barrier to their devotional life."[26]

It is argued that simply editing out male pronouns will not erase the language problems because these problems lie at the level of the authors themselves. "Go back to the original *koinê* Greek where Paul writes 'in his own hand,' and there he is, still talking about subjugating women. What do we do with that? Despise Paul? Leave the church? Rewrite the Bible?"[27]

Though the translators do not explicitly say so, this last option appears to be the one that they take. This approach is justified by a decidedly existentialist approach to Scripture, "letting the language inspire the questions to which our faith will supply the answers." Quoting Elisabeth Schüssler Fiorenza, the translators argue that "inspiration—the life-giving breath and power of Sophia-Spirit—does not reside in texts: it dwells among people. She did not cease once the process of canonization ended. She is still at work today."[28]

The task of translating thus becomes "more a matter of overhauling theologies rather than tinkering with texts."[29] This represents a significant difference between the INT and the NTPI. While the two introduce many of the same inclusive changes, the justification that they advance in favor of these changes differs significantly. The NTPI editors tend to justify their inclusive language with references to alternate meanings of Greek or Hebrew words, with the fundamentally gender-neutral sense of masculine metaphors or with appeals to contemporary English usage. The translators of the INT, on the other hand, are more forthcoming in their belief that the biblical writers were at times simply wrong and that theological assertions coming from a first-century androcentric perspective must be "corrected" in light of a feminist worldview. The original sense of a passage is often subordinated to the pressing need to "overhaul theologies."

This philosophy gives the translators of the INT permission to take significant liberties with the text. Not only are masculine pronouns eliminated but also anything that smacks of exclusion. While the NTPI adds wives' names in contexts where origin or generation is the issue, the INT includes them wherever possible. The genealogy in Matthew not only lists the names of Sarah, Rebecca, Leah and Bathsheba but places them before their husbands' names: "*Sarah and Abraham* begat Isaac" (Mt 1:2 INT). Because of Abraham's prominence in the New Testament, Sarah also plays a leading role: Lazarus is carried to the "arms of *Sarah and Abraham*" in Luke 17:24 INT. Romans 4:1 INT begins, "What shall we say about *Sarah and Abraham*, our ancestors according to the flesh?" Hebrews 11:8 INT appears as "by faith, *Sarah and Abraham* obeyed when they were called."

This egalitarian perspective also appears in passages concerning role relationships in marriage. As noted above, in Ephesians 5:22 (compare Col 3:18) the INT rewrites the text to eliminate any reference to a husband's authority in the home. Indeed, references to marriage are expressed in "partner" terminology in order "to acknowledge and value non-traditional relationships."[30] Homosexual relationships are evidently in view. The first chapter of Romans is rewritten to refer not to homosexual relations per se but to sexual relations contrary to one's own nature: "And their men who would have naturally had sexual relations with women abandoned those ways and became consumed with burning passions for one another" (Rom 1:27 INT). The implication appears to be that homosexual relations are condemned only if one is acting in a promiscuous fashion or against one's "natural" inclination (whether heterosexual *or* homosexual?). Negative female images in general are also eliminated. "Babylon the great, mother of whores" (NRSV) becomes in the INT "Babylon the Great, Source of All Idolatry" (Rev 17:5).

As in the ILL and the NTPI, the translators go beyond gender distinctions when addressing issues of exclusion. Attempts are made not to identify people by their afflictions or infirmities. "The poor" become "those who are poor" (Lk 4:18; 6:20) and "a cripple" becomes someone "unable to walk" (Acts 3:2); "lepers" become "people with leprosy" (Lk 17:12). Similarly, "servant" becomes "attendant," "aide" or "employee," except with reference to service to God, where "servant" is retained (Rom 1:1). The term "slave" is retained in the context of slavery to sin (Rom 6:17), but master-slave relations are translated as "employer" and "employee" (Eph 6:5). As in the NTPI, expressions like "Temple authorities" replace the pejorative use of "the Jews" in the Gospel of John (compare Jn 8:48).

As in other feminist versions, in the INT God language comes under special revision. The translators claim that the title "Lord" (Greek *kyrios*) is offensive to many women, so words such as "Sovereign" or "Savior" are introduced in its place. In those passages where the divine name YHWH lies behind the Greek *kyrios* in the New Testament, the translators use "Our God." When the issue is one of sovereignty, titles like "Most High," "Almighty" and "Sovereign" are introduced. Wanting to deemphasize the idea of fatherhood while retaining the intimacy of Jesus' relationship with God, the translators replace "Father" with "Abba God" in Jesus' prayers (using the Aramaic term for "father," which appears in Mk 14:36). Because of its masculine imagery, the title "king" is often replaced with "ruler." Strangely, the translators replace the word "kingdom" with a neologism, "kindom," in order to stress communal ties.

Masculine titles related to Jesus are also changed. In place of "Son," the terms "Only Begotten," "Firstborn" and "God's Own" are introduced. "Son of Man" as Jesus' self-designation is usually rendered as "Chosen One" or "Promised One." Throughout the Gospels, the translators seek to emphasize Jesus' humanity over his maleness. Male pronouns are deemphasized in regard to Jesus' earthly ministry and then removed altogether in reference to the resurrected Christ. Language related to the Spirit is also altered. Finding justification in the fact that the Hebrew word for God's Spirit, *rûaḥ,* is feminine, references to the Spirit are translated using feminine pronouns (even though the Greek term *to pneuma* is neuter).

Tension arises from the fact that the translators of the INT view the patriarchal culture of the Bible as evil and oppressive.[31] As a result they cannot seem to decide whether to rewrite the text to fit their feminist agenda or to allow it to stand "in its naked and unabashed sexism."[32] For example, in 1 Corinthians 11:1-16 Paul's argument that women should cover their heads in worship becomes instead the Corinthians' own insistence on head coverings (vv. 3-9), to which Paul responds that head coverings are nothing more than a symbol of the woman's prophetic authority. At other times, however, so-called offensive verses like 1 Timothy 2:9-15 are retained: "I don't permit a woman to teach or to have authority over a man. She must remain silent. After all, Adam was formed first, then Eve" (1 Tim 2:12-13 INT). This inconsistency is addressed in the introduction:

> One of the problems we faced . . . was that in our desire to present a non-sexist message of redemption, we ran into the danger of covering over the history of oppression from which we need to be redeemed. In the scriptures, we are confronted not only by God's redeeming Word, but also by the sinful response to that Word, both in the texts and in our lives. The history of exclusion must never be covered over by making the reading comfortably inclusive.[33]

Regardless of one's opinion about the legitimacy of the changes introduced by the INT, the editors' inability to decide what their translation is intended to be represents a major inconsistency. For these translators, in some places the Bible is a record of sexism and oppression from which we must be freed; in other places it is God's message of freedom from such sexism. So how is a reader to know which is which? Which parts are the authoritative word from God? Which are the fallible (and evil) word from men (males)? This is particularly confusing when a single author—Paul in this case—is allowed to speak as an enlightened feminist in some contexts and as an oppressive sexist and misogynist in others. The translators state that "the history of exclusion must never be covered over by making the reading comfortably inclusive." But that is exactly what they do, make the Bible comfortably inclusive, in Ephesians 5:22, Colossians 3:18, 1 Corinthians 11 and a host of other passages. Such a perspective would seem to reveal a very low (or at least very inconsistent[34]) view of the authority of Scripture. In chapter four I define a legitimate translation as one that seeks to capture the author's intended meaning, not one that creates a meaning the translators want the text to have.

Conclusion

This chapter has surveyed three Bible versions that take a radical approach to gender-inclusive language. I have presented the data with only occasional evaluation and critique. Some of the individual features of these versions are considered in connection with various aspects of gender-inclusive language in chapters four through seven. Their reimaging of God language is evaluated in chapter seven.

The significant departure that these feminist versions make from the historical and cultural context of the biblical world raises important questions concerning what a Bible translation should and should not be. Are these versions legitimate translations? Or are they radical rewritings of the biblical text? Is it legitimate to alter the human author's intended meaning in order to achieve some deeper "spiritual" or existentialist meaning? Chapter four examines the issue of what constitutes a legitimate Bible translation.

Part 2

CRITIQUE

Four

WHAT IS A BIBLE TRANSLATION?

THE GOAL OF A TRANSLATOR SHOULD BE TO REPRODUCE THE MEANING OF a text that is in one language (the *source language*), as fully as possible, in another language (the *receptor language*). Herbert M. Wolf writes, "The goal of a good translation is to provide an accurate, readable rendition of the original that will capture as much of the meaning as possible."[1] To do this effectively, the translator must understand both the meaning of the original text and the manner in which the target audience is likely to comprehend that meaning in the receptor language.[2]

Is a "Literal" Translation Best?

There is a very common perception among readers of the Bible that the more "literal" a translation is, the more accurate it will be. "Literal" in this sense usually means corresponding as closely as possible to the *form* of the original Greek or Hebrew text. This is also called "word-for-word" translation because the goal is to find an equivalent word in English for each word in Greek or Hebrew.

The problem with such an approach is that no two languages correspond exactly to each other. Each uses its own unique set of words, phrases and idioms to communicate a particular meaning. Agreement in form or wording does not necessarily mean agreement in meaning. Anyone who has ever studied a second language soon learns this. For example, the Spanish phrase "¿Cómo se llama?" translated "literally" comes out something like "How do you call yourself?" Yet no one would translate the sentence this way. In good idiomatic English it *means* "What is your name?" Though not a word-for-word equivalent, this is the correct meaning.

John Beekman and John Callow provide some humorous examples of just how misleading a literal translation can be. In some languages of northern Ghana the phrase meaning "he got married" translates literally into English as "he ate a woman." In this case a literal translation retains the form but completely misses its meaning. In another West African language a literal translation of Jesus' words to James and John, "Are you able to drink the cup that I drink?" (Mk 10:38), comes across as one drunkard challenging another to a drinking contest.[3] To translate "literally" in that language would portray Jesus and his disciples as drunkards! Eugene Glassman provides an example from the Urdu language. The phrase literally translated "My throat has sat down" means "I have lost my voice."[4] (The phrase "I have lost my voice" is actually an English idiom for "I cannot speak because of some irritation in my throat.")

This difference between form and meaning is easily illustrated in the biblical text. In table 4.1 a Greek expression is followed by a "word-for-word" equivalent and the actual meaning in English (thousands of similar examples could be provided).

A quick glance at these examples confirms that English and Greek use very different constructions to express the same meaning. *Form* does not here conform with *meaning*. Though contemporary literal translations do not usually translate in such a wooden, literal manner, obscurity or mistranslation can result from an overly literal approach. Compare, for example, the renderings of 2 Corinthians 10:13 in the ASV, the NASB and the NIV.

Greek expression	"Literal" rendering	Meaning in English
en tō speirein auton	"in the to sow him"	"as he was sowing" (Mt 13:4)
eti lalountos tou Petrou	"yet of speaking of Peter"	"while Peter was speaking" (Acts 10:44)
Pater hēmōn ho en tois ouranois	"Father of us, the in the heavens"	"Our Father in heaven" (Mt 6:9)
eis to stērichthēnai hymas	"for the to be established you"	"so that you might be established" (Rom 1:11)
oute halykon glyky poiēsai hydōr	"nor salt sweet to make water"	"nor can a salt spring yield sweet water" (Jas 3:12)

Table 4.1

> ASV: But we will not glory beyond our measure, but according to the measure of the province which God apportioned to us as a measure, to reach even unto you.
> NASB: But we will not boast beyond our measure, but within the measure of the sphere which God apportioned to us as a measure, to reach even as far as you.
> NIV: We, however, will not boast beyond proper limits, but will confine our boasting to the field God has assigned to us, a field that reaches even to you.

The NASB improves on the very literal ASV by translating "glory" as "boast," "according to . . . the province" as "within . . . the sphere," and "even unto you" as "as far as you." Yet even the NASB is practically incomprehensible. What does it mean to "not boast beyond . . . measure"? What is "the measure of the sphere"? The NIV shows that this phrase means confining boasting "to the field God has assigned to us" and not boasting "beyond proper limits." Although the NASB is closer to the *form* of the original Greek,[5] the NIV more clearly represents the *meaning*. It therefore constitutes a more accurate translation. The addition of words or the alteration of Greek forms (for example, substituting a noun for verbs) in the NIV might bother some readers. It should not. This is the nature of translation. Indeed, in many cases it is the *only* way to translate accurately. Eugene Nida makes this point clear:

> Perhaps some of our confusion comes from a purely quantitative perspective. We begin to think of translation in terms of the number of corresponding words. Such a mechanical view of things—straining at gnats and swallowing camels—is practically useless. It really should make no difference to us whether a translation of a term in Greek consists of one or five words; or whether, on the other hand, we render an entire phrase in Greek by a single word in an aboriginal language—a thing which often does occur. We are not concerned primarily with counting words and parts of words. *Our objective must be in finding the closest equivalence in meaning.*[6]

The quest for "literalness," though noble in principle, often results in poor translation. In John 2:4 Jesus' addressing his mother as "woman" (NKJV, NASB, NRSV), though literal, sounds rude to English ears. Unless Jesus intended to express disrespect for his mother, this translation is poor, since it miscommunicates to most readers. The NIV's "dear woman" mutes the sense of disrespect and so captures the sense of the original better. The CEV's "mother" is also appropriate, since it creates in the mind of the modern reader the same impression that the Greek "woman" did for first-century readers.

Similar examples could be multiplied. In the NKJV the Galatian believers have received the Spirit by the "hearing of faith," an incomprehensible English phrase (Gal 3:2, 5). The NRSV changes the nouns "faith" and "hearing" to a participle and a verb, respectively, for the more accurate rendering "by believing what you heard" (compare NIV).

English versions seek to stay literal by consistently translating a particular Greek or Hebrew grammatical form with the same English construction. One of the most problematic Greek forms is the genitive case. Beginning Greek students are often taught that the genitive case in Greek is the case of possession and may be translated with the English preposition "of." For example, in the Greek phrase *ho logos tou theou* ("the Word of God") the Greek genitive *tou theou* is translated "of God." The error occurs, however, when Greek students start thinking that the English word "of" represents a "literal" translation of the Greek genitive case. In reality, the Greek genitive has a much wider range of senses. Compare some examples of genitives (in italics below) in the NKJV and the NIV:

NKJV	**NIV**
you were sealed with the Holy Spirit *of promise* (Eph 1:13)	you were marked in him with a seal, the promised Holy Spirit (Eph 1:13)
that the God of our Lord Jesus Christ, the Father *of glory* . . . that you may know what is the hope *of His calling* (Eph 1:17-18)	I keep asking that the God of our Lord Jesus Christ, the *glorious* Father . . . in order that you may know the hope *to which he has called you* (Eph 1:17-18)
upholding all things by the word of *His power* (Heb 1:3)	sustaining all things by *his powerful* word (Heb 1:3)

In many instances the word "of" is a perfectly acceptable translation of the Greek genitive case. But careful examination confirms that in these examples the retention of the word "of" in the NKJV (compare NASB) results in an obscure or misleading translation. What, for example, does "the Holy Spirit of promise" mean? Here it means the Holy Spirit *who was promised,* or, as the NIV has it, "the promised Holy Spirit." We have here a descriptive genitive.[7] The NKJV phrase "Father of glory" may suggest that God in some sense begets glory. This is probably an attributive genitive, meaning "the glorious Father" (so NIV). The NKJV's "hope of His calling" seems to suggest that believers hope they will be called. But we are already called! The genitive here is probably a genitive of production,[8] "the hope produced by his calling." In the fourth example, the NKJV's "word of his power" is almost nonsensical (word that his power possesses?). This is another descriptive genitive, "powerful word." While in many respects the NKJV is a fine translation, its consistent retention of the preposition "of" for the genitive case represents a misguided attempt at literalism. This is because the English form "of" does not correspond exactly with the meaning of the Greek genitive.[9]

Commenting on this kind of literal approach, Norman Mundhenk points out:

A translator who gives the wrong meaning in this way has fallen into

> a very common trap: he thinks that as long as he keeps the "same" words he cannot be too far wrong with the meaning. Instead, what he has done is not translation at all—he has put a new, and therefore wrong message into the Bible. Whenever this happens, the problem has become very serious indeed.[10]

An overly literal approach can contribute to a misunderstanding of the biblical text, as the preceding examples show. Such misunderstandings are most obvious in the case of idioms. The Hebrew phrase translated literally to "cover his feet" in 1 Samuel 24:3 (ASV, KJV) actually means to "relieve himself" (for example, RSV, NASB, NIV, NKJV). Of course the English here is itself a euphemism; in another language the phrase would have to be translated differently. In this case a literal "translation" would be a mistranslation, since a normal English reader could not comprehend the sense from the Hebrew idiom.

In reality all Bible versions, to one degree or another, use both literal and idiomatic language. Even the most literal translations must at times abandon a word-for-word policy to accurately communicate meaning. In the example above both the NKJV and NASB use "relieve himself" (although the ASV and the KJV retain the literal "cover his feet"). Similarly, in John 2:4, Jesus' words in Greek read literally, "What is to you and to me?" The NASB has "what do I have to do with you?" and the NKJV, "what does your concern have to do with Me?" The Hebrew idiom "speak to the heart" (Is 40:2) in the NASB is "speak kindly" and in the NKJV is "speak comfort." The Hebrew phrase "an ox of the stall" (Prov 15:17), referring to an animal being fattened for slaughter, is rendered "fattened ox" in the NASB.[11] The issue is not whether a translation sometimes introduces idiomatic language (all do), but to what extent *meaning* is allowed to take precedence over *form*.

Formal Equivalence and Dynamic Equivalence

Corresponding to this distinction between form and meaning are two basic philosophies of translation. Formal equivalence ("literal" or "word-for-word" equivalence) seeks to stay as close as possible to the *form* of the original Greek or Hebrew. "Dynamic equivalence" (also called "idiomatic" and more recently "functional" equivalence) focuses first and foremost on the *meaning* of a text. From what has been said above, it should be clear that the primary goal of a good translation must always be meaning rather than form. Indeed, though we speak of a "translation debate" between these two methodologies, from the perspective of linguists and international Bible translators the debate was over long ago. The technical writings and research emerging from major international translation organizations like Wycliffe Bible Translators and the United Bible Society view it as a given that dynamic or functional equivalence is the only legitimate method of true translation. Precise formal equivalence is little more than imitation of a source language's form, not true translation into a receptor language. Evangelical scholar D. A. Carson noted in 1987 that "as far as those who struggle with biblical translation are concerned, dynamic equivalence has won the day—and rightly so."[12]

This is not to suggest that formal equivalence versions have no place in Bible study. They are very useful tools (especially for those with only a basic knowledge of the original languages), since they give the reader a view of the formal structure of the Hebrew or Greek. They can be helpful in (1) identifying the structure of the original text, (2) identifying Hebrew or Greek idioms and formal patterns of language (some of which have cultural significance), (3) doing word studies, (4) identifying potential ambiguities in a text and (5) tracing formal verbal allusions (which might be obscured by idiomatic renderings). Literal versions are therefore tools (rather than translations) that can provide students with a check on the idiomatic renderings of other versions. Every serious student of the Word should own and use them. I encourage all my students to use a variety of Bible versions and to compare formal and functional translations. In this way they can see what the Greek or Hebrew *says* (its basic wording and grammatical structure) as well as what it *means*. The error, as we have seen above, is assuming that the form is the meaning and that "literal" means "accurate."

I am not suggesting that the form of the Hebrew or Greek should be disregarded. Retaining formal characteristics sometimes helps clarify the meaning of the text (but note that meaning still takes precedence). Greek word order, for example, is very flexible, and words can appear in almost any position in a sentence for emphasis.[13] Sometimes retaining this word order in translation brings out the sense of the original more clearly. The Greek word order in Luke 1:42, for example, is "blessed are you among women." Though English normally puts the subject first ("you are blessed among women"), most translations retain the Greek order to retain the poetic rhythm and the emphasis on "blessed" (for example, KJV, NIV, RSV).

Similarly, in John 1:4 the Greek word order is "in him life was." The Greek emphasis on "in him" is retained in most English translations: "In him was life" (KJV, NIV, RSV and others). The order of "was" and "life" had to be reversed, however, to make readable English, illustrating the fact that *form must give way to meaning*. In 1 Corinthians 2:7 ("for Christ did not send me to baptize") the word "not" appears first in the Greek for emphasis. It would be impossible to place the word first in English and retain the meaning. One could indicate emphasis through italicization, "for Christ did *not* send me to baptize," but this also illustrates our principle that a different English form is required to capture the Greek meaning.

In some cases it can be helpful to reflect certain formal characteristics of the Greek or Hebrew, but good translation never sacrifices meaning for form. Some Bible translators have adopted the slogan "as literal as possible, as idiomatic as necessary." *Inasmuch as there is no loss of meaning,* a translation should correspond as closely as possible to the form of the Greek or Hebrew. As soon as formal equivalence results in a loss of meaning, however, the translator must find a more appropriate word or phrase in the receptor language corresponding to the *meaning* of the original language. Eugene Glassman sums up this point well:

> Inherent in the definition of both *translate* and *interpret* . . . is the concept that regardless of the *form* used, what is carried across from one language to another is the *meaning* of the original writer or speaker. If that meaning is lost—whether by addition, omission or distortion—then neither translation nor interpretation takes place.[14]

The main problem with the "as literal as possible" approach is that translators, especially those who are very familiar with the original

Greek and Hebrew, often assume that their literal translation is perfectly clear to the common reader, although it represents very awkward or obscure English. A good illustration of this can be seen in the retention of the word "of" for the genitive case in the examples cited above. Those of us who spend our lives studying Greek and Hebrew and literal Bible translations come to read, think and speak in biblical idiom. We need to remember that, in many cases, these words and expressions do not represent real (clear, readable, contemporary) English. After translating a passage, a translator should stop and ask, "Is this how the biblical writer would have said this if he were writing in contemporary English?" The policy "as literal as possible, as idiomatic as necessary" could be sharpened to "as idiomatic as necessary to achieve clear and readable English."

Form, Meaning and the Inclusive Language Debate

The priority of meaning over form has great importance for the gender-inclusive language debate. Opponents of inclusive language sometimes take an overly literal approach, insisting on the retention of forms in order to maintain "accuracy" in translation. Wayne Grudem, for example, criticizes the NIVI for substituting English plural forms for Greek or Hebrew singulars, thereby changing "what the Bible said for what it did not say." He writes, "I strongly disagree with this procedure. The evangelical doctrine of Scripture is that every word of the original is exactly what God wanted it to be."[15]

While I would agree that "every word of the original is exactly what God wanted it to be," we are not talking about original texts here but about English translations of those texts. And every Bible translation involves word substitution, that is, substituting Greek and Hebrew words and phrases for English ones. Every translation must change what is *said* (in Hebrew and Greek) to capture what is *meant.* If changing a singular to a plural captures the sense of the original, then it represents an accurate translation.

The guidelines established at the Conference on Gender-Related Language in Scripture demonstrate this same confusion of form and meaning. Guideline A.2 mandates that "person and number should be retained in translation." Yet in many cases this is impossible. For example, the Hebrew term for "heaven(s)" *(shāmayim)* is actually a dual form and so "literally" should be translated "two heavens." Yet no one would consider translating Genesis 1:1 as "in the beginning God created 'the two heavens' and the earth." *'Elōhîm,* the Hebrew word for "God," is actually plural in form. Although the term sometimes carries the plural sense "gods" (for example, Ex 18:11; 20:3), in most cases it must be translated with the singular "God." Genesis 1:1 would seem heretical if the plural were retained: "In the beginning *the gods* created the heavens and the earth."

The same phenomenon occurs in the New Testament, where certain Greek words, like those for "Sabbath" and "heaven," often appear in plural forms. Retaining the plural in English translation would have Jesus proclaiming that "the kingdom of *heavens* is at hand" (Mt 3:2) and that he is the "Lord of the *Sabbaths*" (Mk 2:7).[16] Similarly, neuter plural nouns in Greek often take singular verbs. A "literal" translation of 1 John 3:10 would read "the children of God *is* manifested." Collective nouns and compound subjects can also take singular verbs in Greek. All three of these constructions appear in a striking passage in James 5:2-3, where a "literal" translation would read: "Your riches [collective noun] *has rotted* and your garments [neuter plural] *has* become moth-eaten, your gold and silver [compound subject] *has rusted*." This English monstrosity results from retaining Greek number in translation.

Grammatical Versus Biological Gender

The inability to retain form is also significant with reference to gender itself. This is because languages like Greek and Hebrew have both grammatical gender, which is really just a formal characteristic of words, and biological gender, which refers to sexual identity. While all Hebrew and Greek nouns have grammatical gender (masculine or feminine in Hebrew; masculine, feminine or neuter in Greek), only rarely do they have biological gender. For Greek terms like *anēr* ("man" or "husband") and *gynē* ("woman" or "wife"), biological gender coincides with grammatical gender. In other cases, grammatical and biological gender are at odds.[17] The masculine Greek noun *diakonos* ("deacon," "minister" or "servant") is used to refer to the woman Phoebe in Romans 16:1. The Hebrew term for "preacher" *(qōhelet)* applied to Solomon in Ecclesiastes 1:1 is feminine, but no one would translate "the preacher . . . she said." The Greek term for "child," *teknon,* is neuter, yet we do not use the word "it" to refer to children. Similarly, the Greek word for the Holy Spirit, *to pneuma,* is neuter. But because the Spirit is a person, we use "he," not "it."[18] The Hebrew terms for "spirit" *(rûaḥ)* and "soul" *(nep̄esh)* are feminine, but no one would suggest that the immaterial or spiritual part of human beings is essentially feminine.

In all these cases the form indicates grammatical rather than biological gender, and pronouns associated with this form must often be altered in English translation to capture the meaning of the Greek or Hebrew. Similarly, when the term "man" is used to mean "humanity" or "human being," its masculine form is obviously a grammatical feature rather than a sexual indicator. Not all persons are biologically male.

Those who produced the gender guidelines would probably argue that examples like these are precisely the "unusual cases" allowed for by the principle. But the point remains the same: The guideline "person and number should be retained in translation" is flawed because it mandates a particular form without considering the meaning in context. A sound principle should state something like this: *If retaining the form found in the original source language (whether person, number, gender, tense, voice, mood and so on) results in any loss of meaning in the receptor language, then that form should be altered to capture the sense intended by the original author.*

Thus to mandate a particular form without consideration of the meaning is inherently flawed. If a plural form in English conveys accurately the sense of a singular form in Greek or Hebrew, then that plural represents an accurate translation. The inverse is also true. If a plural form in English misconveys the sense of a plural form in Greek or Hebrew, then that English rendering, though formally equivalent, represents a mistranslation of the original. Mandating forms without consideration of meaning is always dangerous. This topic is addressed at greater length in chapter five.

The literalist argument of mandating form can actually be turned on its head and used against traditional translations. I surveyed various Bible versions and found that in hundreds of cases, English versions add the words "man" or "men" where there is no corresponding Greek or Hebrew term. For example, in the NIV there are 1,357 verses where the English words "man" or "men" appear with no corresponding term in the Greek or Hebrew text.[19] Similarly, in the RSV there are 1,032 such verses and in the NASB, 917. The NRSV is by far the most "accurate" in this regard, since there are only 344 verses where English "man" or "men" appear with no equivalent word in Greek or Hebrew. Those who are so concerned about retaining the form of the original Greek or Hebrew should be outraged at such "additions" to God's Word. Of course in reality there is no problem at all with adding the English terms "man" or "men" *when these words accurately convey the sense of the original Greek or Hebrew*. It is the meaning rather than the form that must be retained in translation.

Every Translation Is an Interpretation

The importance of capturing the meaning instead of merely reproducing the form points to another important principle related to Bible translation: Every translation is an interpretation. When confronted with an original text, the translator must interpret the meaning of the original text before he or she can translate the meaning of it into another language.

Some literal translations insist that the translator intentionally avoid interpreting the text being translated. The surface structure of the text is retained in order to encourage the reader to interpret the text.[20] This, however, is a misunderstanding of the translation process. If the translator, through sound exegesis, has determined the most likely meaning of the text, why should this meaning be withheld from the reader? Intentional ambiguity invites misinterpretation. A translator should leave the meaning ambiguous only when (1) the original author was intentionally ambiguous or (2) the meaning of a text is so obscure that any interpretation is highly speculative. In the latter case, marginal notes are usually necessary to alert readers to the difficulty in arriving at a solution.

The fact that all translation is interpretation places an enormous responsibility on the translator, whose goal is to encourage the average reader to comprehend texts accurately. This is admittedly a difficult and painstaking task. If the translator interprets too little, the Bible will remain a closed book for most readers. Interpreting too much, on the other hand, risks imposing the interpreter's bias on the biblical text. The goal must always be to determine the sense intended by the original author and then to express that sense in language the common reader can readily understand. This brings up two important dimensions of the translation process—the world of the original author and the world of the contemporary reader.

Seeking the Author's Intended Meaning

Every piece of literature, whether ancient or modern, was produced in a particular historical context, or life setting. Understanding this context is essential for proper interpretation. It is impossible, for example, to comprehend the full significance of Lincoln's Gettysburg Address without understanding something of the momentous events of the American Civil War and Lincoln's role in that war. It is no different with the books of the Bible. Each biblical document must be understood within its own historical, cultural and religious context. Each of the letters of Paul, for example, was written to a particular church or individual at a particular point in Paul's ministry to address particular concerns or questions in that church. To understand Paul's writings, the reader must enter as fully as possible into the thought world of Paul and his readers.

For this reason the first goal of Bible study must always be exegesis, which means seeking to determine as accurately as possible the author's intended meaning. What did this text presumably mean to the original author and to the original readers? This question is answered by analyzing the language of the text in its own historical and literary context. This is not an easy task, since the world we live in differs from the world of the original readers (historically, culturally, socially, politically, geographically). There is always a danger of reading the text through our own cultural eyes and so misunderstanding the author's original meaning.

For example, a modern reader might assume that sanitation is the issue when the Pharisees accuse Jesus' disciples of eating with unwashed hands (Mt 15:2), or that the "whitewashed tombs" of Matthew 23:27 are attempts at concealment (since to whitewash often means "to conceal" or "gloss over" in English). In fact the issue in Matthew 15 is ceremonial uncleanness, and tombs were painted white in Palestine to reveal their location so as to avoid ceremonial defilement by those who might accidentally touch them. Reading the Bible with understanding is not simply drawing out a first impression and then deciding it is the most natural and therefore the correct reading of the text. It is entering the very different world of the text and hearing a message that may be alien to our twentieth- (or twenty-first-) century ears.

If the first step of Bible study is to understand the author's intended meaning in the author's own cultural context, then the primary goal of translation must be to reproduce that meaning as clearly as possible for the contemporary reader. The translator must seek to enable the modern reader to hear the text as people living in the first century heard it. This means retaining the historical and cultural aspects of the original as much as possible while translating the language into contemporary idiom.

If obscurity and poor English are the failings of a literal translation, freer translations sometimes err by moving too far from the author's cultural context or by adding meaning that was not in the mind of the original author. The popular Living Bible (LB) at times loses the cultural setting in its attempt to use contemporary language. Translating "lamps" as "flashlights" (Ps 119:105 LB), a "holy kiss" as "handshakes" (1 Pet 5:14 LB), and "kissed" as "embraced him in friendly fashion" (Mt 26:49 LB) all move away from the historical context and hence away from the author's intended meaning.

There is also the danger of adding meaning not present in the original. In 1 Kings 20:11, for example, we find in the Living Bible, "Don't count your chickens before they hatch!" But the Hebrew proverb in this passage is "One who puts on his armor should not boast like one who takes it off" (NIV). We can be sure that King Ahab did not have chickens in mind when he spoke these words! As the TEV puts it, "A real soldier does his bragging after a battle, not before it." Even this, however, is not quite accurate. Although it conveys the general truth of the proverb more clearly, it loses the image of taking off armor. I prefer the NIV rendering (compare NRSV, NKJV), since proverbs, by their very nature, are meant to be understood through reflecting on the analogy drawn. Reflection on the proverb and an examination of the context makes its meaning clear. Perhaps the best translation would be something like "one should not boast while putting on armor before a battle but while taking it off afterward!" This retains the imagery and also makes the meaning clear. In any case, the Living Bible translation is inaccurate not because it is idiomatic but because it goes beyond the author's intended meaning.

The need for translators to capture the author's meaning has great significance for the gender-inclusive language debate. It is beyond dispute that the cultural contexts in which the Bible was produced (both Old and New Testaments) was patriarchal. Men generally took leadership roles in society, in the home and in religious life. If the goal of Bible translation is to retain the author's original meaning in its own cultural context, then it is important to retain patriarchal references in Bible translation.

Feminist versions (such as those surveyed in chap. three) often err seriously in this regard. In attempting to project the egalitarianism that they believe should characterize the church today, they have a tendency to distort the patriarchalism of the biblical period. When the NTPI begins Matthew's genealogy with "*Abraham and Sarah* were the parents of Isaac" (Mt 1:2), it ignores the Jewish culture of Matthew's day, where genealogical records were patriarchal, listing the male heads of the household. The INT strays even farther from the cultural context by placing Sarah's name first: "Sarah and Abraham begot Isaac." By following the Greek text and listing only the male names, translators of more accurate versions are not suggesting that Sarah was of no significance or that women are inferior to men, but only that in the cultural and historical context in which Matthew was written, it was through the male head of the household that the genealogy was traced.

It is important to maintain this cultural distance in order to accurately reflect the author's intent. By including Sarah, Rebekah and Leah, these versions actually obscure the very real significance of Matthew's inclusion of other women: Tamar, Rahab, Ruth and Bathsheba.

Similarly, when rendering passages that address male leadership in the home, these two translations stray from the author's original intent. Whereas the NRSV renders Ephesians 5:22, "Wives, be subject to your husbands as you are to the Lord," the INT translates, "Wives, be committed to your husbands as you are to Christ." As we have seen, the NTPI goes even farther: "Those of you who are in committed relationships should yield to each other as if to Christ."

The question of whether Paul's commands here are meant to be universal mandates for the church of all time or are culturally specific to his first-century context is an important one. Although it is legitimate to debate the contemporary significance of these commands, the goal of Bible translation should be to capture the author's intended meaning in its own cultural context. It seems impossible to deny that in Ephesians 5, Paul's intention is to exhort wives to submit (or defer) to the authority of their husbands. Our Bible translations should reflect this command, together with all of its historical and cultural "baggage." Translations should reflect the meaning that the author intended, not the contemporary significance that Christians believe the text has for today.

We can illustrate this principle with another example. Most churches today do not require women to cover their heads during worship, despite Paul's mandate to do just that in 1 Corinthians 11. Most believe that Paul's command here is culturally specific, relating only to its first-century cultural context. Though these believers do not directly obey this command, they draw a universal principle from the passage relating to respect or submission (depending on the interpretation that is taken). Yet it would be wholly inappropriate to translate this passage in a way that eliminates any reference to head coverings. To do so would be to miss Paul's intended meaning in its cultural context. We must translate in a way that reflects the author's own context. Then through careful examination of cultural and historical factors, we must determine which aspects of these commands are directly applicable today and which must be applied at the level of principle.[21]

Who Is the Reader?

If the historical and cultural world of the original author represents one side of the translation process, the world of the reader represents the other. This brings up an important question: *Who is the reader?* Literal translations cater especially to the educated Christian public, using words and phrases that are incomprehensible to the wider public. I personally have few problems understanding the language of the KJV, the NASB or the NKJV, since I have spent most of my life immersed in their language and idiom. I think and speak in "Christianese." Yet the Bible was written for everyone. There is significant precedent for translation that is understandable to common people.

Jerome's Vulgate was so called because it was written in the "vulgar" (common) language of the people. William Tyndale is reported to have said to an opponent that "if God spare me I will one day make the boy that drives the plough in England to know more of Scripture than the pope himself!"[22] John Wycliffe was criticized by his opponents for having translated the Scripture so that it became "more open to the laity, and women who could read, than it used to be to the most learned of the clergy."[23] The King James translators themselves defended using the language of the common people. The preface to the original KJV reads:

> Translation it is that openeth the window, to let in the light; that breaketh the shell that we may eat the kernel; that putteth aside the curtain, that we may look into the most holy place; that removeth the cover of the well, that we may come by the water; even as Jacob rolled away the stone from the mouth of the well, by which means the flocks of Laban were watered. Indeed without translation into the vulgar [common] tongue, the unlearned are but like children at Jacob's well without a bucket or something to draw with.[24]

This idea of rendering God's Word into the language of the people has its primary precedent in the Bible itself. It was once believed that the language of the New Testament was a unique kind of Hebraic Greek or even a "Holy Ghost language" created especially for biblical revelation. Study of Egyptian papyri over the past one hundred years has demonstrated conclusively that New Testament Greek is actually an example of Koine (or "common") Greek, the everyday language of the people that spread throughout the Mediterranean region following the conquests of Alexander the Great (late fourth century B.C.).[25] There is nothing archaic, solemn or mystical about the kind of language used by the inspired authors of the New Testament. It is the Greek of the street. This says a great deal about the nature of God's revelation. Just as God took on the form of common humanity when he revealed himself as the living Word, so his written Word was revealed in language that the person on the street could understand. This fact alone should convince us to translate Scripture into contemporary, idiomatic English—not an imitation English that artificially mimics patterns and structures of either Greek or Hebrew.

The fact that the "average reader" plays a crucial role in the translation process has significance for the gender-inclusive language debate. Even if translators are perfectly comfortable with masculine generic terms like "man" and "he," they must consider how these terms will be heard by their readers. A translation should seek to give the contemporary reader the same impressions that the original readers presumably had. Take, for example, the Greek plural noun *adelphoi*, usually translated "brothers." We may assume from the context of Paul's letters that his readers heard this address with a full sense of inclusion, referring to both male and female believers.[26] If, when hearing the English translation "brothers," contemporary readers perceive them to be male believers, then this English term is a poor translation. This is because it does not communicate to the common reader the same sense that Paul's readers had when they heard it. It matters little at this point whether the translator considers "brothers" to be an acceptable generic term or whether the term has a long and noble history in the English language. If many or most contemporary readers misunderstand its sense, it represents a poor translation.

The Meaning of Words

Since words make up the basic building blocks of any language, it is worthwhile to examine briefly the nature of words and their meanings.

The study of word meanings, or "lexical semantics," has received a great deal of attention from biblical scholars recently.[27] The findings of these scholars will prove particularly significant to the discussion of gender-inclusive language in the following chapters.

Words generally have a range of "senses" (a "semantic range"). Some translations stay as literal as possible by translating a Hebrew or Greek word or phrase, inasmuch as possible, with the same English word or phrase each time it occurs. From the perspective of lexical semantics, this can create serious difficulties. One of the most common mistakes made in the analysis of biblical words is assuming that words carry a single all-encompassing meaning. This is sometimes identified as the "literal" or "root" meaning of a term. This meaning is then assumed to be present in every use of that word.

In reality, most words in every language can be used in a variety of *senses*. A dictionary definition of the adjective "fresh"[28] might look something like this:

1. New to one's experience; not encountered before: He came up with a fresh idea.

2. Novel, different: That is a fresh approach to the problem.

3. Recently made, produced or harvested; not stale or spoiled: I love fresh bread.

4. Not preserved, as by canning, smoking or freezing: Is that fresh fruit or canned?

5. Not saline or salty: That is a freshwater lake.

6. Not yet used or soiled; clean: I need fresh linen in my room.

7. Additional, new: Fresh evidence emerged late in the trial.

8. Having the glowing, unspoiled appearance of youth: She has a fresh face.

9. Revived or reinvigorated, refreshed: The general desperately needed fresh troops.

10. Fairly strong, brisk: That's a fresh wind!

11. Bold and saucy, impudent: That man is fresh!

Notice that this word (actually called a "lexeme," that is, a lexical unit) can have a variety of senses depending on the context. Another way of approaching this is to say that the lexeme "fresh" has various *referents*—

objects or concepts in the real world—to which it may point or refer.

Is there one "root meaning" that connects all these senses? Someone might suggest the idea of "newness," but this would not apply at all to senses 5, 10 or 11, and would not help very much to explain senses 4, 6 or 8 ("fresh linen" could be old but clean; "fresh fruit" need not be newly picked; a youthful appearance can hardly be called "new"). Though it is certainly true that many of these senses share some features in common, each represents a distinct "sense" of the same lexeme.

The range of senses that a word can carry are called that word's *semantic range.* (Semantics is the study of meaning, so this means the range of potential meaning that a lexeme can carry.) The semantic range of the adjective "fresh" would include all of the senses above (as well as some I have not noted).

The idea that words have a range of senses is of course very basic English. Unfortunately it has often been ignored in the study of the biblical languages. Take, for example, the Greek word *sarx.* It is often said that the "literal" meaning of *sarx* is "flesh." In one sense this is true, if "literal" means nonfigurative. The Greek term originally referred to soft body tissue covering the bones. Yet in the New Testament, the term is used with a wide range of senses. Compare the following verses from the NASB:

And the rest were killed with the sword . . . and all the birds were filled with their flesh *[sarx].* (Rev 19:21)	*Sarx* here means "soft body tissue," "flesh
For no one ever hated his own flesh *[sarx],* but nourishes and cherishes it. (Eph 5:29)	*Sarx* here means "physical body."
And unless those days had been cut short, no life *[sarx]* would have been saved. (Mt 24:22)	*Sarx* here means "life" or perhaps "individual persons."
And the Word became flesh *[sarx],* and dwelt among us. (Jn 1:14)	*Sarx* here means "a human being."
If somehow I might move to jealousy my fellow countrymen *[sarx].* (Rom 11:14)	*Sarx* here means "family," "race," "nation" or "countrymen."
It is not children of the flesh *[sarx]* who are children of God. (Rom 9:8)	*Sarx* here means natural or physical descent.
In the days of His flesh *[sarx],* He offered up both prayers . . . (Heb 5:7)	*Sarx* here means "earthly life" or "lifespan."
The spirit is willing, but the flesh *[sarx]*	*Sarx* here means something like "limited

is weak. (Mt 26:41)	human ability" or "human will."
For if you are living according to the flesh *[sarx]*, you must die. (Rom 8:13)	*Sarx* here means something like "sinful nature" or "sinful sphere of existence."
These indulged in gross immorality and went after strange flesh *[sarx]*. (Jude 1:7)	*Sarx* here means sexual behavior or proclivity; "going after strange sarx" is practicing deviant sexual behavior.

These various senses of the Greek lexeme *sarx* make up part of its first-century semantic range. The word may carry any of these senses, depending on the context in which it is used.

The English lexeme "flesh," on the other hand, in everyday English refers almost exclusively to soft body tissue covering the bones or to the skin. People do not normally refer to human beings as "flesh" or to their own race as their own "flesh" or to deviant sexual behavior as "going after strange flesh." Nor is "flesh" as "sinful nature" common, except in Christian circles.[29] To argue that *sarx* literally means "flesh" and must always be translated as "flesh" is to confuse the various senses of a word in one language (*sarx* in Greek) with the senses of a different word in a different language ("flesh" in English). Words do not generally have a single "root" (essential, true) meaning, but a range of potential senses. Furthermore, the various senses of words in different languages seldom overlap exactly.

Context determines which sense the author intended. It should be obvious from the preceding English and Greek examples that the *context* in which a word is used determines which sense the author intended. This does not suggest that a word can mean anything at all. The semantic range (the various ways the word is used in the contemporary language) limits the potential senses. But within that semantic range, context determines which sense is intended.

The NASB, attempting to follow a "literal" philosophy, translates *sarx* as "flesh" in all of the examples above except Matthew 24:22 and Romans 11:14, where it uses "life" and "countrymen" respectively. Even in these verses, however, a marginal note tells the reader that the word literally means "flesh." Such a note (though perhaps helpful for a word study) opens the way for misunderstanding. If the term "literal" here means "nonfigurative," then the note is simply telling the reader that this same lexeme can sometimes appear with the sense "soft body tissue." This does little to illuminate its meaning in this context. If "literal," on the other hand, means "actual" or "essential" meaning, then the note is simply wrong, demonstrating a misunderstanding of lexical semantics. The "actual" meaning of a word is its meaning in context. In Revelation 19:21 *sarx* means "soft body tissue" ("flesh"), but in John 1:14 it means "a human being." In Romans 8:13 it means "sinful nature." It is linguistic nonsense to speak of a "literal" or "essential" meaning apart from its context because words carry meaning *only* in context. Returning to our English example, this is like saying that the word "fresh" literally means "new," and so a "freshwater lake" is a lake with new water in it. This is obviously absurd. The word "fresh" means whatever sense it carries in the particular context in which it is used.

This point has important implications for Bible translation. There is no reason for always using one particular English word to translate a particular Greek or Hebrew word, especially if another word captures the sense of the Greek or Hebrew word better in a particular context.[30] Since every Greek word has a semantic range and that range of senses seldom overlaps exactly with any single English word, various English words *must be used* to translate accurately. To translate *sarx* as "flesh" in every case is to impose the wrong sense of the word (and hence the wrong meaning) on a particular context. That is mistranslation.

This point also has significance for the inclusive language debate. The English word "man" and the Greek word *anthrōpos* are two different lexemes in two different languages with two different semantic ranges. To say that the Greek word *anthrōpos* means "man" and thus should be translated "man" is both simplistic and, in some contexts, inaccurate. *Anthrōpos* is a Greek word with its own range of senses, which may or may not overlap in a particular context with the semantic range of the English "man." The only way to determine for sure is to examine the semantic range of *anthrōpos* in its contemporary setting (first-century Koine Greek), and the semantic range of "man" in its contemporary setting (in this case, late-twentieth-century American English). If in a particular context *anthrōpos* carries the clear sense "human beings" but the English term "man" does not, then other English terms must be used. In some cases the semantic ranges of the two terms simply do not overlap in particular contexts. (This issue is addressed in chapter five.) In the excursus we seek to determine the semantic range of "man" in contemporary English. How is the word heard and perceived today?

A word generally has only one "sense" in any particular literary context. It should be obvious from the preceding examples that a word generally carries only one sense in any particular context. If I say that a particular body of water is a "freshwater lake," I am referring only to the fact that the water is not salty; I am not also saying that it is new. If I tell you that I eat only fresh fruit, I may mean "newly picked" *or* "not canned," but it is unlikely that I mean both. This is because sentences in the real world (usually called "utterances"[31]) appear in particular contexts, and the author or speaker generally has one thought in mind when forming that utterance. The only exception to this occurs when a speaker makes an intentional double-entendre, or play on words. If I poked one of my students with a stick as I said, "Are you getting my point?" I might be using the word "point" with a double meaning. Apart from puns and similar wordplays, speakers and authors generally have only one sense in mind when they use a word.

This point is also important for the inclusive language debate. It is sometimes argued that terms like *'ādām* and *anthrōpos* always carry male overtones or connotations, even when they are used with reference to human beings.[32] But this argument confuses two distinct senses of a single lexeme. When a Biblical writer uses the term *anthrōpos* in a particular context (for example, "an *anthrōpos* is more valuable than a sheep"), that writer usually has in mind either a male human being or a person in general. He does not mean both (unless an intentional double-entendre is present). The claim that a male overtone or connotation is necessarily present in these terms confuses the sense of a word in a particular context with its broader semantic range.

The meaning of words changes over time. We have been speaking of the semantic range of words, but we should actually be referring to the *contemporary* semantic range, since the meaning of words often changes over time. Take, for example, the English word *gay.* Because of the contemporary dominance of the sense "homosexual," the former sense of "cheerful" or "carefree" has almost disappeared from the language. To use the term with the sense "cheerful" is to invite misunderstanding. This, of course, is one of the greatest problems with the language of the King James Version. Word meanings have changed significantly since the seventeenth century, and words that occur in the KJV may well be misunderstood. In James 5:11 (KJV) we read that "the Lord is very pitiful." Such language (though heresy today) was perfectly acceptable in 1611, when the term still carried the sense "full of pity" or "compassionate."

This also has significance for Bible translation. First, the translator must seek to determine as precisely as possible the semantic range of biblical words in their original historical context. The meaning of many Greek words changed from the period of classical Greek to the Koine of the first century A.D. Many pastors and teachers have fallen into the error of assuming that the Greek word for the church, *ekklēsia,* actually means "the called-out ones," since its etymology (*ek* = "out"; *kaleō* = "call") might suggest a "calling out." In fact, this sense, if it ever existed, had long since disappeared from the meaning of the word by the first century, when it was used in the sense of a "gathering" or "assembly."[33] The meaning of the Greek word in the New Testament must be determined not from its history or its etymology but from its contemporary semantic range and from the New Testament contexts in which it is used.[34]

The fact that the meaning of words changes over time has significance not only for the original meaning of words in the biblical languages but also for the other side of the translation process: the world of the reader. Translators must be attuned to the changing state of the English language—the way words are heard and understood—and must be prepared to adjust and revise their translations as word meanings change. This is a crucial issue in the gender-inclusive language debate. How much has the meaning of the generic masculine "man" changed in the English language? Is this an artificial change that is being imposed by a select few in the interest of an agenda? Or is it a more general tendency among the reading public? This issue is addressed in the excursus that follows chapter five.

Words have connotative as well as denotative meanings. A final point that must be made is that words can carry connotative as well as denotative meaning.[35] The word "dog" denotes in English a furry, four-footed animal. The Greek word for dog *(kyōn)* denotes the same thing. Yet when Paul warns the Philippians to "watch out for those *dogs"* (Phil 3:2), the *connotation* of the word is much more negative. First-century Jews detested dogs and applied the term to the hated Gentiles. The word "dog," therefore, had a particular connotative, as well as denotative, value. The same thing occurs in English, where connotative values are given to people and things. Peter Cotterell and Max Turner point out that for English speakers the fox is cunning, the mule is stubborn, and the elephant never forgets. Mothers-in-law are figures of fun and stepmothers are inevitably cruel.[36] These are connotative values for British and American culture that go beyond the denotative value of the words themselves.

The translator must constantly consider that Greek or Hebrew words may have connotative as well as denotative meaning. They also must be aware that the English words they are using have particular connotative meanings for their readers. A good example of this is John 2:4, discussed at the beginning of this chapter. While the connotation of addressing your mother as "woman" in Greek is positive, in English it is negative. The translator must recognize that this negative connotation can cause the meaning of the text to be misunderstood and misconstrued. Recently I was given a piece of Islamic literature arguing that the Bible is inferior to the Qur'an because John 2:4 says that Jesus rudely called his mother "woman." The writers of this literature did not recognize that the connotation of the contemporary English word "woman" is very different from the Koine Greek *gynē*.

This point too has implications for gender-inclusive language. In a review of the 1992 revision of the Good News Bible, *Expository Times* editor C. S. Rodd writes concerning the use of inclusive language:

> "The masculine embraces the feminine," it used to be asserted, and no one was worried about this. Now that we have become more self-conscious about the gender of nouns and pronouns, however, the *connotation* of the words has altered, and masculines are felt to be restricted to males.[37] (italics mine)

This again highlights the need for translators to know their audience. If many or most readers draw the wrong connotation from a particular word or phrase, then that rendering represents a poor translation. Obviously it is impossible to discern and account for all connotative value in language. Connotation can be personal and individual as well as societal (the word "dog," for example, might even today connote a very negative image for one person [who has been bitten!] and a very positive one for another). However, when a large percentage of the translator's target population gives a particular connotative value to a word, the translator must take notice and adjust the translation accordingly.

Conclusion

This chapter on Bible translation recognizes the impossibility of translating a text from one language (the source language) into another (the receptor language) without interpreting that text. Languages, by their very nature, are idiomatic—unique in their use of words, phrases and clauses to express meaning. Translating is more than simply replacing each word in the original language with an equivalent word in the receptor language. It is finding the appropriate word or idiom in the receptor language that carries over the sense of the original. For this reason, form must not take precedence over meaning in Bible translation.

A similar principle of meaning over form also applies to individual words. Words do not have a single all-inclusive meaning that can be applied to every use of that word. They have a contemporary semantic range, a range of potential senses common to a particular language at a particular time. The literary context in which the word is used determines which sense the author intended. Since words in different languages have different semantic ranges (ranges that seldom overlap exactly), it is wrong to insist on using the same English word to translate each occurrence of a Greek or Hebrew term. In each instance, an English word (or words) must be chosen that captures the sense of the Greek or Hebrew in the context in which it is used.

These principles concerning the nature of language and translation have an important role in evaluating the accuracy of gender-inclusive language in Bible translation.

Five

INCLUSIVE LANGUAGE RELATED TO HUMAN BEINGS

Generic "Man" and "He"

IN CHAPTER FOUR IT WAS POINTED OUT THAT TRANSLATORS FACE TWO critical factors as they seek to translate a passage accurately from the source languages of Scripture (Hebrew, Greek and Aramaic) into a receptor language (English in this case). The first factor is the meaning of the text in its own cultural and historical context. How did the author intend the passage to be understood? How was it perceived by its original readers? The second factor is the sense perceived by the target readers in their own cultural and historical context. Translators must seek language that will encourage the modern reader to hear the text with the same perception that the original readers had. Bridging the gap between the ancient context and the modern reader is the great challenge of translation. If translators fail to determine accurately the sense of the original, meaning is lost at the initial stage of the process. If they interpret the passage accurately but then fail to pass that interpretation on to the reader, obscurity and misunderstanding can result.

These two issues, as applied to the inclusive language debate, are the primary concerns of chapters five and six. Is the meaning of the original text compromised when inclusive terms like "person" and "human being" are used to render masculine generic terms in Hebrew and Greek? Opponents of inclusive language often say yes; supporters say no. Much of this chapter is devoted to an examination of the legitimacy or illegitimacy of various techniques used to achieve gender inclusion.

The second issue concerns the perception of readers. Do English masculine generic terms such as "man" and "he" convey the inclusive sense inherent in their Greek counterparts? This question is examined in the excursus following this chapter.

When "Man" Means "Human Being"

Much of the discussion related to gender-inclusive language centers on using inclusive terms to replace masculine generic terms in Hebrew and Greek. Do these inclusive terms accurately convey the sense of the original? To answer this question, we must first determine the generic nature of these Greek and Hebrew terms.

Hebrew 'ādām and Greek anthrōpos. Both Hebrew and Greek use masculine terms to refer to males exclusively and also to refer to human beings in general. The primary Hebrew term for this inclusive sense is *'ādām;*[1] the primary Greek term is *anthrōpos.*[2] Another way of saying this (as explained in chap. four) is that the semantic ranges of *anthrōpos* and *'ādām* include various potential senses: "a male," "a human being," "humanity" and so on.

In many Old Testament contexts *'ādām* clearly carries the sense of "person." When the Lord says, "I will blot out man *['ādām]* whom I have created" (Gen 6:7 RSV), it is both males and females who will be judged. The phrase "whoever sheds the blood of *man*" (Gen 9:6 RSV) means "whoever sheds the blood of a *human being.*" A quick glance through a concordance reveals just how common this use of *'ādām* is.

Similarly, in many New Testament contexts, the Greek term

anthrōpos carries the senses "human being" or "humanity" rather than "male." Matthew 12:12 in the NIV reads, "How much more valuable is a man *[anthrōpos]* than a sheep!" The NIVI captures the sense of the Greek when it renders the sentence, "How much more valuable is a human being than a sheep!" In fact, the translation "human being" is more precise, since the contrast here is between people and animals, not between men and women. Such examples could be multiplied. In Mark 10:27, the disciples ask, "Who then can be saved?" Jesus responds, "With *man,* this is impossible, but not with God" (NIV). The NIVI reads, "*Humanly,* this is impossible." Again, by substituting the adverb "humanly" for the prepositional phrase "with man" (which functions adverbially), the NIVI captures better the sense of the Greek original, which has the meaning "by human ability."

Romans 3:28 reads in the NIV, "For we maintain that a *man* is justified by faith apart from observing the law." The NIVI avoids the possible implication that Paul is speaking only of males by translating, "For we maintain that a *person* is justified by faith apart from observing the law." Similarly, in 2 Corinthians 5:11, where the NIV reads, "Since, then, we know what it is to fear the Lord, we try to persuade *men,*" the NIVI has "we try to persuade *people.*" The record of Paul's missionary journeys in Acts confirms that he proclaimed the gospel to both men and women In all of these examples, the NIVI captures more precisely the sense of the original Greek.

The preceding examples go a long way toward explaining why the Conference on Gender-Related Language in Scripture (chap. one) adopted guideline A.5: "In many cases, *anthrōpoi* refers to people in general, and can be translated 'people' rather than 'men.' The singular *anthrōpos* should ordinarily be translated 'man' when it refers to a male human being."

While this guideline allows for the use of inclusive renderings such as "people" for the plural *anthrōpoi,* it says nothing about inclusive language for the singular *anthrōpos.* It only affirms the exclusive use of *anthrōpos* (that it should be translated "man" when it refers to a male). What if *anthrōpos* refers to a person of either gender? This rather glaring omission led many of those reading the guidelines to look to guideline A.3, which does speak of the singular "man" in English. Guideline A.3 originally read, "'Man' should ordinarily be used to designate the human race or human beings in general." For many readers this statement implied that whereas the plural *anthrōpoi* may be translated "people," the singulars *anthrōpos* and *'ādām* should be translated "man." Yet in several of the examples cited above (and dozens more could be added), it is the singular that is functioning generically as "a human being," "a person" or "humanity."

As a result of the confusion that the wording of this guideline caused, it was revised. The phrase "or human beings in general" was dropped and the guideline now reads, "'Man' should ordinarily be used to designate the human race." This is a significant concession. The guideline now appears to allow for hundreds of cases where the NIVI has replaced generic "man" with more inclusive terms such as "person(s)" and "human being(s)." At the same time, a positive statement about the inclusive use of the singular *anthrōpos* is still strikingly absent. There seems to be a marked reticence by the authors of the guidelines to affirm positively that *anthrōpos* and *'ādām* are accurately and precisely translated as "person" or "human being" in many contexts.

As revised, guideline A.3 seems to apply only to those few cases where "man" is used of the human race, as in Genesis 1:26-27: "Then God said, 'Let us make *man* in our image.'" Even the other examples provided in the guideline (Jn 2:25; Ezek 29:11) no longer seem to fit the revised version. When John says that Jesus "knew what was in man," he means that Jesus knew what was in the hearts of *people*. There does not seem to be a corporate sense of "human race" here. Similarly, Ezekiel 29:11 is an oracle against Egypt that reads, "No *foot of man* shall pass through it" (RSV). This, of course, means "no *human foot*" (NRSV). It does not refer to corporate humanity.

A more difficult question is whether the remaining part of the guideline, " 'man' should ordinarily be used to designate the human race," represents a valid principle. The issue of using "man" in statements of representative leadership or corporate humanity is addressed later in this chapter.

Hebrew 'îsh and Greek anēr. Whereas *'ādām and anthrōpos* often carry an inclusive sense, the Hebrew term *'îsh* and the Greek *anēr* (root *andr-*) appear less commonly with this sense. It is wrong to assume, however, that these terms *cannot* carry an inclusive sense. For example, in a context such as Deuteronomy 24:16, even the very literal NKJV translates *'îsh* as "person": "A *person* shall be put to death for his own sin." In many other contexts there is little doubt that both males and females are intended. Exodus 12:4 addresses a small household's sharing its Passover lamb with another household and mandates that "you are to determine the amount of lamb needed in accordance with what each person [*n*ᵉ*pāshōt 'îsh,* literally 'soul of man'] will eat" (NIV). While women may generally eat less than men, they would surely have been included in the count. Similarly, in the gathering of manna it is commanded that "each one *['îsh]* is to gather as much as he needs" (Ex 16:16 NIV).

When tumors break out among the citizens of Gath because of the presence of the ark of the covenant, it is almost certainly the "people *['îsh]* of the city, both young and old" (NIV), rather than the "men" (RSV, NKJV, NASB), who are afflicted (1 Sam 5:9). After Samuel explains to the people *(hā'ām)* the rights and duties of kingship, he dismisses each "one" (*'îsh,* RSV, NASB, NIV) to their own tent (1 Sam 8:22). In Solomon's prayer of dedication for the temple, he refers to prayer "by anyone *[ādām]* . . . when each one *['îsh]* knows his own burden" (2 Chron 6:29 NKJV; compare 1 Kings 8:38). In Psalm 62:12 we learn that the Lord rewards "each person *['îsh]* according to what he has done" (NIV; compare NKJV). Jeremiah predicts that following the destruction of Jerusalem "everyone *['îsh]* will say to his neighbor, 'Why has the LORD done so to this great city?'" (Jer 22:8 NKJV; compare NIV; NASB). The destruction itself will take place "so that everyone *['îsh]* may turn from his evil way, that I may forgive their iniquity and their sin" (Jer 36:3 NKJV; compare RSV, NIV). It should be noted that all of these examples cite noninclusive translations (that is, those that normally retain generic "man": RSV, NASB, NKJV, NIV) to illustrate this inclusive sense of *'îsh*. Many more examples could be provided.[3]

In other cases it is difficult to discern whether to take *'îsh* as inclusive or exclusive. In Exodus 32:28, did three thousand "men" (NASB) or "people" (NIV) die in the plague following the golden calf incident? Similarly, did the judgment for David's census in 2 Samuel 24:15 result in the death of seventy thousand "men" (NKJV) or seventy thousand "people" (RSV, NIV, NASB)? In both cases the latter seems the more natural reading. In Exodus 33:8, 10, was it the "people" (NIV, NASB) or the "men" (RSV, NKJV) who stood at the entrance of their tents when Moses entered the tent of meeting? In these examples (and many more could be cited[4]), it is difficult to determine whether the author had men or people generally in mind, but a strong case can be made for the latter. The "noninclusive" versions are divided. Some might argue that in such cases we should simply default to the generic "man." The problem is that in these contexts the English word "man" clearly sounds exclusive. It is essential that the hard work of exegesis be done on a case-by-case basis in order to avoid passing on the wrong meaning to the reader.

The Greek noun *anēr* also appears less commonly with an inclusive sense than its counterpart *anthrōpos,* usually carrying the sense of either "male human being" or "husband." In a number of contexts, however, the referent appears to include both men and women.[5] The *Exegetical Dictionary of the New Testament* points out that *anēr* "can denote any human being."[6] For example, in Matthew 12:41 Jesus says, "The men [*andres,* NRSV; NIVI 'people'] of Nineveh will arise at the judgment with this generation and condemn it; for they repented at the preaching of Jonah" (RSV). Since females were certainly among those converted at Nineveh, the sense here appears to be "people." Similarly, in Matthew 14:35 it seems likely that it was the "people" (NRSV, NIVI) of Gennesaret, not the "men" (RSV, NIV), who brought their sick to Jesus. In Ephesians 4:13 NIV Paul speaks of the time when "we all reach unity in the faith . . . and become mature" (literally, "come . . . to a perfect man [*anēr*]"). Since Paul is speaking to women as well as men ("we all"), he would seem to have in mind human maturity rather than specifically male maturity.[7]

In proverbial statements *anēr* also appears to carry an inclusive sense. When Paul quotes from Psalm 32:1-2 in Romans 4:7-8, he follows the Septuagint (LXX—the Greek Old Testament) in using *anēr:*

"Blessed is the man *[anēr]* whose sin the Lord will never count against him" (Rom 4:8 NIV). The Hebrew text here has *'ādām,* which, as we have seen, often carries an inclusive sense. From Paul's perspective God's forgiveness comes to men and women equally (Gal 3:28), so an inclusive sense for *anēr* is probably intended. James also uses *anēr* in an inclusive sense. In James 1:12 he writes, "Blessed is the man *[anēr]* who endures trial" (RSV), and in 1:20 he points out that "the anger of man *[orgē andros]* does not work the righteousness of God" (RSV). It is obviously human anger, not male anger, to which James is referring (the NIVI correctly translates as "human anger"). Similarly, in James 3:2 we find, "If anyone is never at fault in what he says, he is a perfect man *[anēr]*" (NIV). The proverbial nature of the sentence, together with the indefinite pronoun "anyone" in the conditional clause, suggests that the referent is generic.

In other cases, a decision on whether males or males and females are intended is very difficult. Were only men among the invited guests in the parable of the great banquet (Lk 14:24)? Perhaps, but this is not certain. Did Peter address all of his "fellow Jews" (NIV) or only the "men of Judea" (RSV, NRSV) on the Day of Pentecost (Acts 2:14)? It is interesting that here an "inclusive" version (the NRSV) interprets *anēr* with reference to males only, while the original NIV uses more inclusive language. Both versions are obviously grappling with the sense of the original, not seeking to impose an agenda on the text.

There are many other places where the interpreter must make a difficult decision. Had the church in Acts 4:4 grown to five thousand "men" (NIV, RSV, NLT, GW, NCV) or five thousand "persons" (NIVI; NRSV, TEV, CEV)? The inclusive versions are divided.[8] Does God reserve for himself seven thousand "men" in 1 Kings 19:18 or seven thousand "persons"? The Hebrew text does not specify, and all English translations refer to "all those whose knees have not bowed down to Baal." "All" presumably means everyone, both men and women. When Paul cites the passage in Romans 11:4, he follows the Septuagint in introducing the plural *andres.* Whereas the RSV rendered the verse, "I have kept for myself seven thousand men," the original NIV took into account the Hebrew text and translated, "I have reserved for myself seven thousand who have not bowed the knee to Baal" (Rom 11:4 NIV). Evidently the original NIV translators concluded that *andres* here meant "persons," not "men."

The relative rarity of these inclusive senses for *'îsh* and *anēr* explains why the Conference on Gender-Related Language produced guideline A.4: "Hebrew *'îsh* should ordinarily be translated 'man' and 'men' and *anēr* should almost always be so translated." This is still a flawed guideline, however, since statements such as "should *ordinarily* be translated" or "should *almost always* be so translated" provide no real guidance concerning when it is appropriate to translate these terms in this way. To be more precise, the principle should state something like "*'îsh* and *anēr* should be translated 'man' or 'men' *when they refer to males,* and they may be translated 'person(s)' or 'human being(s)' *when they refer to humans in general.*" Stating the principle this way, however, eliminates the need for having a principle at all, since this is the way every word in Hebrew or Greek should be treated. Whatever the word means in context is how it should be translated. When *anthrōpos* refers to human beings, it may be translated "human being," and when *anēr* refers to human beings, it may be translated "human being." The imposition of a particular translation without consideration of individual contexts smacks of an agenda beyond the accurate interpretation of Scripture.

One objection to introducing "persons" or "human beings" in these contexts might be that "man" and "men" are perfectly acceptable generic terms and so should be retained in translation. The acceptability of these terms, however, is not a decisive reason for retaining them. If inclusive terms reproduce more precisely and accurately the sense of the Greek or Hebrew terms in context, then they should be adopted. The question remains, however: Is "man" still perfectly acceptable as a generic term? This is a difficult issue because it concerns the different perceptions individuals have when they hear the word. Is the term perceived today as inclusive (including men and women) or as exclusive (including only males)? This question is examined in the excursus following this chapter.

In a number of the passages cited above, the English term "men" clearly does not convey the same inclusive sense intended by the

Hebrew or Greek author. A clear example of this appears at the feeding of the five thousand in John 6, where Jesus instructs his disciples using the Greek plural *anthrōpoi:* "Have the people *[anthrōpoi]* sit down" (Jn 6:10 NIV). All modern translations that I have surveyed use "people" here. Only the KJV translates, "Make the men sit down." The two translations clearly have different senses. The KJV suggests that only males are being addressed. It is possible, of course, that this is the correct interpretation and that Jesus instructed only the men to be seated. In this case either (1) the women and children were left standing or (2) there were no women or children present.[9] Neither scenario seems likely. The former would contradict Mark 6:39 and Luke 9:15, where "all" are seated; the latter would contradict Matthew 14:21, where women and children are mentioned.

That John intended the term to be inclusive is also suggested by his change to the more exclusive term *hoi andres* ("the men") in the following phrase, "So they sat down, the men numbering about five thousand" (Jn 6:10).[10] If Jesus instructed all the people to be seated, as seems likely, the English translation "men" for *anthrōpoi* is clearly wrong, since it gives the impression that women and children were excluded. The important point is that the English term "men" is not capable of conveying the generic and inclusive sense of *anthrōpoi* in this context. *Anthrōpoi* is a more inclusive term than "men."

This illustrates one of the principles established in chapter four, that the semantic ranges of words in different languages seldom overlap exactly. To mandate that a particular word (such as "man" or "men") in one language must be used for a particular word in another (such as *anthrōpos* and *anthrōpoi*) is invalid and inevitably promotes inaccurate translations.

In some cases it is very difficult for translators to determine whether the Greek or Hebrew term is meant to be inclusive or exclusive. For example, what does *anthrōpoi* mean in John 4:28? Did the Samaritan woman go into town and tell the "people" (NIV, RSV, TEV) about Jesus, or did she tell the "men" (KJV, NKJV, NASB)? Similarly, was it the "people" (NASB, RSV, TEV, NIV) who saw the sign Jesus had done in John 6:14, or only the "men" (KJV, NKJV). Since "men" clearly sounds exclusive in these contexts, the translator's decision is critical for an accurate translation. Translators must make decisions on a case-by-case basis, using all the historical and linguistic tools available to them.

When "He" Means "He or She"

One of the most difficult issues in gender-inclusive translation is how to render the masculine singular personal pronouns "he," "him," "his." Even when "man" can be avoided quite easily with an inclusive term such as "person" or with indefinite pronouns such as "anyone," the translator must still deal with the resumptive pronouns that follow. For example, in the sentence "A *person* must control *his* temper if *he* is going to succeed," the word "person" is inclusive but the two personal pronouns that follow are masculine. As mentioned in chapter two, some translations that remove generic "man" often retain the masculine resumptive pronouns. The REB reads in Psalm 1:1-3: "Happy is *the one* who does not take the counsel of the wicked . . . *he* is like a tree . . . *he* too prospers in all *he* does." Most inclusive versions, however, seek ways to avoid masculine generic pronouns, since (it is argued) these too can be perceived as exclusive.

Masculine generic pronouns in Greek, Hebrew and English. Both Hebrew and Greek use masculine pronouns in a generic sense (meaning "he or she"). For Hebrew, these masculine pronouns are *hûʾ* ("he"), *hēmâ* and *hēm* ("they"), and the suffixes *-ô* and *-hû* ("him" or "his"). In Greek, the masculine generic personal pronouns are *autos* ("he" or "it") and *autoi* ("they"). In English subject pronouns must be stated ("*he* ate"). But Hebrew verbs in themselves carry their own person, number and gender (*ʾākal;* the verb alone means "*he* ate" [third person, singular, masculine]). Greek verbs carry person and number but not gender (*ephagen,* "he, she or it ate" [third person, singular]).

When Jesus says, "Blessed are the meek, for they *[autoi]* will inherit the earth" (Mt 5:5 NIV), it is clear that the masculine pronoun "they" *(autoi)* functions generically, referring to men and women. This is no problem for an English translation, since plural personal pronouns in English do not carry gender distinction. "They" can refer to men, women or both. The problem arises from the fact that *singular* personal pronouns in English, like their Greek and Hebrew counterparts, *do* carry gender ("he," "him," "his"; "she," "her," "hers"). There is no neutral singular pronoun such as "they" in English ("it" obviously does not work for human beings). When Jesus says, "No one can come to me unless the Father who sent me draws him [*autos*[11]]" (Jn 6:44 NIV), the Greek term *autos* is clearly functioning generically, meaning "him or her." The issue that pervades the inclusive language debate is whether the English personal pronouns "he," "him" and "his" carry this same inclusive sense. Should translators use masculine "he" in a generic sense, or should they use more neutral expressions such as "he or she"? Those opposed to inclusive language say emphatically that "he" is a perfectly legitimate generic term. Those supporting inclusive language respond that "he" carries an exclusive sound in contemporary English and so misses the sense intended by the author.

Even supporters of generic "he" tacitly admit that there are problems with its use. Wayne Grudem writes, "Everyone seems to agree that gender-neutral terms are preferable to 'he, him, his' when they can be used without awkwardness and without loss of meaning (and I too would agree)."[12] The key question, then, is not whether gender-inclusive terms are inherently inaccurate but whether they can be used with clarity and precision.

English handbooks on masculine generic pronouns. Many handbooks of English style address the problem of the masculine generic "he." Some acknowledge its controversial nature but then affirm its accuracy. The third edition of Strunk and White (1979) reads:

> The use of *he* as a pronoun for nouns embracing both genders is a simple, practical convention rooted in the beginnings of the English language. *He* has lost all suggestion of maleness in these circumstances. . . . It has no pejorative connotation; it is never incorrect. Substituting *he or she* in its place is the logical thing to do if it works. But it often doesn't work, if only because repetition makes it sound boring or silly.[13]

Other handbooks take a more inclusive approach, warning the writer against using "he" in generic contexts. The 1989 edition of *St. Martin's Handbook* reads:

> Remember to avoid using masculine pronouns to refer to antecedents that include or may include both males and females. For example, the sentence *Every attorney values his client's testimony* implies that only men are attorneys. Such a sentence can be revised in several ways: by eliminating the pronoun, by using both masculine and feminine pronouns, or by shifting to the plural.[14]

The preceding example may thus be manipulated as follows: (1) *Every attorney values a client's testimony* (eliminating the pronoun), (2) *Every attorney values his or her client's testimony* (using both masculine and feminine pronouns), or (3) *All attorneys value their client's testimony* (shifting to the plural). Another technique not mentioned but sometimes utilized is called "singular they": *Every attorney values their client's testimony.* These techniques and others are employed by contemporary Bible translators.

While acknowledging the existence of the last option, the "singular they," handbooks frequently reject it outright or warn against its use in formal writing. This is because a singular antecedent ("every attorney," in this case) is technically supposed to be followed by a singular pronoun ("his"). Strunk and White explicitly argue that the plural pronoun "they" is "not to be used when the antecedent is a distributive expression such as *each, each one, everybody, every one, many a man.* Use a singular pronoun." They go on to add that "a similar fault is the use of the plural pronoun with the antecedent *anybody, anyone, somebody, someone.*"[15]

Other style books allow the singular "they" in speech but warn against its use in writing. *Little, Brown* (1983) notes:

> In speech we often solve the problem of the generic *he* by combining a plural pronoun with an indefinite pronoun, as in *Everyone brought their books to class.* But this construction violates the expectations of most readers, so it should be avoided in writing.[16]

St. Martin's Handbook similarly cautions, "You will probably hear—and perhaps use—such sentences in conversation, but you should be careful about using them in writing."[17]

A number of stylists have challenged this negative assessment of the singular "they," pointing out that in many cases this construction works as well as the generic "he," or better.[18] Consider, for example, the following sentences, in which pronouns have indefinite antecedents:[19]

1. Anyone can do it if *they* try hard enough.
2. Who dropped *their* ticket?
3. Either Mary or John should bring a schedule with *them*.

For many readers, "they" sounds correct in these sentences. One reason is that although the subjects are singular, their indefiniteness carries a sense of plurality (indefiniteness implying more than one possibility). According to many handbooks, however, the above sentences should have been completed with "he," since their antecedents are singular. Even the third sentence, strictly speaking, should be completed with "him," since antecedents joined by "or" are viewed as singular.[20] For most readers, however, following the "rule" in this case produces a sentence that sounds incorrect. Many other examples could be provided where the masculine singular, though technically correct, sounds wrong. George Jochnowitz describes an incident in which his daughter brought to his attention what she called a grammatical error in the 1940 edition of Margaret Mitchell's *Gone with the Wind*. The passage read, "Everyone was very polite and kind to her because he felt sorry for her" (p. 36). When Jochnowitz consulted the original 1936 edition, he found that the passage originally read "*they* felt sorry for her." Evidently a copyeditor "corrected" Mitchell's grammar to "he," thus creating the jarring phrase that offended his daughter.[21] In a case like this, the "rule" of grammar produces a construction that sounds wrong to most readers. A singular indefinite subject followed by "they" would commonly be viewed as correct.

Investigators have pointed out that the singular, indefinite "they" has a long and distinguished history in the English language. The *Shorter Oxford English Dictionary* notes that since at least 1526, "they" and "them" have been used "in ref. to a sing. noun made universal by *every, any, no,* etc., or applicable to either sex (= 'he or she')."[22] Examples of this usage appear in writers such as Shakespeare, Swift, Austen, Shelley, Dickens, Trollope, Shaw and others.[23] According to Ann Bodine, this construction was commonly accepted as correct prior to the nineteenth century. It is only in the last two hundred years that prescriptive grammars and handbooks have attempted to eliminate its use. Bodine writes that

> despite almost two centuries of vigorous attempts to analyse and regulate it out of existence, singular "they" is alive and well. Its survival is all the more remarkable considering that the weight of virtually the entire educational and publishing establishment has been behind the attempt to eradicate it.[24]

She criticizes these handbooks for being prescriptive rather than descriptive, mandating what should be done instead of reporting what is actually done by educated writers and speakers. Miriam Meyers confirms the legitimacy of this criticism by supplying an extensive list of examples of singular "they" taken from speech and writing in the media and elsewhere.[25]

Bodine also challenges the logic of grammarians who claim that "he" should be used instead of "they" because it agrees in number with the singular antecedent. This logic is flawed, she points out, because while agreeing in number with the antecedent, "he" disagrees in gender. "They," on the other hand, agrees in gender but disagrees in number. Both "he" and "they" thus have one incongruity with their antecedent. Logically, neither should function better than the other.[26]

Finally, empirical studies have also confirmed that "they" is commonly used and accepted as a generic singular pronoun. Experiments on preference of usage have found that writers using a generic pronoun choose generic "he" or singular "they" with about equal frequency.[27]

We can conclude (with appropriate caution) that the singular "they," though rejected by many grammars and style books, represents a widely used and often preferable generic pronoun that can take the place of generic "he" in many cases. Though some Bible versions seem to avoid it, others make use of it. We will therefore examine its potential use in the discussion of alternatives to masculine generic "he" below.

This discussion of singular "they" illustrates an important point. Simply because an English handbook mandates a particular usage does not mean that usage is correct. Handbooks by their very nature are conservative, seeking to prescribe grammatical forms traditionally considered to be appropriate among educated people. As language changes, however, and as educated and refined writers and speakers adopt new forms, handbooks (just like dictionaries) must be revised to reflect these changes. Otherwise they become hopelessly outdated, prescribing grammar that is viewed by writers and readers as archaic, awkward or obscure.

Common Techniques for Avoiding the Masculine Generics "Man" and "He"

In addition to utilizing inclusive terms such as "person" and "human being," gender-inclusive versions have adopted a variety of techniques for avoiding the masculine generics "man" and "he." This section briefly examines the legitimacy of some of these techniques.

Using indefinite pronouns. One popular technique for avoiding the generic "man" is using indefinite pronouns such as "someone," "anyone," "everyone," "one" and "whoever." Proverbs 29:20 reads in the RSV, "Do you see a *man* who is hasty in his words?" The verse is rendered by the NRSV as, "Do you see *someone* who is hasty in speech?" The NIVI reads, "Do you see *one* who speaks in haste?" Proverbs 21:16 RSV reads, "*A man* who wanders from the way of understanding." The NRSV translates inclusively, "*Whoever* wanders from the way of understanding." Deuteronomy 27:15 in the RSV reads, "Cursed be the *man* who makes a graven or molten image." The NRSV translates, "Cursed be *anyone*." In Mark 4:23 RSV Jesus says, "If *any man* has ears to hear, let him hear." The NRSV reads, "Let *anyone* with ears to hear listen!" John 1:9 reads in the RSV, "The true light that enlightens *every man* was coming into the world." The NRSV renders, "The true light, which enlightens *everyone,* was coming into the world." James 1:19 RSV reads, "Let every *man* be quick to hear, slow to speak, slow to anger." The NRSV reads, "Let *everyone* be quick to listen, slow to speak, slow to anger."

These examples demonstrate that proverbs, legislative texts and general instruction are especially well rendered by indefinite pronouns. No one should object to these translations. The indefinite pronoun functions effectively in this case because "man" carries precisely this general and indefinite sense. These translations actually produce greater precision by clarifying that the references are not to males but to people in general. A striking example of this is found in Exodus 35:22, where the RSV reads, "So they came, both men and women . . . every *man* dedicating an offering of gold to the LORD." The antecedent reference to "men and women" shows that "man" *('îsh)* here carries a generic sense. The NRSV renders the last phrase correctly as "*everyone* bringing an offering of gold to the LORD." The original NIV had already translated, "*They all* presented their gold as a wave offering to the LORD."

In this example and many others, the introduction of an indefinite pronoun produces smoother and clearer English. In many places idiomatic versions such as the NIV had already introduced indefinite pronouns, not because of an inclusive intention but because they represented better English. James 1:19, for example, already appeared in the NIV as "*everyone* should be quick to listen." This is not to suggest that the indefinite pronoun is always a good choice. Care must be taken to retain a masculine reference if in context "man" applies only to males and if an indefinite pronoun would misrepresent this sense.

Switching from a singular to a plural construction. This method for avoiding masculine "he" and "man" works because the English plural pronoun, unlike the singular, does not carry gender distinctions. Sometimes the plural is used to bring out the general or proverbial sense of generic "man." Psalm 10:3 RSV reads, "The *man* greedy for gain curses and renounces the LORD." In the NRSV this becomes "*those* greedy for gain." The NIV's "blessed is *the man* who fears the LORD" (Ps 112:1) is revised in the NIVI to "blessed are *those* who fear the LORD." Proverbs 11:17 NIV, "*a kind man* benefits himself, but *a cruel man* brings trouble on himself," becomes in the NIVI "*those who are kind* benefit themselves, but *the cruel* bring trouble on themselves." These examples demonstrate that in many cases a plural construction, like an indefinite pronoun, captures well the sense of instructional, legal and proverbial material. This is because this material, although couched in singular forms, is *notionally* plural, referring to people in general.

The plural is often utilized so that resumptive pronouns can be rendered with the gender nonspecific "they." Genesis 6:3 appears in the RSV as "My spirit shall not abide in *man* for ever, for *he* is flesh."

The NRSV translates, "My spirit shall not abide in *mortals* forever, for *they* are flesh." Job 15:14 in the RSV reads, "What is man, that *he* can be clean?" The NRSV renders, "What are mortals, that *they* can be clean?" The RSV's "fret not yourself over *him* who prospers in *his* way" (Ps 37:7) becomes in the NRSV, "Do not fret over *those* who prosper in *their* way." "*He who* spares the rod hates his son" (Prov 13:24 RSV, NIV) becomes "*those who* spare the rod hate their children" (NRSV, NIVI). When translated for proverbial material and general statements of truth, plural constructions capture the same basic sense as the singular.

Grudem, on the other hand, repeatedly rejects this method of attaining gender inclusion, claiming that it distorts the meaning of the text. He criticizes the NRSV at James 5:14-15 for changing the RSV's singular reference to plural. The RSV reads, "Is any among you sick? Let *him* call for the elders of the church, and let them pray over *him*." The NRSV revises, "Are any among you sick? *They* should call for the elders of the church and have them pray over *them*." Grudem claims that "James wrote about a private home with one person sick, but now it looks like a hospital ward!"[28] While one can appreciate Grudem's sense of humor, his conclusion represents an extremely wooden, literal approach. Any normal reader would recognize that the NRSV is speaking about individual cases of sickness, not an epidemic. If I said to a congregation of believers, "Those in need of encouragement should stay after the service for prayer," no one would misunderstand my statement, thinking I was referring to groups rather than individuals. James is not referring to a single specific individual who is sick but to *individuals* (note the plural) who are sick. As in the examples above, the instruction is generic and therefore *notionally plural*. There is no loss of meaning when a plural pronoun is introduced.

Translators who choose to retain the singular form at James 5:14-15 can translate as the NIVI does: "Is *any one* of you sick? Call the elders of the church to pray over you and anoint you with oil in the name of the Lord." Gender inclusion is achieved here by using the indefinite pronoun "one" (the Greek itself uses the indefinite pronoun *tis*) and by introducing a second-person imperative ("call") for the Greek third-person imperative ("let him call"). In either case there is no loss of meaning.

This same overly wooden approach applies to many of Grudem's criticisms. Is the individual application really lost, as he claims, in the NRSV translation of John 15:5, "*those* who abide in me and I in them bear much fruit" instead of "*he* who abides in me and I in him" (RSV)?[29] The substantival participle *ho menōn* (literally, "the one who abides") is clearly functioning generically in the sense of "those individuals," and the NRSV captures this generic sense well with "those." Grudem complains that the NRSV translation results in a "loss of a sense of individual application," but this is special pleading. If I tell my class that those who fail the exam will fail the course, it is obvious to all that I am speaking about individuals failing, not groups. No one would complain that by using the word "those" I am threatening to fail the class en masse. No normal reader approaches the English language in this way.[30]

In some cases the collective sense of the singular is evident from the context. Grudem criticizes John 14:23 in the NRSV for changing a singular reference in Greek to an English plural. Compare the RSV with the NRSV:

> RSV: If a *man* loves me, *he* will keep my word, and my Father will love *him*, and we will come to *him* and make our home with him.
>
> NRSV: *Those* who love me will keep my word, and my Father will love *them*, and we will come to *them* and make our home with *them*.

Grudem writes:

> The problem is that Jesus did not speak with plural pronouns in this verse; he used singulars. And there is a difference in meaning. There is a loss of individuality in application, because "those" and "them" are groups of people. The words of Jesus no longer speak of the Father and the Son coming to an individual person, but to a group of people, perhaps a church.[31]

But as Grant Osborne points out, the immediate context suggests that Jesus' reference is collective, referring to *all* the disciples.[32] The question that prompted this response by Jesus was posed by Judas (not Iscariot): "But, Lord, why do you intend to show yourself to *us* and not to the world?" (Jn 14:22 NIV). Jesus' response concerns *those disciples* who will keep his word. Incidentally, it should be noted that in this example the RSV, which Grudem cites as the accurate counterpart to the NRSV, is also wrong according to such a literalist approach, since no word for "man" appears in the Greek. The Greek actually says, "If anyone *[tis]* loves me," using the indefinite relative pronoun *tis* ("anyone," "whoever"). An overly literal reading produces at least as much possibility for misunderstanding "man" as exclusively male as for causing the "individual-versus-group" confusion that Grudem asserts.

Although the plural often captures the inclusive and generic sense of the masculine singular in Greek or Hebrew, it is not always an appropriate choice. Grudem correctly points out the confused sense that results when a plural is used for a singular in Psalm 19:12. In the NIV, after a series of lines praising the precepts and ordinances of the Lord, the psalmist reflects on his own sinfulness: "The ordinances of the LORD are sure. . . . They are much more precious than gold. . . . Who can discern *his* errors?" (Ps 19:9-12 NIV).

The NIVI (compare NRSV) translates the last line "but who can detect *their* errors," inadvertently suggesting that it is God's ordinances that contain errors. This is clearly a slip in the translation process. Other inclusive versions such as the CEV, NCV and the NLT avoid the problem by rewording the verse in different ways ("their own," "our" and "my").[33] This is not a problem inherent in inclusive renderings but a mistake made by the NIVI and the NRSV.

Using singular "they" with indefinite pronouns. Another way to avoid masculine singulars is to use an indefinite pronoun followed by the singular "they." The CEV does this in John 14:23, the passage cited above: "If *anyone* loves me, *they* will obey me. Then my Father will love *them*, and we will come to *them* and live in *them*." Although some English handbooks reject the use of the singular "they," it nevertheless has a long history of usage and is widely accepted as clear and accurate.

Most inclusive versions make use of the singular "they." At Ecclesiastes 3:13 the NIV reads, "That everyone may eat and drink, and find satisfaction in all *his* toil." The NIVI reads, "That everyone may eat and drink, and find satisfaction in all *their* toil." The reader should compare these two sentences and decide which one is preferable. I suspect most readers would prefer the singular "they." More examples of "singular they" include Psalm 62:12 (NIVI), "Surely you will reward each person according to what *they* have done"; John 3:4 (NIVI), "How can anyone be born after having grown old? Surely *they* cannot enter a second time into *their* mother's womb to be born"; Revelation 3:20 (NIVI), "If anyone hears my voice and opens the door, I will come in and eat with *them*, and *they* with me"; James 1:19 (NIrV), "Everyone should be quick to listen. But *they* should be slow to speak."

In these passages singular indefinite pronouns confirm for the reader that "they" and "them" are being used as singulars. Although English grammar technically may require a singular pronoun, most English speakers prefer the sound of a plural pronoun. For example, in Exodus 9:19 (NCV) we read that "the hail will fall on every person or animal. . . . If *they* have not been brought in, *they* will die." Though the pronoun should be singular (compound subjects divided by "or" take a singular verb), to most readers "they" sounds correct.

It is significant that the Hebrew text itself sometimes uses a similar construction, following a generic singular with a plural construction. In Psalm 39:6 generic "man" *('îsh)* is followed by a plural verb. The NRSV reads, "Surely everyone *['îsh]* goes about like a shadow . . . for nothing they [plural verb in Hebrew] are in turmoil." The NIV actually changes the Hebrew plural back to a singular in order to agree with the singular *'îsh:* "*He* bustles about, but only in vain."

Changing from a third-person singular pronoun to a first-person plural or second-person plural pronoun. Another technique used to avoid both generic "man" and "he" is to switch from a third-person construction to a first- or second-person one. Neither the first person (singular: "I," "me," "my," "mine"; plural: "we," "us," "our," "ours") nor the second person ("you," "your," "yours") carries any gender distinction in English. Thus the RSV renders Proverbs 20:24 as "*A man's* steps are ordered by the LORD," while the NRSV renders it, "*All our* steps are ordered by the LORD." What appears in the NIV as "what does *man* gain from all his labor" (Eccles 1:3) is translated in the NJB as "what profit can *we* show for all our toil."

The second-person plural pronoun appears in the NIVI at Matthew 15:11: "What goes into *your* mouth does not make *you* 'unclean.'" The

NIV renders the verse, "What goes into *a man's* mouth does not make *him* 'unclean.'" Similarly, Galatians 6:1 RSV reads, "If a *man* is overtaken in any trespass." NJB renders it as "if one of *you* is caught doing something wrong." Romans 12:7 NIV, "if [his gift] is serving, *let him serve*" becomes "if [your gift] is serving, *then serve*" in the NIVI.[34]

Grudem rejects this technique, claiming that it produces inaccurate readings. He criticizes the second-person rendering of the NRSV in James 1:19-20: "For *your anger* does not produce God's righteousness." The RSV has, "For *the anger of man* does not work the righteousness of God." Grudem writes:

> With the NRSV, readers might well think that James is speaking only about the anger of Christians, those within the believing community whom he is addressing. But in fact James is making a more general statement about the anger of human beings. James did not say "your anger"; he said "the anger of man."[35]

Grudem levels the same criticism at the NRSV rendering of James 2:14 and Galatians 6:7. While James 2:14 RSV reads, "What does it profit, my brethren, if *a man* says *he* has faith but has not works?" the NRSV has "What good is it, my brothers and sisters, if *you* say *you* have faith, but do not have works?" Similarly, in Galatians 6:7 the RSV rendering, "Whatever a *man* sows, that will *he* also reap," becomes in the NRSV "*You* reap whatever *you* sow." Grudem claims the NRSV promotes a misinterpretation: "Readers will probably think that Paul is speaking only of something that is true of Christians. . . . But in fact Paul is making a much more general statement about human conduct, and about people generally."[36]

Grudem's concern for misinterpretation is laudable, but he does not take adequate account of the generic sense of "you" that is intended by the translators. Whereas the first definition of "you" in my dictionary is a pronoun that is "used to refer to the one or ones being addressed," the second is a pronoun "used to refer to an indefinitely specified person; one."[37] For example, "you can't win for losing."[38] This kind of indefinite and general reference appears to be what these authors intended.

Consider the contemporary proverb "You get what you pay for." If

I opened a sermon with this statement, nobody would think I was saying that only the Christians present in the audience get what they pay for. The two forms of the proverb, "You get what you pay for" and "A man gets what he pays for," have the same semantic content. Both *mean* that a person gets what he or she pays for. The first statement could perhaps be misunderstood to mean *you* get what you pay for, but *I* often get cheated ("you" referring to the person being addressed). The second could be misunderstood to mean *a man* gets what he pays for, but *a woman* is often cheated. Both statements have a degree of ambiguity that must be clarified by the context. Yet *in context,* both can represent accurate translations for the generic use of *anthrōpos*. Like plural forms and indefinite pronouns, the second-person pronoun can function well in generic proverbs and instructional statements.

It is of course possible that a reader approaching the NRSV in a very literal manner would completely miss the indefinite sense intended by the translators. (This is perhaps why this method of achieving gender inclusion is among the least utilized today.) It is equally possible, however, that someone approaching the RSV in the same literal manner might miss the generic sense of "man" and "he." When James wrote *orgē . . . andros* ("the anger of man") in 1:20, he did not mean the anger of males but the anger of human beings. Surely all would agree that to avoid such literalist confusion on either side, the phrase is best translated "human anger." In fact, this is how the NIVI renders the verse: "For *human anger* does not bring about the righteous life that God desires" (James 1:20 NIVI). Any literalist misunderstanding in the NRSV's "you" and the RSV's "man" is avoided with a clear, accurate and inclusive translation. This example again makes it clear that in some cases a gender-inclusive translation renders the original more accurately than a noninclusive one. This point is discussed in greater detail later in this chapter.

Once again, guidelines adopted by the Conference on Gender-Related Language in Scripture appear to be misguided. Guideline A.1 is a positive one, affirming the use of masculine singular pronouns: "The generic use of 'he, him, his, himself' should be employed to translate generic 3rd person masculine singular pronouns in Hebrew, Aramaic and Greek." Guideline A.2 is a negative one, rejecting the two main techniques for replacing masculine pronouns: "Person and number should be retained in translation so that singulars are not changed to plurals and third-person statements are not changed to second-person or first-person statements, with only rare exceptions required in unusual cases."

The only plausible reason for retaining masculine pronouns is that they more accurately represent the meaning of the original. Yet it has been demonstrated that this is simply not the case. Retaining masculine terms will likely create more confusion than introducing inclusive language, particularly in view of the kind of literalist reading that some have advocated.

Both of these guidelines are classic examples of confusion between form and meaning. It was demonstrated in chapter four that retaining the Greek or Hebrew forms in Bible translation is irrelevant if the meaning of the original is lost. Insisting on formal equivalence can result in confusion or ambiguity because English, Hebrew, Aramaic and Greek are different languages that use different forms to express the same meaning. Some Hebrew plural terms, such as *shāmayim* and *'elōhîm,* must be translated with singular terms: "heaven" and "God." Neuter plural nouns often take singular verbs in Greek but must be translated with plurals in English. There is no exact correspondence in form.

The New Testament writers sometimes change forms. Further evidence that guidelines A.1 and A.2 are flawed is that they are contrary to the pattern of the biblical writers themselves. On a number of occasions Paul changes singulars to plurals when quoting from the Old Testament. Compare the Old Testament texts in table 5.1 with Paul's New Testament quotations.

In all three passages the apostle Paul translates Hebrew singulars with Greek plurals, thus breaking guideline A.2. Someone might argue that Paul is not translating the Old Testament but merely applying singular Old Testament references to groups of people in the New Testament. But an examination of their contexts suggests that these Old Testament passages are indeed generic, referring to people in general. Psalm 36, for example, is an oracle against the sinfulness of wicked

Old Testament Text	New Testament Citation
Is 52:7 How lovely on the mountains are the feet of *him* who brings good news.	Rom 10:15 As it is written, "How beautiful are the feet of *those* who bring good news!"
Ps 36:1 There is no fear of God before *his* eyes.	Rom 3:10, 18 As it is written . . . "There is no fear of God before *their* eyes."
Ps 32:1 Blessed is *he* whose transgressions are forgiven, whose sins are covered.	Rom 4:6, 7 David says the same thing . . . "Blessed are *they* whose transgressions are forgiven, whose sins are covered."

Table 5.1

people (see the plurals in verses 10-12). Psalm 32 concerns believers who have received forgiveness from God. It is significant that in Psalm 32:1, Paul is quoting from the Septuagint, which itself had introduced the plural construction. The Septuagint translators evidently recognized that although the verse was singular in form, its generic message was accurately conveyed with a plural construction (compare Ps 33:20-21 LXX [34:19-20]).[39] It is also significant that in Isaiah 52:7 the original NIV had already translated the Hebrew singular with a plural: "How beautiful on the mountains are the feet of *those* who bring good news." In the absence of an inclusive agenda the translators recognized the generic nature of the Hebrew singular.

The real question that must be asked, therefore, is not whether person or number should always be retained but whether in each case their retention or alteration results in a loss of meaning. On the one hand, will introducing inclusive language result in a loss of the sense intended by the original author in the source language? On the other hand, will retaining "man" and masculine pronouns result in loss of the inclusive sense for the reader in the receptor language?

Summary. This section has examined various techniques for introducing inclusive language for generic "man" and masculine generic pronouns. The careful use of these methods can accurately capture the sense intended by the original author. The variety of methods available to translators means that it is seldom necessary to retain masculine terms when the author intended an inclusive sense. When one particular version (say, the NRSV) fails to render accurately the sense of the original, other versions (such as NIVI, NLT, CEV, TEV) usually capture it well. For example, the NRSV renders Luke 14:27 "whoever does not carry *the* cross" in place of the RSV's "*his* cross." While the Greek refers to an individual's own cross, the NRSV seems to suggest Christ's cross. The NIVI appropriately translates "and those who do not carry their cross." The NLT reads "if you do not carry your own cross." Similarly, in Revelation 21:3, the choice of "mortal" for *anthrōpos* in the NRSV is probably inappropriate ("the home of God is with mortals"), since the end of mortality is the whole point of the eternal state.[40] Though "mortals" is synonymous with "human beings" in terms of present human existence, it is a less-than-adequate term for the glorified state. The NIVI more appropriately renders it, "Now the dwelling of God is with human beings."

All of this suggests that there is nothing inherently inaccurate about gender-inclusive language when it is used with appropriate caution and with as much understanding as possible of the historical and cultural context. It is a very common fallacy among those who oppose inclusive language to find a few inaccuracies in one version and then jump to the conclusion that the methodology itself is flawed. This is not valid. Inclusive language must be evaluated on a case-by-case basis to determine if it enhances or hinders the meaning of the original.

Unnecessary or Inappropriate Use of Gender-Inclusive Language

Where only males are intended. Translators have introduced inclusive language in some contexts where only males are intended. This is fairly common in the NRSV and the CEV, which have more comprehensively inclusive agendas than most other contemporary versions. Examples of this appear occasionally in the Psalms, especially when the psalmist is described by his enemies. The NRSV sometimes alters the third person to the first or second person. Compare the RSV and the NRSV translations below:

> RSV: My enemies say of me in malice: "When will he die, and his name perish?" (Ps 41:5)
>
> NRSV: My enemies wonder in malice when I will die, and my name perish. (Ps 41:5; compare CEV "when will you die?")
>
> RSV: Many are saying of me, there is no help for him in God. (Ps 3:2)

NRSV: Many are saying to me, "There is no help for you in God." (Ps 3:2; compare Ps 34:6; 35:25; 71:11)

Since both psalms are identified in their titles as psalms of David, there seems to be no reason to alter the masculine reference. Even if David is not named (the authenticity of some of these superscripts is questionable), the masculine pronouns indicate that the author is speaking as a man. This does not mean that the psalm has no application for women. But something is lost to a comprehension of the historical context when the masculine reference is removed. Incidentally, in these examples other inclusive versions often retain masculine pronouns (see NIVI, NLT, NCV, REB, NJB). The error here is made by the NRSV translators and is not something inherent in gender-inclusive versions. A similar slip is made by the NIVI and CEV translators at Luke 5:18, where the paralytic is said to be carried to Jesus by "some people" instead of by "some men." While the parallel accounts in Matthew and Mark do not specifically refer to "men," Luke here uses *andres* (plural of *anēr*). Since the four were undoubtedly men, there is no reason to alter the text. All other inclusive versions retain "men" (NRSV, NLT, TEV, NJB, NAB, NCV).

In other cases, the use of inclusive language appears to be unnecessary, but the change in meaning is very slight. In 1 Samuel 4:10 NRSV it is "everyone" who flees home instead of "every man" (RSV). Since only males were soldiers, this change is unnecessary. Similarly, in 2 Samuel 4:2 the NIV text reads, "Now Saul's son had two men who were leaders of raiding bands." The NIVI drops "men who were" and reads simply, "Now Saul's son had two leaders of raiding bands."[41] While no one could argue that this change represents a serious inaccuracy, I do not find these choices to be wise. Since the following context identifies these leaders as men, and since the NIV represents good English, there is no reason for the alteration. In chapter two it was suggested that form should be retained if and when there is no loss of meaning. By introducing an unnecessary formal change here, the translator takes one (albeit small) step away from the meaning intended in the Hebrew text.

In 1 Corinthians 13:11 the NRSV reads, "When I was a child, I spoke like a child . . . when I became an adult" (RSV "a man"). The word translated "adult" is *anēr,* which usually means a male human being. While it is certainly true that in this passage Paul is contrasting childhood with adulthood, since he is speaking as a man it would seem slightly more accurate to translate *anēr* as "man."

A number of similar examples can be cited. In Luke 14:16 (NIV) Jesus says that "a certain man *[anthrōpos tis]* was preparing a great banquet." The NRSV reads "*someone* gave a great dinner" but then follows with the resumptive pronoun "he" throughout the story. Since in Jesus' story the "someone" was a man and since "a certain man" is perfectly acceptable English, the change was unnecessary. The NIVI, incidentally, retains the NIV reading "a certain man." Similarly, in Acts 9:7 "the men *[andres]* traveling with Saul" on the road to Damascus become in the NIVI "*those* traveling with Saul." Since the Greek here is *anēr* and since it seems unlikely that women would be present on such an occasion, "men" should have been retained. Inclusive versions such as NRSV, CEV and NLT all retain "men" here.

In some cases, although changes appear to be unnecessary, they produce slightly better English style or enhanced clarity. In 1 Corinthians 3:21, the NIV's "so then, no more boasting about men!" becomes in the NIVI "no more boasting about human leaders." Though only men seem to be in view (1 Cor 1:12: Paul, Cephas, Apollos), the NIVI rendering helps clarify the nature of the Corinthian boasting. Similar examples will be provided below.

In other cases a decision is more difficult. In 1 Kings 9:5 NIV Solomon is told, "You shall never fail to have a man *['îsh]* on the throne of Israel." The NRSV, NIVI and NLT all have "successor" instead of "man." Since the line of male heirs is intended, there is little reason to alter the masculine reference. (The NJB retains "man.") At the same time, though "successor" is not gender specific, it is a more precise term in the context of succession than "man." It also seems to me to represent slightly better English style. Since anyone familiar with Israel's history and culture would recognize that a male heir is in view, the translation "successor" may actually be the better one.

Where the principle is general but the illustration envisions a male. In some cases the author intends the reference to be general but envisions an illustration or application that involves a man. For example, Andreas Köstenberger points out that in James 1:23, James is undoubtedly thinking of a man: "Anyone who listens to the word but does not do what it says is like a man *[anēr]* who looks at his face in a mirror." This is a difficult call. Though the verse is teaching a general proverbial truth about people, not males specifically, James's use of *anēr* suggests that his illustration envisions a male. It would seem best to retain the specific gender in this case. While most inclusive versions use inclusive language in these passages, the NAB retains "man."

This principle also applies to parables that refer to male characters. The CEV deletes masculine pronouns from the parable of the sower (Mt 13:3-9) and refers to a "wise person" rather than a "wise man" who built his house on the rock (Mt 7:24). I find these choices to be inappropriate. When a general principle is illustrated with a specific illustration, the specifics related to gender should be retained. Just as the reference to a "woman" who loses a coin in Luke 15:8-10 should remain feminine, so the masculine references to the sower should be retained.

In some texts, especially legislative ones, women could conceivably be included but the author was surely thinking of men. For example, the statements about homicide and kidnapping in Exodus 21:12-19 surely envision men, as does the reference to two men fighting in verses 22-25. The NRSV is inclusive throughout, even though the word *'îsh* is used in the passage.

Where language is intentionally patriarchal. Because the original biblical contexts were patriarchal in nature (see discussion in chap. four), Bible translations should retain cultural references in order to convey accurately the author's intended meaning. As we have seen, feminist versions such as the INT and the NTPI often distort the meaning of the original text by seeking to abolish all traces of patriarchy.[42] Even the more moderate gender-inclusive versions occasionally mute the patriarchal culture of the Bible. The CEV, for example, repeatedly translates commands for wives to "submit" *(hypotassō)* to their husbands as exhortations to "put your husband first" (Tit 2:5; Eph 5:22; Col 3:18 CEV). This seems to be an excessive weakening of the force of the Greek verb. The CEV also removes all masculine references in regard to qualifications for church leadership (elders and overseers) in 1 Timothy 3:1-7 and Titus 1:5-9. Whether or not women today should fill such leadership roles is open to discussion, but it is hard to deny that in these contexts Paul was speaking about men. A contemporary translation should retain the patriarchy implicit in the text.

In many other cases, discerning whether the biblical text is meant to be patriarchal is difficult. We must be cautious in assuming too quickly that women would not have been included in certain passages. It might be presumed, for example, that passages related to inheritance refer only to men. Yet Numbers 36:8 speaks of women inheriting land in Israel. This same point applies to a variety of vocations and ministries. Since prophets in the Old Testament could be either men or women, the masculine references to false prophets in Deuteronomy 13 may well be generic and are so interpreted by some versions (NIVI, NLT, NRSV, TEV, CEV). In other passages, the masculine (generic?) term "herdsmen" is rendered as "herders" by inclusive versions (Gen 13:7-8; 26:20; NRSV, NIVI), since in that culture women also functioned in this role (see Gen 29:6, 9). In each of these cases, the historical and literary context must be carefully examined to determine whether an inclusive translation is warranted. One benefit of using a more inclusive term such as "prophet" or "herder" is that it allows for the possibility of women being included without actually specifying them. This leaves the translation with the level of ambiguity that is present in the Hebrew text.

Psalm 1, which is commonly cited to illustrate gender-inclusive language, also raises difficult questions about culture and patriarchy. The text begins with the term "man" *('îsh)* and follows it with masculine pronouns: "Blessed is the *man* who does not walk in the counsel of the wicked. . . . But *his* delight is in the law of the LORD. . . . *He* is like a tree planted by streams of water, which yields its fruit in season and whose leaf does not wither. Whatever *he* does prospers" (Ps 1:1-3 NIV).

The NIVI, like most inclusive versions, uses plural references: "Blessed are *those* who do not walk in the counsel of the wicked. . . . But *their* delight is in the law of the LORD. . . . *They* are like trees planted by streams of water, which yield their fruit in season and whose leaves do not wither. Whatever *they* do prospers."

The plural is appropriate because the psalm clearly carries a general and proverbial sense, referring to individuals who delight in God's law. A more difficult question is whether, in a patriarchal culture where only men studied the law, the author could have envisioned a woman in this situation. One possible solution is to argue that since it was never God's intention to exclude women from the study of God's Word, the psalmist—writing by inspiration of the Holy Spirit—actually intended *'îsh* to be understood in an inclusive sense. The translation "those" allows for women even though it does not specify them ("man or woman" would specify them). Again, however, a decision is very difficult. Some might argue that it is best to retain masculine references because, as far as we can determine, the actions described here were performed in the psalmist's context only by males. It should be left to notes in study Bibles or other reference aids to explain that in the present age the text applies also to women. Others would argue that since the text clearly applies to women today, a neutral rendering such as "those" allows for this application without compromising the original meaning.[43]

Summary. The examples cited in this section illustrate the point that translators adopting moderate inclusive language, like all translators, must make hard decisions that sometimes result in inaccuracies. All translations are produced by fallible human beings and must constantly be examined for accuracy. This is why a continual examination and revision process is necessary for all Bible versions. Some of the rhetoric arising from the present debate runs counter to this important principle. The statement issued by the International Bible Society on May 23, 1997, affirmed that "the present NIV would continue to be published unchanged." If this statement means that all revision efforts have ceased, it represents a serious setback for those seeking to maintain the accuracy and contemporary relevance of this excellent version.

As we have seen, the most problematic passages for translators are those in which it is very difficult to determine whether or not the author intended masculine terms to be inclusive. Given the patriarchal nature of the biblical culture, this can be a very difficult call in many contexts.

The most appropriate and accurate translation is produced by sound principles of interpretation that are applied on a case-by-case basis, not by any political, social or theological agenda.

When Gender-Inclusive Language Enhances Meaning

While the immediately preceding examples demonstrate that forcing inclusive language onto a passage can result in a less accurate translation, earlier examples cited in this chapter revealed that the introduction of gender-inclusive language often results in a more accurate translation, since inclusive terms tend to be more precise than their noninclusive counterparts. Whereas the English "man" can mean "male" or "human being," "person" confirms that in this context the latter is intended. More precision is achieved.

Improving awkward or archaic expressions. Another way that gender-inclusive language may enhance translation is by producing clearer and more idiomatic renderings. For example, certain Hebrew and Greek idioms utilize the terms "men" or "sons" in ways that do not translate well into English. The "son of" idiom in Hebrew and Greek is addressed in chapter seven.

Grudem complains that the NRSV's replacing "men of war" in Numbers 31:28, 49 (RSV) with the term "warriors" results in an inaccuracy, since Israel's army was made up exclusively of men.[44] While Grudem is certainly correct concerning the nature of Israel's army, "warriors" (NRSV, NAB) and "soldiers" (NIV, TEV, CEV) are much more common English terms for members of an army than the odd and archaic "men of war." (The term "man-of-war" in my dictionary is defined as a warship.) If I stated that brave American soldiers won the Battle of the Bulge in World War II, no one would accuse me of using excessive gender-inclusive language. The historical context makes the sense "male soldiers" patently obvious. The introduction of inclusive language, perhaps inadvertent in this case, produces a better English rendering.

In John 3:1 the NIV reads, "Now there was a man of the Pharisees named Nicodemus." The NIVI reads simply, "Now there was a Pharisee named Nicodemus." The literal translation "a man of the Pharisees" is very awkward English. I have never referred to someone as "a man of the Baptists" or "a man of the Methodists." I would rather say "a Baptist" or "a Methodist." The inclusive translation here represents a significant improvement in English style. Andreas Köstenberger, on the other hand, complains that by eliminating the word "man," the NIVI blunts an important connection with the use of the same word *anthrōpos* in the previous verse, where we learn that "he [Jesus] did not need man's testimony about *man,* for he knew what was in a *man*" (Jn 2:25 NIV).[45]

Köstenberger's concern is legitimate. Having to use an awkward English expression in order to retain a verbal allusion creates tension, and something will always be lost in the translation. There is another complicating factor. The sense of *anthrōpos* in 2:25 and its sense in 3:1 are not the same. In 2:25 the term means "persons," whereas in 3:1 it seems to carry the sense "a male person." Despite this change in sense, the verbal connection with verse 25 appears to be present.[46] Perhaps the best resolution here is to use the term "person" in both verses: "for he knew what was inside a person" (2:25) and "there was a certain person, a Pharisee named Nicodemus" (3:1). The content of John 3 (the masculine pronouns and so on) make it obvious that Nicodemus was a male, so there is no loss of meaning. Such a translation retains both the inclusive sense of *anthrōpos* in 2:25 and the verbal connection with 3:1.

Where the referents are males but the statement concerns their humanity. In some cases the referents are male, but an inclusive translation sharpens the sense of the original. In Numbers 8:17, for example, the NIV reads, "Every firstborn male in Israel, whether man or animal, is mine." The NIVI renders, "Every firstborn male in Israel, whether human or animal, is mine." While the referent here is obviously male, translating the Hebrew *'ādām* as "human" sharpens the author's contrast between animals and humans.

Another example of this appears in James 5:17, where the original NIV reads, "Elijah was a man just like us." The NIVI translates, "Elijah was human just as we are." While at first glance someone might argue that there was no reason to change the NIV, since Elijah was indeed a man, a moment's reflection confirms that the NIVI is a better rendering.

The point is not that Elijah was a "male" like us (many of James's readers were not males) but that he was subject to the human weaknesses that we all have. While the referent in this case happens to be a male, the sense of *anthrōpos* in this context is "a human being." An inclusive rendering more accurately conveys this sense.

Similar examples could be multiplied. When Cornelius falls down to worship Peter (Acts 10:26), he responds, "Stand up; I too am a man" (RSV). The NRSV has Peter say, "Stand up; I am only a mortal." Grudem argues that the NRSV is a poor translation because the term "mortal" shifts the emphasis from one's humanity to one's mortality (that is, one's liability to death).[47] Here, however, Grudem has identified the wrong lexical form. It is true that the English adjective "mortal" focuses on one's mortality (the first definition in my dictionary is "subject to death").[48] But the NRSV uses the noun, not the adjective. The only definition of the noun "mortal" in my dictionary is "a human being," and this is exactly what *anthrōpos* means in Acts 10:26. The NIVI appropriately translates, "I am only human myself," and the NLT reads, "I'm a human being like you!" All of these versions (including the NRSV's "a mortal") are better than the RSV's "a man," since they bring out more clearly the contrast in context between a human being and a god. Again, a clear and inclusive translation more accurately reflects the author's intent.

Where traditional versions inappropriately introduce the term "man." In many cases the word "man" has been introduced into traditional versions where no parallel term appears in the Hebrew and Greek (for more on this, see chap. six). These may or may not be accurate translations, depending on the context in which the term is used. For example, in Matthew 5:15 the RSV reads, "Nor do men light a lamp and put it under a bushel, but on a stand, and it gives light to all in the house" (compare KJV, NASB). The Greek verb is in the third-person plural form, *kaiousin* ("they light"), which carries no gender distinction. C. S. Rodd points out that the original permits the inclusion of women and that in the culture of Jesus' day it is likely that women were mainly the ones to light the lamp in the home.[49] The inappropriate introduction of "men" probably obscures the cultural context. Translations such as the NIV had already introduced "people" here (NKJV "they"; NRSV "no one").

When "Man" Carries the Sense of Corporate Humanity or Representative Leadership

Passages in which "man" refers to corporate humanity or to Adam as representing the human race are among the most difficult to translate. This is a particular problem in the case of the Hebrew term *'ādām*, which can carry at least three distinct senses: "Adam" (the first man), "man" (exclusive of females) and "humanity." The term in Genesis 1:27 clearly has this third sense: "So God created man *['ādām]* in his own image, in the image of God he created him; male and female he created them" (NIV; compare Gen 5:1-2). While some inclusive versions retain the term "man" here (NJB, NAB), others use terms such as "human beings" (REB, NIVI, TEV), "humans" (CEV), "humankind" (NRSV) and "people" (NLT). Grudem takes great exception to the NRSV rendering:

> Throughout the NRSV the human race is no longer called "man." The majestic, noble name which God gave us as humans at the beginning of creation—the great and wonderful name "man"—is no longer our name in the Bible. . . . Feminist pressure has renamed the human race. We are now to be called "humankind," instead of the name God gave us.[50]

While rhetorically powerful, Grudem's statement clouds the essential issue by using an English translation ("man") when referring to a Hebrew term *('ādām)*. In the Genesis story God does not give humans the wonderful (English) name "man," he gives them the Hebrew name *'ādām*, which is a different word in a different language with a different semantic range. If we take Grudem's statement seriously, then we have all changed the noble Hebrew name *'ādām* into a corrupt Anglo-Saxon name: "man."

Of course what Grudem is actually arguing is that in the original text, the same Hebrew word is used for the first man ("Adam"), the male person ("man") and the human race ("mankind"), and so translators should use the same English word. Even this, however, is not an exact parallel, since we transliterate *'ādām* as "Adam" but then translate it as "man" for the other two senses.

The problem is that if the English term "man" does not carry the same inclusive sense that the Hebrew term *'ādām* had, then it would convey the wrong sense for the passage for many readers. Grudem's argument is something like saying that in John 2:4 Jesus addresses his mother with the noble name "woman," so this word should be retained in English translations, even if it sounds offensive to English ears. But Jesus did not call his mother "woman" in contemporary English, he called her *gynē* in Koine Greek.[51] If the English word "woman" conveys a very different sense to the modern reader than the Greek word *gynē* conveyed to first-century readers, then it represents a poor translation and should be replaced with a different term.[52]

Grudem argues that since *'ādām* was used in Hebrew both for "a male human being" and for "humanity," we should choose a noun in English that is capable of this same dual role. He writes that "the problem is that 'humankind,' 'human beings' and 'human' are not names that can also refer to men in distinction from woman, and thus they are a *[sic]* less accurate translations of *'ādām* than the word 'man.'"[53]

Such a statement not only confuses form and meaning but also imposes an impossible standard on Bible translation. Grudem is suggesting that when translating a lexeme with two distinct senses in the source language, translators should find a parallel lexeme with the same two distinct senses in the receptor language. But the semantic ranges of words in different languages seldom overlap exactly. It is the sense of the Greek or Hebrew word in a particular context (not its other possible senses in other contexts) that must be the controlling factor in determining which English word to choose. Grudem's argument is akin to saying that because the Greek word *anēr* can mean both "man" and "husband" we should adopt an English word that carries these same two senses. Since the English word "man" can, in some contexts, mean "husband," then *anēr* should be translated "man" whenever it appears, even in contexts such as John 4:17: "I do not have a man *[anēr]*." This argument is obviously fallacious. We translate *anēr* as "husband" in John 4:17 because that is its sense in this context. It matters little that elsewhere *anēr* means "man." The semantic ranges of "man" and *anēr* do not overlap exactly. The goal must be, always, to find an English term that most accurately captures the sense of that Greek or Hebrew term in each particular context.

An even more fundamental problem with Grudem's claim is his assumption that God was necessarily speaking Hebrew when he named the human race. How do we know what language God and Adam spoke together? The language used by the author of Genesis could well have arisen millennia after the creation of the world, and the Hebrew *'ādām* could itself be a translation (with cultural and societal baggage) of an entirely different term. All languages arise and develop within cultures. This makes it especially dangerous to assume that the male connotations associated with one sense of *'ādām* ("a male human being") should necessarily be imposed on a different sense of the same lexeme (*'ādām*, "humanity"). How do we know that these two referents (the man and humanity) were even identified with the same lexeme in the language of Eden?[54]

As we saw in chapter four, distinct senses of a lexeme do not necessarily impose their meaning on each other. Bread that is "fresh" is not also nonsaline (as in "fresh" water). We cannot assume that the lexeme *'ādām* always contains male connotations simply because it is used in some contexts with reference to the first (male) human being.[55]

Passages such as Genesis 1:27 raise complex issues in relation to representative leadership and authority, and I do not pretend to have all the answers. Translators will continue to struggle with accurately rendering *'ādām* in Genesis 1:27, 5:1-2 and many other passages because of the continuing debate about its precise sense in these passages. Whatever decision these translators make, they will probably have to include marginal notes to explain the other options.

Some have argued that "man" is the only appropriate English term to represent the sense of "corporate humanity." Yet this sentence itself defines the less precise term "man" with the more precise term "humanity." It seems to me that "humanity" captures this corporate solidarity quite well. It is sometimes argued that since Adam was created first and since Eve was created from a part of him (Gen 2:21-22), the female is to be subsumed under the broader category of the male. "Man" (the male) in some sense encompasses both males and females. But this does not seem to be what the Genesis account teaches. Maleness is not the primary category under which the female emerges. Rather, the man is incomplete without the woman (Gen 2:18). After their creation the two stand beside each other as equals and as whole persons; neither is subsumed as merely "a part" of the other. While Adam's priority in creation may perhaps mean that he is to function as leader in the relationship (1 Tim 2:12-13), it does not necessarily follow that the woman must be subsumed under the name given to the male. Rather, the two are mutually dependent on one another (1 Cor 11:11-12), both standing as whole persons before God. Both are persons, not "men."

Conclusion

This chapter has examined many examples of gender-inclusive language in contemporary versions and has determined that techniques used in these versions to achieve gender inclusion can accurately convey the sense intended by the original author. As repeatedly noted throughout this chapter, the effectiveness of these techniques in individual cases does not mean that they are always appropriate or that masculine terms should always be replaced with inclusive ones. When the author intended an exclusive sense, that exclusion should be reflected in the translation. On the other hand, when an inclusive sense is intended, the expression that best captures that sense represents the best interpretation.

The point is that decisions must be made on a case-by-case basis through sound exegesis, not with a sweeping condemnation of certain techniques. The guidelines established at the Conference on Gender-Related Language in Scripture are seriously flawed in that they condemn the use of such techniques with little or no consideration of context or of contemporary English usage.

Contemporary English usage is dealt with in the excursus that follows this chapter. Chapter six considers other examples of gender-inclusive language, especially as related to terms such as "brother(s)," "father(s)" and "son(s)."

Excursus
Contemporary English Usage: Are "Man" and "He" Inclusive Today?

The conclusion reached in the previous chapter, that Greek and Hebrew terms like *anthrōpos* and *'ādām* can carry an inclusive as well as exclusive sense, will not be enough to convince many that terms like "human being" should be adopted in Bible translation. It could be argued, for example, that "man" and "he" are perfectly acceptable generic terms in English, and so should be retained. It is to the question of contemporary English usage, therefore, that we briefly turn.

"Man" as Male and Female

The *Oxford English Dictionary* (OED), which describes both the etymology of words and also their contemporary usage, and is descriptive rather than prescriptive, points out that in Old English "human beings" was the prevailing sense of the word "man." This inclusive sense has gradually weakened, however, in favor of the sense "male":

> In the surviving use, the sense "person" occurs only in general or indefinite applications (e.g. with adjs. like *every, any, no,* and often in the plural, esp. with *all, any, some, many, few,* etc.); in modern apprehension *man* as thus used primarily denotes the male sex, though by implication referring also to women.
>
> The gradual development of the use of the unambiguous synonyms *body, person, one,* and (for the plural) *folk(s), people,* has greatly narrowed the currency of *man* in this sense; it is now literary and proverbial rather than colloquial.[1]

Webster's New Riverside University Dictionary notes that:

> The use of *man* in its primary sense of "an adult male human being" makes this term unacceptable to many when the sense intended is "a human being, regardless of sex." Consequently, such terms as *men and women, human beings,* and *persons* have come to be used as substitutes for *man* in the latter sense.[2]

If nothing else, these statements suggest that "man" and "men" as generic terms are in significant decline in contemporary English. Of course one cannot make such a determination from dictionary definitions alone. While seeking to follow contemporary English usage, dictionaries often prescribe usage rather than describe the present state of the language. They also often include senses of words that are archaic or rarely used by the general public. It is necessary therefore to evaluate contemporary English usage through empirical studies of English usage and perception. There has been a significant amount of research in this area.

I must admit that I first approached this research with a good deal of skepticism. I assumed that these studies would be conducted by feminists and would therefore reflect a feminist bias. Of course it must be admitted that no researcher approaches their study with a clean slate. Even in the most scientific of fields "unbiased research" is an oxymoron. The question, however, is not whether a particular investigator holds a particular perspective (all investigators do), but whether their study is fair and objective in collecting, analyzing and evaluating the data. I examined studies published in a variety of fields—not just women's studies, but also psychology, sociology, linguistics, communication, English grammar and learning theory. I also looked for authors who wrote like scholars, rather than apologists and polemicists. Even with these cautions and reservations, the evidence appears to be overwhelming that a large percentage of the population perceives masculine generic terms as exclusive rather than inclusive, that is, referring primarily or exclusively to men.

Studies of Generic "Man"

Joseph Schneider and Sally Hacker (1973) gave college students hypothetical chapter titles for a textbook on sociology and asked them to bring in pictures that could be used in the chapter. Among students who were given titles using generic "man," such as "Industrial Man" and "Economic Man," 64 percent of the pictures submitted showed only men. When gender-neutral terms like "Industrial Life" and "Economic Life" were used, only half of the pictures contained only male images. This represented a statistically significant 39 percent increase in the number of women portrayed.[3] Lavisa Wilson (1978) conducted a similar study on teachers, asking them to mark which of a set of pictures (containing a man and a woman, two men, or two women) applied to stimulus words like "repairman," "salesmen," "men of good will," "early men," "stone age men," "craftsmen," "policemen," as well as gender-neutral equivalents like "cavepeople," "salespeople," "police officers," etc. Wilson found that teachers were more likely to select pictures of men and women when generic terms were used.[4] J. A. Sniezek and C. H. Jazwinski (1986) similarly found that when subjects were asked to draw pictures of "man," "people," and "men and women," pictures of "man" had significantly more males than those drawn for "people."[5] In another study these researchers determined that when occupations and their accompanying explanations use generic masculine terms, 92.9 percent of names requested for that category were masculine.

Studies of children have produced similar results. Alleen Nilson (1973) found that young children thought that "man" meant male people in sentences such as "man needs food."[6] Linda Harrison (1975) asked junior-high students to draw pictures of "early man," "mankind," "early humans" or "early men and women." The least number of women were drawn in the "early man" category, and (not surprisingly) the most women were drawn for "early men and women."[7] In another study, Linda Harrison and Richard Passero (1975) read elementary school children sentences which contained either inclusive words like "people," "salespeople" and "pilgrim ancestors" or masculine generic terms like "man," "manmade" and "pilgrim forefathers." When asked to circle pictures which indicated the referents of these sentences, females were circled more often for the inclusive sentences.[8]

These studies indicating that children often misunderstand generic "man" as male-only have important implications for the uproar over gender-inclusive language in children's versions like the International Children's Bible (ICB) and the New International Reader's Version (NIrV). If children are even more prone than adults to misunderstand masculine generics, one would think that the choice to use more inclusive terms in these versions would be appropriate.

There seems little doubt from these studies that when "man" is used as a generic term, it is often misunderstood to refer only to males. At the least, a certain level of confusion and ambiguity often results. This confusion has been illustrated by many writers. Psychologist Wendy Martyna points out the startled laughter that greets such sentences as "Menstrual pain accounts for an enormous loss of manpower hours," or "Man, being a mammal, breastfeeds his young." Compare the sentence "Humans, being mammals, breastfeed their young." The latter is obviously a more clear and unambiguous statement. Note the subtle ambiguity in phrases like "a man for all seasons," and "no man is an island." The former is specific (male), the latter is general.[9] Similar results related to perception and usage have been demonstrated concerning the use of generic "he."

Studies of Generic "He"

In an experiment conducted by Wendy Martyna, students were asked to judge whether pictures of either a male or a female could apply to sentences containing generic "he," "they" or "he-or-she." For example, a student would be given a sentence like "When someone listens to the record player, he will often sing along." The student would then be shown a picture of either a male or female performing this action and asked whether the picture applied to the sentence. While male pictures were judged unequivocally to be applicable to sentences containing all generic forms, and female pictures to be applicable to sentences containing "they" or "he-or-she," 20 percent of the students reported that female pictures did not apply to sentences containing the generic "he."[10] A subsequent study found 40 percent did not find females to be applicable.[11] While twenty percent may not seem like a very large percentage, it must be recognized that these respondents reported that generic "he" did not include women. This is very significant when we realize that twenty (or even forty) percent of readers might miss the point of a biblical passage where generic "he" is used. The issue is not merely one of offending female readers, but of providing a clear and precise translation.

In another study, Donald Mackay and D. C. Fulkerson (1979) asked subjects whether sentences using "he" as a generic pronoun (e.g., "A bicyclist can bet that he is not safe from dogs") could be applied to females. Errors in comprehension of the sentences containing generic "he" occurred 87 percent of the time. Ninety-five percent made at least one comprehension error, and 80 percent of the subjects made no correct responses (believing all generic "he" references to refer to males only).[12] Virginia Kidd conducted a similar experiment in which students were asked whether the antecedent of a sentence containing masculine generic pronouns was male, male or female, or female. Significantly more students chose male. Kidd concluded that "the use of a male pronoun as the generic is not generally interpreted as representative of a neutral antecedent. . . . The masculine pronoun as the generic simply does not accomplish the purpose for which it is intended."[13]

Many other studies could be cited which demonstrate similar results.[14] Overwhelming empirical evidence would appear to confirm that when masculine generic terms are used, women and girls are perceived as being included significantly less often than men and boys. It is not only women who have these perceptions. Both women and men reported that they usually pictured men when they read or heard the masculine generic.

The Problem of Ambiguity and Confusion

The problem with masculine generic terms is not that they *cannot* be perceived as inclusive. The above studies indicate that in many cases they are perceived as such. The problem is rather the level of ambiguity and potential confusion which results. Referring back to her 1977 study, Martyna notes the ambiguity of generic "he":

> Not only do some students comprehend it as specifically male, and other students as a human referent; but the same students render contradictory

judgments, deciding in one instance that "he" includes "she," and in another that it does not.[15]

Even in clearly generic contexts (e.g., "When someone is near a hospital, he should be quiet"), "he" was found to be ambiguous, allowing both specific and generic interpretations to be drawn. Martyna concludes, "My research does not argue that *he cannot* function generically, but that it allows both specific and generic interpretation, even in a context which should force a generic inference."[16]

Writing from a philosophical perspective, Janice Moulton also argues that "he" and "man" do not function as true generics: "If 'he' and 'man' are genuinely gender-neutral, then they ought to be applicable to any person regardless of gender." Yet few would say without irony, "She's the best man for the job," or "He's the best" of a female.[17] The famous syllogism "All men are mortal; Socrates is a man; therefore Socrates is a mortal" becomes confused if one introduces "Sophia is a man" as the middle sentence.[18] Although in the first sentence "men" is perceived by the reader to mean "human being," the sense "male" has obviously intruded into the second sentence since the female name Sophia sounds wrong. Someone could argue, of course, that "Sophia is a man" is a perfectly acceptable sentence, since "man" here means "human being." This may be true for the author's intent; but the sentence still sounds wrong to the reader. The perception of "male" thus results in confusion and ambiguity. Other examples of the failure of gender neutrality occur in sentences like "Man has two sexes," and "Some men are females."[19]

This level of confusion and ambiguity again has significant implications for the use of masculine generics in Bible translation. Are these translations leaving themselves open to misinterpretation?

Seeking the *Best* Translation

The fact that "man" *can* still be perceived as a generic term is an argument utilized by opponents of gender-inclusive language. Grudem writes that "the claim that the English language will no longer allow the generic use of 'he, him, his' is simply false."[20] He then notes that this sense appears in all the dictionaries he surveyed. Later in the same article he writes, "Someone may object that we *cannot* use 'man' to mean 'the human race' or 'human being,' because that is no longer correct English. But this objection is unfounded." He then points out that 86 percent of the usage panel of the *American Heritage Dictionary* approved the use of the word "man" in the sentence "The Great Wall is the only man-made structure visible from space," and that 81 percent approved the sentence "If early man suffered from a lack of information, modern man is tyrannized by an excess of it."[21] In another place Grudem provides an extensive list of examples of generic "man" and "he" from the popular press and contemporary literature.[22]

In response, it must first be noted that Grudem is building a straw man. No one is arguing that "man" and "he" *cannot* be used or perceived in English as generic terms. Nor is anyone suggesting that the dictionaries have stopped listing "human being" as one of the senses of "man." As noted before, however, mere appearance in a dictionary does not necessarily indicate common usage.[23] Nor does the usage preference of a dictionary panel necessarily reflect that of the ordinary person. A conclusion on the latter must be reached through empirical studies like those previously cited. It should also be noted that these same dictionaries generally qualify the generic sense of "man" by pointing out that it is often inappropriate or open to misunderstanding.

The question that Grudem should have asked is not *can* "man" still mean "human being," but rather is this the *best* rendering? We are not seeking a merely acceptable translation, but the most accurate one for our target audience. One could say, for example, that in most cases the archaic language of the KJV *can* still carry its original meaning. I am sure every English reader would understand the sentence "Thou shalt love thy neighbor . . . " (Mt 5:43 KJV), and certainly most readers would comprehend "And if any man will sue thee at the law . . . " (Mt 5:40 KJV). But are not the better translations, "You shall love your neighbor . . ." (Mt 5:43 RSV) and "if someone wants to sue you . " (Mt 5:40 NIV)? The simple fact is that language changes over time, and translations must be updated to reflect these changes. While for many readers "man" still carries an inclusive sense, for many others it suggests exclusion where the original text intended inclusion. When more inclusive language (1) accurately retains the meaning of the original and (2) conveys inclusion to *both* these groups of readers, it would seem more appropriate and more accurate. If failure to update a translation results in misinterpretation by many average readers, that translation is flawed.

Is Education the Solution?

In another article on the NIVI controversy, Grudem addresses the claim that women will feel excluded when they hear masculine terms:

> Our response to women who say they do not feel included by such language should be to teach them that such usage does *not* in fact "exclude women." . . People who aren't aware of an inclusive, generic meaning for "he, him, his" can learn it in a moment.[24]

This is an extraordinarily condescending statement. It is saying essentially that we will choose the meanings we want English words to have and will then "educate" you concerning these meanings. We will make English "he, him, his" inclusive by informing you that they *are* inclusive. This is like saying that all we have to do is educate everyone that "gay" *really* means "cheerful" and the problem of its semantic shift will go away. Or it is like saying that the KJV is a perfectly acceptable contemporary translation if we will only provide lists of definitions for its archaic words and encourage readers to learn these meanings. An even closer analogy is the wooden, literal approach to translation that argues that if we can get everyone to start thinking in biblical idioms (for example, using "of" for all Greek genitives; translating every Greek or Hebrew term by a single English term;[25] and in this case, using masculine generics), then everyone will begin to interpret biblical texts accurately.

Not only is Grudem's statement condescending, but it simply will not work. As noted above, Ann Bodine and others have shown that for two hundred years English usage handbooks have been trying to mandate the singular "they" out of the English language by telling writers and students that it is inaccurate and wrong. Yet it is even more widely used and accepted today than ever. Prescribing what should be used must eventually give way to describing what *is* being used. If generic masculines are on their way out in contemporary English, Bible translations must translate accordingly or become archaic, outdated and inaccurate.

Six

INCLUSIVE LANGUAGE RELATED TO HUMAN BEINGS

Other Generic Terms

CHAPTER FIVE EXAMINED THE USE OF THE MASCULINE GENERICS "MAN" and "he" and the inclusive terms that are used to replace them. Chapter six surveys a variety of other masculine generic terms, especially those expressing familial relationships (brothers, fathers, sons). Other generic terms, such as masculine participles, adjectives and pronouns, are among the least controversial of generic terms and are touched on only briefly.

"Brothers" or "Brothers and Sisters"?

The Greek masculine noun *adelphos* can carry the sense of a physical "brother" but in the New Testament is more often used figuratively of the kinship between believers. Traditional English translations have rendered the Greek singular as "brother" and the plural *(adelphoi)* as "brothers" (NIV) or "brethren" (NASB, RSV, NKJV, KJV). In many contexts, however, the author is clearly addressing both men and women.[1] A striking example of this is Philippians 4:1-2, where Paul, after addressing the Philippian congregation as *adelphoi* (4:1), encourages two women, Euodia and Syntyche, to live in harmony with each other (4:2).

The semantic range of the Greek term *adelphos* in the New Testament includes the following senses:

1. Physical brother(s): "As Jesus was walking beside the Sea of Galilee, he saw two *brothers,* Simon called Peter and his *brother* Andrew" (Mt 4:18 NIV).

2. Male fellow believer(s): "Paul, an apostle of Christ Jesus by the will of God, and Timothy our *brother*" (2 Cor 1:1 NIV).

3. A male or female believer (in the singular): "Whoever loves his *brother* lives in the light, and there is nothing in him to make him stumble" (1 John 2:10 NIV).

4. Male and female believers (in the plural): "Therefore, I urge you, *brothers,* in view of God's mercy, to offer your bodies as living sacrifices" (Rom 12:1 NIV).

When the latter two senses are intended, the most accurate translations are "brother or sister" and "brothers and sisters," not "brother" or "brothers." Far from being "loose translations" or radical attempts to update the male-dominated culture of the New Testament, these translations are *exactly what the term meant in its first-century context.*

Surprisingly, even the NRSV, which consistently translates *adelphoi* as "brothers and sisters," errs linguistically by repeatedly noting in the margin "Gk *brothers.*" With this note the translators appear to be saying that although they have rendered the term "brothers and sisters," the Greek term actually means "brothers." A linguist would wonder at such a conclusion. As chapter four demonstrated, words get their meaning not from some all-encompassing "root meaning" but from their contemporary semantic range and from the context in which they are used. Since the sense "brothers and sisters" is part of the semantic range of *adelphoi* and since the context here clearly indicates that this sense is intended, "brothers and sisters" is an accurate and precise translation. It is exactly what the Greek term means.

Several objections might be brought forward against this conclusion. First, it might be said that "brothers" is a more literal translation because it, like *adelphoi,* consists of one word instead of three. But this objection, as we have seen, confuses form with meaning. As Eugene Nida points out, it may take a whole sentence in one language to convey the sense of a single word in another.[2]

A second objection might be that the English term "brothers" (or "brethren") is just as inclusive as Greek *adelphoi* (that is, it has the same semantic range) and so is a perfectly legitimate translation. It is true that one of the definitions of "brother" in my dictionary is "a fellow member of the Christian church."[3] But the question is, Does the word carry this inclusive sense for most readers? I am not familiar with any empirical studies of "brothers" that are similar to studies examining the generic "man" (surveyed in the excursus), but students have told me that the term does not sound inclusive to them. If one of the pastors in my church made the following announcement, "*Brothers,* please stay for a meeting with the elders immediately following the service," I suspect only the male half of his congregation would feel welcome. When Paul addressed his congregations as *adelphoi,* on the other hand, women obviously felt included. The semantic ranges of *adelphoi* in the first-century church and "brothers" in the contemporary church are not the same. Whether or not English "brothers" still sounds inclusive to many people, there can be no doubt that "brothers and sisters" sounds more inclusive and thus captures the sense of *adelphoi* better.

A third objection might be that the Greeks had a word for "sister" *(adelphē),* so the New Testament writers could have written "brother or sister" or "brothers and sisters" if that is what they meant (see Jas 2:15; 1 Cor 7:15).[4] This argument, however, is not valid. If the single word *adelphoi* in context clearly carries the sense "brothers and sisters," economy of language will dictate that the writer will *normally* choose the shorthand expression *adelphoi* over the more cumbersome *adelphoi kai adelphai.* The fact that Greek allows for a fuller expression does not mean that a writer will necessarily use it, especially if the shorter expression carries the same sense in a particular context.

A fourth objection might be that the term "brothers" should be retained because, in light of the patriarchal culture, Paul is really only addressing the men of the church. The women would receive the message through their husbands or fathers. I find this hard to believe, especially in light of Philippians 4:1-2 and the broader context of Paul's missionary activity. Whatever one thinks of the leadership role of women in the early church, there is no doubt that Paul proclaimed the gospel to women, taught them, established churches with them and viewed them as his coworkers (Phil 4:3; Rom 16:1-2, 3, 6, 7; Acts 16:15). It seems very unlikely that he would refrain from addressing them in his letters.

Inclusive versions have sometimes adopted a variety of terms for translating *adelphos* and *adelphoi* when they appear in inclusive contexts: "friends," "dear friends," "Christian friends," "believers," "Christians" and so on. Although these terms capture the sense of "fellow believer," they lose the further dimension of family identity that the Greek and English terms convey. Fellow believers are not just friends, they are spiritual family. It would seem, therefore, that the best translation in these contexts would be "brother or sister" for the singular *adelphos* and "brother and sister" for the plural *adelphoi*. Of the inclusive translations I have surveyed, the NIVI, NRSV, NCV,[5] NIrV and GW consistently render *adelphoi* accurately as "brothers and sisters," avoiding less familial terms.[6]

Once again a guideline adopted at the Conference on Gender-Related Language in Scripture appears to be misguided. Guideline B.1 originally read, "'Brother' *(adelphos)* and 'brothers' *(adelphoi)* should not be changed to 'brother(s) and sister(s).'" But if "brother(s)" no longer carries the inclusive sense that *adelphos* and *adelphoi* had in the New Testament, it is difficult to understand why it should not be changed. When words like "gay" (Jas 2:3 KJV), "bowels" (Phil 2:1 KJV) and "girdle" (1 Sam 18:4 KJV) no longer carried the senses they once had, closer English equivalents were introduced. This is a very basic principle of Bible translation.

As with the problems associated with guideline A.3 (chap. five), the difficulties with this guideline eventually resulted in its revision. Dan Wallace, New Testament professor at Dallas Theological Seminary, sent Wayne Grudem examples from secular Greek where *adelphoi* clearly meant "brothers and sisters." For example, a passage from the Oxyrhynchus Papyri (713.20-23; A.D. 97) reads, "My father died leaving me and my *adelphoi* Diodorus and Theis as his heirs, and his property devolved upon us." While Diodorus is a man's name, Theis is a woman's name. The Greek term is thus fully inclusive in this context, meaning "brother and sister" or "siblings." The English term "brothers" does not have this same sense. We would never say "my brothers Bob and Kathy."

Writing to the participants of the conference, Grudem conceded that when Paul wrote to his churches, he would have understood *adelphoi* to mean "brothers and sisters."[7] The guideline was therefore changed to read: " 'Brother' *(adelphos)* should not be changed to 'brother or sister'; however, the plural *adelphoi* can be translated 'brothers and sisters' where the context makes clear that the author is referring to both men and women."

The changed guideline is a significant concession. It is essentially saying that the NIVI and other gender-inclusive versions were perfectly legitimate and accurate in translating *adelphoi* as "brothers and sisters" in these contexts. Indeed, Grudem now writes that "in the case of *adelphoi* these more recent translations seem to have made a genuine improvement in accuracy."[8]

While this is an important clarification, the first half of the guideline is still questionable. When the singular *adelphos* clearly refers to any believer, whether male or female, should it not be translated "brother or sister"? In Matthew 5:22 NIV Jesus says, "But I tell you that anyone who is angry with his brother *[adelphos]* will be subject to judgment." The sense here is clearly anger toward any fellow believer, not just a male. The NIVI appropriately translates "brother or sister."

Fathers, Ancestors and Parents

The Greek and Hebrew terms usually translated "father(s)" (Hebrew *'āb, 'ābôt;* Greek *patēr, pateres*) have a significantly wider semantic range than their parallel terms in English, including not only "fathers" (male parents) but also "parents," "ancestors" and even "predecessors." Similarly, the terms usually translated "son(s)" (Hebrew *bēn, bānîm;* Greek *huios, huioi*) have a broader semantic range than their English counterparts, including not only "sons" but also "children," "offspring" or "descendants." These distinct semantic ranges should immediately warn us against mandating a single English translation ("sons" or "fathers") for a particular Greek term. From the perspective of the receptor language, it can be said that English commonly uses more precise terms than Greek with reference to lineage and ancestry.

Ancestors and forefathers. When it is clear that former generations rather than immediate parents are in view, most inclusive versions translate the Hebrew terms *'āb* and *'ābôt* (plural of *'āb*) and the Greek terms *patēr* and *pateres* (plural of *patēr*) as "ancestor" and "ancestors." In 1 Samuel 12:6 (NRSV), for example, Samuel says to the people, "The LORD is witness, who appointed Moses and Aaron and brought your ancestors *['ābôt]* up out of the land of Egypt." Since Samuel is speaking of many generations past and since it was both men and women who came out of Egypt, it would seem that "ancestors" represents the clearest, most accurate translation, especially since the English translation "fathers" (KJV, RSV, NASB, NKJV) used in this sense is archaic. Though we might speak of "our pilgrim fathers" (who are not even related to us), I cannot envision a context in which I would say that my fathers are from Germany. Rather, I say that my ancestors are from Germany.

While "ancestors" is clearly the best translation when all ancestors, both male and female, are in view, in other contexts a decision is more difficult. Ancestry in ancient Israel was generally viewed in the context of patriarchy. Genealogies, land rights and inheritances were usually traced through the father. In Genesis 47:29-30 (NIV), for example, Jacob says, "When I rest with my fathers *['ābôt]*, carry me out of Egypt and bury me where they are buried." Jacob is here referring to both his father Isaac and his grandfather Abraham. Genealogical descent is viewed as a line of "fathers": from father to father to father. While "fathers" therefore captures something of the historical context of these passages, it represents very awkward and archaic English. "Ancestors," on the other hand, is much better English but misses something of the historical context.

Here we are confronted with a real tension in Bible translation. One solution is to use the term "forefathers," which is good, if somewhat archaic, English. (The original NIV, while translating *'ābôt* as "fathers"

264 times, uses "forefathers" 80 times.[9]) Yet it does not fully capture the sense of *'ābôt,* since "forefathers" and "ancestors" are almost exact synonyms in English.[10] If I were to say "my forefathers are from Germany," I would be describing all my ancestors, not just male heads of household.

This tension is not easily resolved, and it is true that something will always be lost in the translation. In chapter four it was pointed out that both idiomatic and "literal" translations have a role to play in Bible study, since idiomatic translations usually capture better the sense of the original in contemporary English, whereas literal translations provide a better view of the form and structure of the Hebrew or Greek. Perhaps it would be best in this case for idiomatic translations to use the term "ancestors" (or perhaps "forefathers") and more literal ones to retain "fathers." Students comparing both would see the nearest English equivalent ("ancestors"), while also recognizing the sense of patriarchal lineage ("fathers").

In some contexts, the use of "ancestor(s)" seems inappropriate. In Genesis 17:4 the NRSV reads, "As for me, this is my covenant with you: You shall be the *ancestor ['āb]* of a multitude of nations" (compare GNB). Since Abraham was a patriarch (a male head of a clan) and since references to him as the "father" of both Christians and Jews build on this idea of Hebrew patriarchy (see Rom 4:16-17), it seems appropriate to retain this image of a father figure in English translation. Furthermore, in contemporary English we still use the term "father" in the sense of patriarchal founder (for example, George Washington as the "father" of our country). The NIVI and other inclusive versions (NLT, CEV, NJB, NCV, NIrV) appropriately retain "father" in passages like Genesis 17:4 and Romans 4:16-17.

Parents and fathers. The issue of when to translate *'ābôt* and *pateres* as "parents" is also a difficult one, and it requires careful case-by-case exegesis. If the context suggests that both parents are in view, then of course "parents" is to be preferred to "fathers." On the other hand, if the cultural context of the passage indicates that a male head of the family is intended, then "father" or "fathers" should be retained. The NIVI, for example, retains the term "fathers" throughout much of

Proverbs, evidently from the assumption that the father is functioning as representative head of the family.

Hebrews 12:9 RSV reads, "Besides this, we have had earthly fathers *[pateres]* to discipline us and we respected them." The NRSV renders, "Moreover, we had human *parents* to discipline us." In our contemporary context both mothers and fathers discipline, but it might be argued that the author of Hebrews is thinking of the father as the primary disciplinarian of the family. But this is far from certain. Further complicating the issue is the fact that the more common New Testament term for parents is *goneis,* not *pateres.* Someone might say that if the writer of Hebrews meant "parents" instead "fathers," he would have used *goneis.* This is not valid, however, since *pateres* can and does mean "parents" in some contexts. In Hebrews 11:23 we learn that "by faith Moses, when he was born, was hid for three months by his parents *[pateres]*" (RSV). Unless Moses had two fathers, *pateres* here must mean "parents." All of this confirms that a decision between "parents" and "fathers" must be made on a case-by-case basis through sound exegesis.

One special case of father language appears in the translation of the Hebrew term *yātôm,* which can mean either "fatherless" or "orphan."[11] Grudem points to the NRSV's translation in Psalm 109:9, "May his children be orphans, and his wife a widow," and in Exodus 22:24, "Your wives shall become widows and your children orphans." In these examples the translation "orphan" is less than adequate, since the mother is viewed as still alive. While the term "orphan" can mean the loss of only one parent[12] and the context confirms that this is what is intended, the more common understanding of an orphan is someone deprived of both parents. It would have been more precise for the NRSV to have retained the term "fatherless." Again, however, the problem is not with the gender-inclusive method per se but with an inadequate NRSV rendering (compare NCV, GW, CEV). Both the NIVI and the NLT retain "fatherless."[13] The translators recognized that in these references *yātôm* means "having no father to support the family." They thus remain sensitive to the original cultural and historical context, making a translation decision based on careful exegesis.

Not surprisingly, the guideline adopted for the terms "father" and "fathers" at the Conference on Gender-Related Language in Scripture does not take into account this need for case-by-case exegesis. Guideline B.3 states, "'Father' *(patēr, 'āb)* should not be changed to 'parent,' or 'fathers' to 'parents,' or 'ancestors.'" Such a generalization not only ignores contextual considerations but is simply wrong for a passage like Hebrews 11:23, where *pateres* clearly means "parents." With reference to ancestry, it mandates that the translator use archaic English.

The Language of Sonship

Even before the inclusive language debate developed, Bible versions often introduced terms like "child(ren)" or "descendant(s)" for the Hebrew and Greek terms traditionally rendered "son(s)" *(bēn, bānîm, huios, huioi)*.

"Sons" as descendants. In many Old Testament contexts, the Hebrew plural *bānîm* clearly carries the sense "descendants," not "sons." The "sons of Anak" in Numbers 13:33 (RSV) means the "descendants of Anak" (NIV). "Sons of Judah" in Numbers 26:20 (RSV) means "descendants of Judah" (NIV). Sometimes poetic parallelism makes this meaning clear. First Chronicles 16:13 (RSV) reads, "O offspring of Abraham his servant; Sons *[bānîm]* of Jacob, his chosen ones!"[14] In the New Testament, the Greek term *huioi* can be used in the same way: "So you testify against yourselves that you are the descendants *[huioi]* of those who murdered the prophets" (Mt 23:31 NIV). Of course the reason for these renderings is not to promote gender inclusion but to introduce clear and contemporary English. A striking example of this appears in the lists of exiles in Ezra 2. If a literal rendering were retained, the prolific Parosh would have had 2,172 "sons"!

A special case of descendant terminology occurs in the Hebrew phrase *b^enê-yisrā'ēl* (literally "sons of Israel"). The phrase is translated variously as "children of Israel" (KJV, NKJV), "people of Israel" (RSV) or "Israelites" (NIV, TEV, NAB, NRSV, NJB). Among contemporary translations, only the NASB consistently uses "sons of Israel." All of these translations contain some truth. The Israelites arose from Israel's (Jacob's) sons, so "sons of Israel" and "children of Israel" are historically appropriate. The only problem is that we do not usually use "sons" and "children" with reference to descendants today (although anyone with much exposure to the Old Testament knows the technical meaning of the phrase). Since the nation that arose from Israel's sons was known as "Israel," both "people of Israel" and "Israelites" are accurate and clear English. Again, this is not an issue of gender inclusion but an attempt to update archaic language.

Passages in which male descendants are clearly in view are more difficult. In 2 Chronicles 26:18 (RSV), for example, we read, "It is not for you, Uzziah, to burn incense to the LORD, but for the priests the sons *[bānîm]* of Aaron." Since Aaron's sons were long since dead, *bānîm* here must mean "descendants" (so NIV).[15] Although we are speaking of male descendants, we do not usually use "sons" in this sense in contemporary English. This same difficulty arises in passages related to royal lineage. Second Kings 8:19 NIV reads, "The LORD . . . promised to maintain a lamp for David and his descendants *[bānîm]* forever." In such cases the translator must choose between a rendering that is imprecise with reference to gender ("descendants") and one that is awkward and archaic with reference to contemporary English ("sons"). As in the case of "fathers" used for ancestors, literal and idiomatic versions should perhaps render these passages differently, the former using "sons," the latter using "descendants."

Sons or children? The Hebrew plural *bānîm* (often translated "sons") often refers inclusively to children rather than exclusively to sons. Isaiah 1:2 (NIV) reads, "Hear, O heavens! Listen, O earth! For the LORD has spoken: 'I reared children *[bānîm]* and brought them up, but they have rebelled against me'" (compare Is 1:4).[16] Job 42:16 (NIV) reads, "After this, Job lived a hundred and forty years; he saw his children *[bānîm]* and their children [*bānîm* 'descendants'] to the fourth generation." Since the beginning of the book describes the loss of Job's sons and daughters, these references must be to children and descendants generally rather than to sons exclusively (see Job 1:2-5; 5:4; 14:21).[17] In a passage like Jeremiah 38:23, the context makes an inclusive sense clear: "All your wives and children *[bānîm]* will be brought out to the Babylonians" (NIV). The meaning "children" is particularly evident when the term is used in parallel with an inclusive term like "people" or "nation," as in Isaiah 30:9: "These are rebellious people *['am]*, deceitful children *[bānîm]*" (NIV; compare Is 63:8).

The singular Hebrew term *bēn* may also be used in the sense of "child," though this use is disputed. Isaiah 49:15 NIV reads, "Can a mother forget the baby at her breast and have no compassion on the child *[bēn]* she has borne?"[18] In parallel with the inclusive term "baby" (literally "suckling"), *bēn* probably means "child." The context of Ezekiel 18:4 may also suggest an inclusive meaning: "For every living soul belongs to me, the father *['āb]* as well as the son *[bēn]*—both alike belong to me" (NIV). Although the illustration that follows refers specifically to a father and a son (v. 5), the universal reference to "every living soul" may suggest that the prophet is speaking of children, not just male sons (compare Jer 13:14).

In the New Testament too the plural noun *huioi* ("sons") appears to carry an inclusive sense of "children" in many passages. Forty-five times the KJV had already rendered *huioi* as "children." Galatians 3:7 (KJV) reads, "Know ye therefore that they which are of faith, the same are the children *[huioi]* of Abraham" (compare Acts 13:26). Whether the singular *huios* ever means "child" is a more difficult question. In Luke 14:5 (NIV) Jesus says, "If one of you has a son *[huios]* or an ox that falls into a well on the Sabbath day, will you not immediately pull him out?" Similarly, in Matthew 7:9 Jesus says, "Which of you, if his son *[huios]* asks for bread, will give him a stone?" (NIV; compare Lk 11:11). While the point Jesus is making is obviously general, applying to all children, his illustration may be gender specific.[19] Jesus may have been envisioning a particular case where a boy would fall into a well or would ask his father for bread. This is a very difficult call for translators. Since Jesus' intent is not certain, I would be reluctant to call "child" an inaccurate translation. Yet I would prefer the translation "son" because it seems to me more likely Jesus is using a specific illustration to establish a general principle.

Since the plural terms can certainly carry an inclusive sense, we are again surprised to read guideline B.2 from the Conference on Gender-Related Language in Scripture: "'Son' *(huios, bēn)* should not be changed to 'child,' or 'sons' *(huioi)* to 'children' or 'sons and daughters.'

(However, Hebrew *bānîm* often means 'children.')" The last, clarifying phrase suggests that there is one exception to the rule, the Hebrew plural *bānîm,* which can mean "children." Yet the examples above suggest that it is not only the plural *bānîm* but also the Greek plural *huioi* (and possibly the singulars *bēn* and *huios*) that can carry an inclusive sense.

Someone might object that these terms literally mean "son(s)" and so should be consistently translated as such. But this objection demonstrates a misunderstanding of the nature of language and translation (see chap. four). The Hebrew and Greek terms have a much wider semantic range than their parallel English terms. This is most obvious from the range of meanings assigned to the "son of" idiom. Notice how the original NIV (no inclusive agenda) seeks to capture the sense of the Hebrew idiom: "sons of the priests" (Ezra 2:61 RSV) becomes "the priests" (NIV; TEV "priestly clans"); "sons of the singers" becomes "singers" (Neh 12:28; TEV "families of singers"); "son of your bondmaid" (Ex 23:12 RSV) becomes "slave born in your household" (NIV); "sons of your own people" (Lev 19:18 RSV) becomes "one of your own people" (NIV). Translators have struggled with the difficult "sons of the prophets" (1 Kings 20:35 RSV[20]), rendering it variously as "company of the prophets" (NIV), "group of prophets" (TEV), "brotherhood of prophets" (NJB) or "guild prophets" (NAB).

The same phenomenon occurs in the New Testament: "sons of the kingdom" (Mt 8:12 RSV; compare Mt 13:38) becomes "subjects of the kingdom" (NIV; NRSV "heirs of the kingdom"); "your sons" for the Pharisees (Mt 12:27 RSV) becomes "your people" (NIV; TEV "your followers"); "sons of the bridegroom" (Mk 2:19) becomes "guests of the bridegroom" (NIV; NASB "attendants of the bridegroom"); "sons of disobedience" (Eph 2:2; 5:6 RSV) becomes "those who are disobedient" (NIV); "son of peace" (Lk 10:6 RSV) becomes "man of peace" (NIV); "sons of this age" (Lk 20:34) becomes "people of this age" (NIV); "son of perdition" (Jn 17:12 RSV) becomes "the one doomed to destruction" (NIV); the "sons of the prophets" (Acts 3:25 RSV) becomes "heirs of the prophets" (NIV). None of these are attempts at inclusive language but are attempts at capturing the many distinct senses that the Hebrew and

Greek terms can carry. To insist that translators must always use the English "son(s)" results in obscurity or mistranslation (the "sons" of the bridegroom are not his biological sons).

Believers as "sons of God." Sonship to God represents an important subcategory in the language debate related to sons and children. The phrase "son(s) of God" appears with various referents in the Old and New Testaments, including angelic beings,[21] Israel as a nation, the Davidic king,[22] Jesus Christ, and Christian believers. We will deal with the terminology related to Jesus Christ in chapter seven. Our present concern is with the nation Israel and Christian believers.

Israel as a nation is identified as God's "son" in light of its special relationship with him. Deuteronomy 14:1 (NIV) reads, "You are the children *[bānîm]* of the LORD your God." Similarly, in Hosea 11:1 (NIV) we find, "When Israel was a child, I loved him, and out of Egypt I called my son" (*bēn*; compare Ps 82:6). There is surprising unanimity regarding the translation of these passages. With the exception of the RSV and the NASB (which use "sons"), all major translations, whether traditional or inclusive, use "children" in Deuteronomy 14:1.[23] Similarly, all major translations, including the very inclusive NRSV, use "son" in the second part of Hosea 11:1. The reason for this, no doubt, is the presence of the masculine pronoun "him" used of Israel and the desire to introduce a different term to reflect the synonymous parallelism with "child." The primary emphasis in both these contexts, however, appears to be the loving parent-child relationship God has with his people rather than a son's inheritance rights.

Hosea 1:10 (NIV) presents a slightly more difficult situation: "Yet the Israelites will be like the sand on the seashore . . . they will be called 'sons *[bānîm]* of the living God.'" In addition to the NIV, the KJV, NKJV, NASB and RSV use "sons." On the other side, NRSV, NAB, REB, TEV, NLT, CEV and NIVI render "children." Although inheritance of the land and a united kingdom are present in the context (v. 11), so also is the theme of a loving reconciliation of a parent and child (vv. 9-10). Since "children" can reflect rights of inheritance and since "son" can indicate a loving parent-child relationship, the difference in meaning here is very slight.

In the New Testament *huioi* can carry the sense of "children" of God. The KJV frequently translated this way, though later versions often switched back to "sons." Matthew 5:9 (KJV) reads, "Blessed are the peacemakers: for they shall be called the children *[huioi]* of God." Matthew 5:44-45 KJV reads, "Love your enemies . . . That ye may be the children *[huioi]* of your Father which is in heaven" (compare Lk 6:35). This verse is not about the inheritance rights of a son but about a child modeling a father's behavior. Luke 20:36 (KJV) reads, "Neither can they die any more: for they are equal unto the angels; and are the children *[huioi]* of God." The issue here is the immortal nature that God's children (not just sons) inherit from their Father. Similar examples appear throughout the New Testament (Rom 9:26; Gal 3:26; Heb 2:10; 12:7-8). In all of these passages a good case can be made that *huioi* carries the sense of "children."[24]

Grudem argues against this conclusion, claiming that *huioi* should always be translated "sons" rather than "children." This, he says, is because of a clear distinction in meaning between *huios* and *teknon* (plural *tekna*), another Greek term for children:

> The New Testament authors were able to speak of "children" *(tekna)* when they wanted to do so (as in Jn. 1:12, "He gave power to become *children* of God," and Rom. 8:16-17, "bearing witness with our spirit that we are *children* of God"). But in other verses the Bible spoke of us as "sons," and faithful translations should not change this to "sons and daughters" or "children" as the NIVI did in Galatians 4:7.[25]

He goes on to note that the translation "children" in Galatians 4:7 "obscures the fact that we all (men *and* women) gain standing as 'sons' and therefore the inheritance rights that belong to sons in the Biblical world."[26]

Yet the very verses Grudem cites contradict his own argument. He seems to be claiming that (1) the Greek term *tekna* has a sense in these passages that differs from *huioi* (*huioi* emphasizing maleness and *tekna* referring more neutrally to children) and (2) *huoi* is used because it emphasizes heirship. Yet in Romans 8 Paul himself moves back and forth between *tekna* and *huioi*, using them synonymously:

> Because those who are led by the Spirit of God are *huioi* of God . .

> The Spirit himself testifies with our spirit that we are God's *tekna*. Now if we are *tekna*, then we are heirs—heirs of God and co-heirs with Christ. . . . The creation waits in eager expectation for the *huioi* of God to be revealed. . . . The creation itself will be . . . brought into the glorious freedom of the *tekna* of God. (Rom 8:14-22)

Not only are the terms used interchangeably here but *tekna* is specifically used in the statement of heirship! It is as "children" (*tekna,* not just "sons") that we are heirs of God and coheirs with Christ.

Nor does Grudem's distinction between *tekna* and *huioi* hold up elsewhere in the New Testament. Male "sons" are frequently addressed as *teknon,* and at least sixteen times the NIV translates the term as "son(s)."[27] In many contexts, as in Romans 8:14-19, the terms are interchangeable. Revelation 12:5 reads, "She gave birth to a son *[huios]*. . . . And her child *[teknon]* was snatched up to God" (compare Eph 2:2-3). Nor is heirship absent from the meaning of *tekna*. In Mark 12:19 the Sadducees question Jesus concerning the Mosaic law of levirate marriage, where a man dies without leaving a "child" *(teknon)* to carry on his name. Inheritance and carrying on the family name is the crucial issue here. The older brother in the parable of the prodigal son is addressed by his father as *teknon* in the same sentence where the father points out his inheritance: "My son *[teknon]* . . . you are always with me, and everything I have is yours" (Lk 15:31 NIV). Elizabeth and Zechariah long for a *teknon* to carry on the family name (Lk 1:7), and in Acts 7:5 we learn that God promised Abraham the land "even though he had no child *[teknon]*." *Teknon* here is practically synonymous with "heir." Grudem's claim that writers used *huios* instead of *teknon* when they were speaking of heirship is simply wrong (compare Jn 1:12; Rom 9:7-8; 2 Cor 12:14; Gal 4:28; 1 Jn 3:1-2).

One thorny issue for translators occurs in Galatians 4, where critics have argued that "sons" should be retained because of the verbal connection between Jesus' sonship and the sonship of all believers:

> But when the time had fully come, God sent his Son, born of a woman, born under law, to redeem those under law, that we might receive the full rights of sons. Because you are sons, God sent the Spirit of his Son into our hearts, the Spirit who calls out, "Abba,

> Father." So you are no longer a slave, but a son; and since you are a son, God has made you also an heir. (Gal 4:4-7 NIV)

In the Greek, the terms *huios* and *huioi* are used throughout. The NRSV, while retaining "Son" for Jesus, uses "child(ren)" for believers (so also TEV, CEV, NAB, NLT).[28] Grudem argues that "to translate it 'children' obscures the connection with Christ as *son*."[29] While at first I agreed with this suggestion, after studying the various New Testament contexts of sonship, I am not so sure. First, is it really the case that using "children" obscures the connection to Jesus' sonship? Consider the following sentence: "When it comes to eating salsa, I am my father's son; and my own children have inherited this love." Is the genetic connection between myself and my children really obscured because I referred to myself as a "son" and to them as "children"? After all, sons *are* children. To argue that this connection is "obscured" in the NRSV is probably nitpicking. Furthermore, since we have seen above that *tekna* ("children") is just as common a term for inheritance rights in the New Testament as *huioi*, it is not legitimate to argue that *huioi* must be translated here as "sons" to capture the sense of "heirs." Both *tekna* and *huioi* can carry the sense of "children," and both can be related to heirship.

"Sons of men." A special case of sonship language occurs in the idioms "son of man" and "sons of men." The phrase "son of man" in connection with Jesus is discussed in chapter seven. Here it is examined in terms of its application to human beings in general. In most of its Old Testament occurrences, the Hebrew phrase *ben 'ādām* (Aramaic *bar 'ᵉnôsh*) is equivalent to "man" or "human being." It sometimes appears in poetic parallelism beside other Hebrew terms like *'îsh* (Num 23:19; Job 35:8) and *'ᵉnôsh* ("man" or "mortal"; Ps 8:4;[30] Job 25:6), and often refers to the lowliness of humanity in contrast with the transcendence of God.[31] Numbers 23:19 (NIV) reads, "God is not a man *['îsh]*, that he should lie, nor a son of man *[ben 'ādām]*, that he should change his mind."

In other contexts the phrase simply means "human being(s)." In Psalm 107:8, for example, we read in the RSV, "Let them thank the LORD for his steadfast love, for his wonderful works to the sons of men." Viewing "sons of men" as archaic in English, the original NIV usually rendered the phrase as "men"[32] or "mankind."[33] Psalm 107:8 (NIV) reads, "his wonderful deeds for men." The NIVI rendered the phrase "his wonderful deeds for human beings." There should be few objections to this translation because it accurately captures the sense of the original in clear and contemporary English. For many contemporary readers, "son of man" is incomprehensible or obscure.

A special use of the phrase appears in Ezekiel, where it occurs ninety-three times as a designation for the prophet. Surprisingly, most inclusive versions retain the translation "son of man" here (see NIVI, CEV, NLT, GW, NJB, NAB).[34] Perhaps the translators considered the phrase to have acquired a technical sense, and so the odd and unusual English "son of man" was retained. The NRSV uses (perhaps overuses) the inclusive term "O mortal," and the NCV uses "human." These too would seem to be accurate renderings, since the "son of man" address often contrasts the lowly human prophet with the sovereign God.

Other difficult sonship passages. Only case-by-case exegesis can determine whether "sons" or "children" is intended. In Isaiah 51:18, for example, a son's leadership role in the family appears to be in view: "Of all the sons *[bānîm]* she bore there was none to guide her; of all the sons *[bānîm]* she reared there was none to take her by the hand" (Is 51:18 NIV). The NRSV's "children" probably misses the cultural context. Similarly, the loss of a son would seem to be in view in Jeremiah 6:26: "O my people, put on sackcloth and roll in ashes; mourn with bitter wailing as for an only son, for suddenly the destroyer will come upon us." Though of course the loss of a daughter is an equal tragedy in human terms, the context is probably referring to a son who would carry on the family name (compare Gen 22:12, 16; 2 Sam 18:18; Amos 8:10; Zech 12:10). There may also be an allusion to the death of the firstborn sons at the exodus (Ex 11-12). The NRSV's "child," though not ruling out this interpretation, slightly obscures it.

In other passages, it is obvious that males are intended, so it is unnecessary to substitute "children" for "sons." For example, in 1 Kings 1:19, 25, the phrase "sons of the king" is a reference to potential male heirs, and so the NRSV's "children" is a less precise translation. In Genesis 46:8 the NRSV repeatedly translates *bānîm* as "children," even when only male offspring are listed. Since the Hebrew text takes separate note of daughters (vv. 15, 17), *bānîm* is more accurately rendered here as "sons."

It must not be assumed too quickly, however, that in other cases the cultural context rules out a more inclusive meaning. Though sons would normally be the heirs of their father's estate, Numbers 36:8 provides an example of women inheriting land: "Every daughter who inherits land in any Israelite tribe must marry someone in her father's tribal clan" (NIV). Though this might be viewed as an exceptional case, it raises important questions as to how best to translate *bānîm* in such contexts. In Jeremiah 3:19, for example, the NIV uses "sons": "How gladly would I treat you like sons *[bānîm]* and give you a desirable land" (compare NASB, REB). Other translations, however, including the literal KJV and NKJV, use "children" (compare NRSV, NLT, CEV, NJB).

Also difficult are passages referring to instruction, correction and passing on religious traditions or values. Though only boys would have received formal training in Torah during the Old Testament period, girls would certainly have been given informal moral and ethical instruction. How, for example, should Psalm 34:11 be translated? The RSV reads, "Come, O sons *[bānîm]*, listen to me, I will teach you the fear of the LORD." The NIVI and NRSV use "children." Was this instruction intended for young men or for young people? Similarly, should "train up a child in the way he should go" (Prov 22:6 RSV) actually be "train up a boy"? All the traditional versions use an inclusive term, "child" (so KJV, NKJV, NASB), but the Hebrew term is actually masculine (*na'ar*; the feminine form is *na'arāh*). Of course no one has objected to the inclusive rendering in the past because this is the way the KJV translated it! The point is that the (grammatical) gender of the word is not decisive in such cases.

Also difficult are the correction passages of the Old Testament. Were fathers the primary disciplinarians? Were sons or children the recipients of this correction? Deuteronomy 8:5 reads in the RSV, "Know then in your heart that, as a man *['îsh]* disciplines his *son [bēn]*, the LORD your God disciplines you." While the more literal translations retain the man/son terminology (NASB, NKJV, KJV), many modern translations speak of a "parent" disciplining a "child" (so NLT, TEV, CEV, NRSV).

The NJB (an inclusive version) retains "man" but uses "child." Since the Hebrew *'îsh* usually (but not always) refers to males and since the singular *bēn* almost always refers to a male child, it may be best to view this as a masculine example (father and son) used to illustrate a general parental principle. This kind of passage again illustrates the difficult balance translators face between capturing the original cultural context of Scripture and clearly communicating the message of the text to a modern reader.

Passing on religious tradition is the point of Exodus 13:8, which reads in the RSV, "And you shall tell your son *[bēn]* in that day saying, 'This is done because of what the LORD did for me when I came up from Egypt'" (compare Ex 13:14; Deut 6:20; NIV, NKJV, NASB). More inclusive translations generally speak of telling your "child" (NLT, CEV, NRSV, NIVI).[35] Similarly, Exodus 10:2 in the RSV calls on the Israelites to "recount to your son and grandson [literally 'son's son'] how ruthlessly I dealt with the Egyptians and what signs I wrought among them" (compare NKJV, NASB). Here the NIV already had the inclusive "children and grandchildren" (compare NLT, CEV, NRSV, NIVI). Since the context of such instruction appears to be Israel's annual festivals—which the whole family would probably attend—the translations "children and grandchildren" may capture the cultural sense accurately (see Ex 13:8, 14).

The use of "son(s)" in the book of Proverbs represents another special case. In the context of the book, there are two different types of passages: in one type, "my son(s)" is addressed and given instruction, and in the other type there is more general proverbial material. Whereas the NRSV uses "child" or "children" throughout, the NIVI retains "son" and "sons" for the instructional material.[36] Proverbs 3:11 (NIVI), for example, reads, "My son, do not despise the LORD's discipline," and 4:1 (NIVI) begins, "Listen, my sons, to a father's instruction." The NIVI revisers evidently believed that retaining the father-son imagery was important to preserving the cultural context.[37] As explained in chapter two, this is particularly appropriate in the "seductress" passages, where young men are being warned away from sexual immorality. The NRSV obscures the male reference by rendering these passages as "my child(ren)." While retaining "son(s)" here, the NIVI often uses "child(ren)" in the general proverbial material. Proverbs 10:1 NIVI reads, "Wise children [NIV 'a wise son'] bring joy to their fathers."[38] Proverbs 17:21 NIVI reads, "To have a fool for a child [NIV 'son'] brings grief." The intention of such proverbial material may well be inclusive, encompassing both sons and daughters.

Also interesting is Isaiah 54:13, where, in an eschatological context, the prophet says, "All your sons *[bānîm]* will be taught by the LORD, and great will be your children's *[bānîm]* peace" (Is 54:13 NIV). The NIV here translates *bānîm* as "sons" in the context of teaching, but as "children" in the context of peace. Surprisingly, the literal KJV and the NKJV use the inclusive "children" for both terms (compare NRSV, CEV). The NASB uses "sons" for both. How are we to judge what the prophet intended? While the Old Testament cultural context might suggest that males are the recipients of the teaching, the eschatological context would incline toward an inclusive sense. In the new covenant context of Jeremiah 31, "all" know the Lord, "from the least to the greatest" (Jer 31:34), and in Joel 2:28-29 it is both "sons and daughters" who receive the Spirit and with it prophetic utterance. Of course the New Testament confirms that in the age of fulfillment, instruction in Scripture is intended for men and women alike (Lk 10:38-42; Acts 2:42; 16:13 and so on).

Other Masculine Generics: Adjectives, Participles and Pronouns

The least controversial inclusive language changes are those related to participles, adjectives and various kinds of pronouns. Although these terms are masculine in the Greek, they are frequently used with an inclusive sense. Since almost all participants in the debate accept the legitimacy of using inclusive language for these terms, they will be surveyed briefly.

Substantival participles. Substantival participles (participles that function as nouns) are very common in Koine Greek. These participles are usually translated into English using a relative clause ("the one who"). For example, 1 Corinthians 3:8 reads in the NRSV, "The one who plants *[ho phyteuōn]* and the one who waters *[ho potizōn]* have a common purpose." Both *ho phyteuōn* and *ho potizōn* are substantival participles. In Matthew 10:37 the NRSV reads, "Whoever loves *[ho philōn]* father or mother more than me is not worthy of me." This kind of translation for substantival participles is very common in both traditional and inclusive versions, and it is generally accepted as fully legitimate. The second half of guideline A.1 established at the Conference on Gender-Related Language in Scripture reads that "substantival participles such as *ho pisteuōn* can often be rendered in inclusive ways, such as 'the one who believes' rather than 'he who believes.'" Since the personal pronoun "he" does not appear in the Greek, there seems no reason to introduce it.

Traditional versions often translated substantival participles using this "he who" phrase, as the RSV at Matthew 10:37, "he who loves father or mother more than me." Other versions had even introduced the word "man" where no corresponding term occurred in the Greek. John 12:35 NIV reads, "The man who walks *[ho peripatōn]* in the dark does not know where he is going." Since the reference is clearly inclusive and since no word for "man" appears in the Greek, there is no reason to introduce it.

Substantival adjectives. Like participles, substantival adjectives often replace nouns in Greek. Even when these terms are intended to be inclusive, the term "man" sometimes appears in translation. Matthew 10:41 in the NIV reads, "Anyone who receives a righteous man [*dikaion,* 'one who is righteous'] because he is a righteous man will receive a righteous man's reward" (compare NASB, KJV). No Greek word for "man" appears in this verse. The NRSV therefore translates, "And whoever welcomes a righteous person in the name of a righteous person will receive the reward of righteousness." Similarly, in John 12:32, while the RSV reads, "And I, when I am lifted up from the earth, will draw all men to myself," the NRSV reads, "And I, when I am lifted up from the earth, will draw all people to myself." The word translated "all men" (RSV) and "all people" (NRSV) is the substantival adjective *pas.*[39] As noted in chapter one, Grudem cites this as an example of the acceptable use of inclusive language, since it improves the accuracy of the translation. He writes, "Everyone should agree that this is an improvement, as are other changes like it."[40]

Other pronouns. Like substantival participles and adjectives, masculine relative pronouns also function generically in Greek. Matthew 11:6 in the NIV reads, "Blessed is the man who *[hos ean]* does not fall away on account of me." The relative pronoun *hos* is used generically of the followers of Jesus, whether male or female. The NASB avoids the term "man" but still translates exclusively with the masculine personal pronoun: "Blessed is he who keeps from stumbling over Me." The NRSV captures better the sense of the original when it translates, "And blessed is anyone who takes no offense at me."

Indefinite pronouns are used similarly. Mark 4:23 (RSV) reads, "If any man *[tis]* has ears to hear, let him hear." The word translated "man" in the RSV is the indefinite relative pronoun *tis,* meaning "anyone" or "whoever." The NIV recognized this inclusive sense and had already translated with "anyone": "If anyone has ears to hear, let him hear." The NRSV avoids the resumptive pronoun "he" by translating, "Let *anyone* with ears to hear listen!" The NIVI switches to a plural construction, "If any have ears to hear, let them hear," whereas the CEV changes to a second person, "If you have ears, pay attention!" All of these versions capture the sense without introducing the word "man." Another example of this can be seen in 1 Corinthians 8:3. Where the NIV has "But the man who *[tis]* loves God is known by God," the NIVI renders "whoever loves God" and the NRSV has "anyone who loves God."

The indefinite pronoun *oudeis* functions in a similar manner.[41] In Galatians 3:11 the RSV reads, "Now it is evident that no man is justified before God by the law." The NRSV reads, "Now it is evident that no one is justified before God by the law." In this case the indefinite pronoun *oudeis,* "no one," is used generically to refer to all people. Again Grudem notes that "these are helpful changes because they use gender inclusive language without sacrificing accuracy in translation."[42]

Guidelines A.6, A.7 and A.8 established at the Conference on Gender-Related Language in Scripture recognize the legitimacy of these translations:

> 6. Indefinite pronouns such as *tis* can be translated "anyone" rather than "any man."

7. In many cases, pronouns such as *oudeis* can be translated "no one" rather than "no man."
8. When *pas* is used as a substantive, it can be translated with terms such as "all people" or "everyone."

In all of these cases, translations like "the one who," "anyone who," "no one" and "all who" render accurately the Greek original in good English while communicating clearly the inclusive nature of the original. Whereas the word "man" is often introduced in traditional translations, no parallel term appears in the Greek. It is interesting that those who vehemently object to adding extra words in order to achieve a gender-inclusive translation seldom object when masculine terms like "he" or "man," which are absent from the Greek, are introduced.

It is also important to note that the sense of these masculine generic terms is really no different from the sense of masculine generic terms like *anthrōpos* and *'ādām*. In the phrase "if someone *[anthrōpos]* is caught in a sin" (Gal 6:1 NIV), *anthrōpos* carries precisely the same semantic content as *tis* in the phrase "if anyone *[tis]* would come after me" (Mt 16:24 NIV). To claim that *anthrōpos* must be translated "man" but *tis* may be translated "anyone" or "someone" is a classic confusion of form and meaning. When *anthrōpos* means "anyone," why not translate it that way?

Conclusion

This chapter has examined masculine generic familial terms traditionally translated "brothers," "fathers" and "sons," as well as other generic terms. Greek and Hebrew terms such as *'ābôt, bānîm, pateres* and *huioi* have significantly wider semantic ranges than their English counterparts. In particular contexts they may be accurately rendered with expressions like "brothers and sisters," "parents," "ancestors," "children" and "descendants." There is no need to appeal to a gender-inclusive agenda to justify these renderings because, in many contexts, they clearly represent a more accurate and precise translation.

Once again, the introduction of inclusive language, perhaps incidentally, has sharpened the precision of Bible translation. This is because in the past translators often followed a simplistic one-to-one correspondence, choosing a single English word for a particular Hebrew or Greek term instead of examining the meaning of the Greek or Hebrew term in context. Hebrew *bēn,* for example, was automatically translated "son," even in idioms where it clearly carried a different sense. The call for inclusive language has forced a greater consideration of the meaning of words and phrases, not just their forms. While great caution must accompany changes that are proposed for a particular passage, it can hardly be denied that inclusive language can and is being used to achieve greater accuracy and precision in Bible translation.

Seven

LANGUAGE RELATED TO GOD & TO JESUS CHRIST

INCLUSIVE LANGUAGE CHANGES RELATED TO GOD ARE THE MOST CONTROversial of all. The moderate inclusive language translations retain all masculine symbols and pronouns related to God (NRSV, NIVI, REB, NJB, NAB, NLT, CEV, GW, NCV, NIrV, ICB). They make no attempt to replace or supplement masculine or father imagery with feminine metaphors and titles (for example, Father-Mother). The feminist versions (ILL, NTPI, INT), on the other hand, frequently introduce such changes. It is necessary, therefore, to conduct a brief examination of inclusive language related to God.

Language Related to God

Feminists who wish to remove masculine references to God strongly stress the fact that God is not a man. This is certainly true and is repeatedly affirmed in Scripture. Numbers 23:19 reads, "God is not a man *['îsh]*, that he should lie, nor a son of man *[ben 'ādām]* that he should change his mind" (NIV; compare Hos 11:9; Job 9:32). This passage means that God is not a human being. God is the sovereign Creator and is distinct from and transcendent above all of his creatures.

It is also a fact that God does not have gender. God is not biologically male or female but pure Spirit (Jn 4:24).

Although God is neither male nor female, he reveals his divine qualities with both masculine and feminine imagery. In the Old Testament, God is a father to his people both as their Creator and as their Redeemer (Deut 32:18; Hos 11). God's fatherhood confirms his love and compassion for his people: "As a father has compassion on his children, so the LORD has compassion on those who fear him" (Ps 103:13 NIV). God is the "father of the fatherless" (Ps 68:5). Like a father, God disciplines his children: "Know then in your heart that as a man disciplines his son, so the LORD your God disciplines you" (Deut 8:5 NIV; compare Prov 3:12). While the Old Testament describes God as father metaphorically, in the New Testament the designation becomes a kind of name. Jesus addresses God as "Father" and calls on believers to do the same. It is by virtue of their relationship with Jesus, the true Son of God, that all believers receive adoption as God's children and can call him their heavenly Father (Gal 4:6; Rom 8:15-16).[1] Masculine imagery related to God is not limited to father language. Titles like "King" and "Lord" draw on masculine symbols, as does the portrait of God as Israel's husband (Is 54:5; Hos 2:2, 7, 16).

Feminine imagery is also used to characterize God. God comforts his people as a mother comforts her child: "As a mother comforts her child, so will I comfort you" (Is 66:13 NIV; compare Ps 131:2; Is 46:3; Hos 11:3-4). A mother's comfort and care is also the issue in Isaiah 49:15: "Can a mother forget the baby at her breast and have no compassion on the child she has borne? Though she may forget, I will not forget you!" (NIV). God is the epitome of a compassionate mother. Female birth imagery is also associated with God's creative power. In Deuteronomy 32:18 God's generating the nation Israel is analogous to a birth: "You were unmindful of the Rock that begot you, and you forgot the God who gave you birth" (RSV). While the Hebrew verb translated "begot" can refer to a father's role in procreation, the verb for "gave you birth" refers to the birth pains of a mother.[2] God's control over nature is portrayed with birth imagery in Job 38:29: "From whose womb comes the ice? Who gives birth to the frost from the heavens?" (NIV).

As many have noted, the wisdom of God is personified in Proverbs as a woman (Prov 1:20; 4:6; 7:4 and so on).[3] Christ likens himself to a mother hen in Matthew 23:37: "O Jerusalem, Jerusalem . . . how often I have longed to gather your children together, as a hen gathers her chicks under her wings, but you were not willing" (NIV).

God as "Father" or "Father-Mother"

If God is not a male and if the Bible in some places uses feminine imagery to describe him, is it appropriate to replace "Father" with terms like "Father-Mother" in Bible translations? A number of arguments may be introduced against this kind of translation.

Differences between similes and metaphors. Some maintain that there is a distinct difference between a simile and a metaphor, a simile expressing the condition of being like something and a metaphor expressing the condition of actually being something. God may be *like* a mother (a simile), but he *is* a father (a metaphor). This distinction, however, does not hold up under scrutiny. Both similes and metaphors are figures of speech that describe a person or thing by comparing it with something else. The two figures of speech differ little in meaning: "God is a fortress" (metaphor) and "God is like a fortress" (simile). A metaphor presents a comparison rather than an ontological reality. To say that God is a fortress does not mean that God is *literally* a fortress but that God is our strength and protection. In short, God is *like* a fortress.

Although a simplistic distinction between metaphor and simile does not adequately characterize the difference between mother and father language for God, it may point in the right direction. In the New Testament the description of God as father goes beyond mere metaphor. Donald Bloesch draws a helpful distinction between metaphor and analogy, noting that "a metaphor connotes a suggested likeness between two things that are manifestly dissimilar, whereas an analogy presupposes an underlying similarity or congruity in the midst of real difference."[4] This is an important distinction. "God is our Father" carries much broader conceptual significance than "God is a fortress." God may be our strong protector, but any other comparison to a fortress is inappropriate. God is our Father, however, in a multiplicity of dimensions.

It may be argued that although this distinction between metaphor and analogy is valid, it does not apply in the present case because mother images related to God can also be called analogies. As in the case of the father analogy, God fulfills a multiplicity of mothering roles (care, comfort, protection and so on). Yet there is a distinct quantitative and qualitative difference between the mother and father metaphors of Scripture. While God is occasionally portrayed with feminine and motherly qualities, he is never actually addressed as "Mother." On the lips of Jesus, however, "Father" becomes the primary term of address to characterize God's relationship with his people.

The ontological aspect of the fatherhood of God. Some have argued that the term "father" should be retained because it is *more* than simply an analogy. It is an ontological reality. We do not come to understand the concept of God as father by comparing him with human fatherhood. Rather, the reverse is true. God is the *fundamental referent* for the term "father," and it is first and foremost through our knowledge of *God* that we give "father" its semantic content. Bloesch writes:

> Such words as Father, Son, and Lord, when applied to God, are analogies, but they are analogies *sui generis*. They are derived not from the experience of human fatherhood or sonship or lordship, but from God's act of revealing himself as Father, Son, and Lord. . . . We come to know the meaning of true fatherhood and true lordship when we realize that God is our heavenly Father and that Christ is our divine Lord. . . . It is not that God resembles a Father, but in calling him Father the Bible challenges the human view of what a father should be.[5]

There is a great deal of truth in this statement. It is certainly the case that "we come to know the meaning of true fatherhood" by looking to God and that the biblical conception of God challenges the human view of what a father should be. The problem is with the suggestion that the meaning of the term "father" is derived from God's fatherhood, that is, that we understand the meaning of "father" first and foremost through our knowledge of God. Our initial apprehension of a father is based on contact with our human father, not God. When we define the term "father," we inevitably start with the biological understanding and move outward. Although God reveals the epitome of "what a father should be," this statement itself places human fatherhood as the original category.

If God had wanted to inform the term "father" with its meaning based solely on his own nature and character, why did he choose a term that already had so much semantic content with regard to human relationships? Why not select an entirely new term (like "Yahweh") that he could define entirely through his own words and deeds?[6] The term "father" immediately and necessarily draws an analogy between God and *the fatherhood we all know* or idealize—that of our own experiences as children and/or fathers. It is certainly true that God epitomizes everything that a father should be: loving, compassionate and strong; protector, provider and disciplinarian. It is also true that God's fatherhood exalts and transforms the concept beyond human dimensions. But it still begins with an analogy, a limited comparison that enables us to comprehend something of the true nature of God. God is not a human father, but we understand a little of his divine nature by envisioning the attributes of an ideal human father.

Bloesch is on to something significant when he points out that God's self-revelation informs and expands our conception of fatherhood and so provides the term "Father" with its own unique semantic content. Edith Humphrey picks up this line of thought when she writes that

> our knowledge about the Father comes not simply from what we know of human fathers, by our own understanding, but by God himself taking up our human language and teaching us the best way to use it. . . . God gives us back our words about him, showing the name that is best suited to his nature, and filling in what that name means.[7]

Notice that Humphrey does not deny that human fatherhood informs our knowledge of the Father. We understand a little bit about God by recognizing that he is *like* an ideal human father (kind, compassionate, caring, protecting, disciplining). But then the self-revelation of God in Scripture expands the sense of the term "Father" beyond merely human categories.

Fatherhood as a symbol of God's self-revelation. This point, it seems to me, brings out the most fundamental (and important) reason for retaining the father language of Scripture: Fatherhood is one of the primary symbols through which God chose to reveal himself. If the Bible is indeed God's word—his self-revelation—then the symbols, analogies and metaphors that the Bible uses are themselves authoritative and so ought to be retained. Bloesch sums this up well:

> The symbols of faith that compose the biblical witness have been elected by God as means of revelation and salvation. In the writing of Scripture the prophets and apostles were guided by the Spirit in their selection of certain foundational symbols and analogies that remain the criterion that guides as well as limits theological speculation. The biblical symbols constitute the parameters of theological thinking.[8]

To reject, alter or downplay the fatherhood language of Scripture is to deny the authority of the biblical text. While it is true that God's Word comes to us through limited human language and in the context of fallible human culture, the cultural symbols used are themselves part of the authoritative revelation. Though finite symbols can never fully describe the nature of a transcendent God, they nevertheless point accurately—if incompletely—toward the truth.

Many scholars claim, on the other hand, that biblical symbols such as Father, Lord and King actually distort and misdirect our understanding of the nature of God. These symbols represent only blurred images of God's true nature and are badly distorted through the lenses of a sinful culture of patriarchy and oppression. All vestiges of this patriarchy must be removed if God is to be truly seen. Bible translation and interpretation must reimagine the symbols to more accurately reflect the nature of God.

It is hardly surprising that the authority of the Bible is questioned by many feminist writers. Elisabeth Schüssler Fiorenza accepts as authoritative only those parts of the Bible that support the struggle for liberation. These passages then become the norm by which to interpret others. She argues that "only the nonsexist and non-androcentric traditions of the Bible and the non-oppressive traditions of biblical interpretation have the theological authority of revelation if the Bible is not to continue as a tool for the oppression of women."[9] When the authority of the Bible is subordinated to concerns for feminist liberation, feminist translators become willing to replace masculine imagery with feminine and androgynous symbols.

The central question, then, concerns the nature and authority of the Bible. Is the Bible merely a culturally relative record of human reflections about God or is it an accurate and authentic self-revelation of God? Are the monarchical and patriarchal descriptions of God inappropriate remnants of sinful human culture or are they the symbols chosen by God and mediated through his Spirit-inspired human agents? It seems to me that an evangelical view of Scripture demands the latter.

It has been argued throughout this book that an accurate Bible translation is one that retains the cultural and historical meaning of the text in language that the contemporary reader can understand. The translator should seek to enable the present-day reader to gain the same impression that the original readers had. When Jesus' disciples heard him address God as "Father," they would have perceived this in terms of human fatherhood—modified and expanded by Jesus' own teaching and by the revelation of God in the Hebrew Scriptures—not in terms of some kind of androgynous "Mother-Father" figure.

Not only did Jesus choose to reveal God as our heavenly Father but he did do so in a cultural context that was even more marked by the oppression and degradation of women than ours is today. Yet he saw no need to alter or remove the metaphor, since it is not the symbol of fatherhood that is inherently oppressive but sinful human fathers who empty the term of positive meaning for some readers. The remedy for this problem is not eliminating Father language for God but allowing the biblical revelation to transform our conception of fatherhood. Garrett Green writes concerning the God of Scripture:

> This God does not jealously hoard his power. As a husband he does not beat his unfaithful wife but cries out with the pain of a jilted lover and redoubles his efforts to win her back (Hos 2). As Father he "did not spare his own Son but gave him up for us all" (Rom 8:32). As Son he did not claim the prerogatives of power and lord it

> over his subjects but "emptied himself, taking the form of a servant. . . . As king he does not isolate himself in heavenly splendor but wills to dwell with his people, to "wipe away every tear from their eyes" and to deliver them from all that oppresses them, even from death itself (Rev 21:4).[10]

Edith Humphrey points out that "here is a poignant reversal of the All-powerful One who yields all, even dying for those whom he loves. This masculinely-pictured God is neither male nor oppressive, but overturns our presuppositions."[11] When Jesus taught us to "call no man your father," he was not calling for the repudiation of human fatherhood but was pointing to God as the model of what it means to be a father. He is not just *a* father, he is *the* Father—the epitome of fatherhood. Those who have been wounded by their fathers do not need to be told that "fathers are just like that." They need to be assured that God's fatherhood as revealed in Scripture can correct this gross distortion and that the Spirit of God can heal the damage that has been done. Humphrey continues, "In this time, of all times, this time of the absent father, and the overburdened super-woman, we need, men need, families need, the corrective image of the Father."[12]

The Dangers of Goddess and Earth-Mother Worship

Though the need to accurately reproduce God's self-revelation in Scripture should be reason enough to retain the masculine God language of Scripture, other reasons can be brought forward. Some claim that the introduction of Mother language enhances our perception of God by providing a fuller description of God's nature. In reality, what often occurs is a distortion and a misrepresentation of that nature. Elizabeth Achtemeier argues convincingly that the portrait of God as Mother inevitably leads to a different religion in which God is neither personal nor transcendent. The Earth-Mother is not transcendent but is the creative life force within nature. From this perspective "all things participate in the life or in the substance and divinity of that deity . . . the creator is indissolubly bound up with the creation."[13] Many of the names suggested as replacements for "Father" in feminist literature have impersonal and pantheistic implications: "Womb of Being," "Womb of

All Creation," feminine "Lifeforce" and "Ground of Being."[14] Feminist scholars often acknowledge and affirm this pantheistic and impersonal shift of meaning. Rosemary Ruether writes that

> the symbolism of the Goddess is not a parallel structure of the symbolism of God the Father. The Goddess does not rule the world; She *is* the world. Manifest in each of us, She can be known internally by every individual, in all her magnificent diversity.[15]

Ruether proposes a synthesis of Canaanite goddess religion and Hebraic prophetic religion, suggesting terms like "God/ess" or "Primal Matrix" as new and nonsexist replacements for Jehovah God or Father God.[16]

This kind of approach is common in radical feminist literature. The denial of patriarchal and authoritarian symbols often leads to a rejection of God's sovereign lordship and transcendence over creation. In true egalitarian spirit God becomes one of us, and we are one with God. For Virginia Mollenkott, the relationship between God and ourselves is one of "mutuality," "reciprocity" and "parallelism."[17] As appealing as this may be for those opposed to all hierarchical structures in life, it is a far cry from the God of Scripture, who is both transcendent and immanent. Though the sovereign Lord of all creation, he stoops down to relate to his creatures in a personal way. As Donald Bloesch puts it, "God is friend, to be sure, but he is Master before he is friend."[18] To deny God's lordship and his kingship is to deny the very essence of Christianity. Feminine images for God, though present in the Bible and useful for enriching our understanding of the breadth of God's character, do not express the unique combination of transcendence and immanence that is God, a being supremely transcendent over his creatures while present and personal with them. Just as the feminine images for God should be retained in those contexts where they appear, so the masculine images should be kept intact and should not be replaced by amorphous or androgynous symbols.

The Language of the Trinity: Father, Son and Holy Spirit

Attempts to remove masculine God language have also been made with reference to the individual persons of the Trinity. A variety of alternatives for Father, Son and Spirit have been suggested, including "God-

Christ-Spirit," "Creator-Redeemer-Sustainer" and others.[19] The most obvious problem with such designations is the one noted above: If the Bible is God's self-revelation, then it is God who has chosen the metaphors through which to reveal himself. Changing the metaphors distorts the biblical revelation. Speaking of the "Creator" and the "Christ" removes the sense of intimacy of relationship that the terms "Father" and "Son" are meant to convey. Lutheran theologian Martha Stortz points out that "it would be easy for a 'Creator' to sacrifice a 'Christ.' Perhaps the category 'sacrifice' would not even apply. It is not so easy for a Father to sacrifice a Son. Yet this is the story of our faith. We could choose another story . . . but then we would have to choose another faith and another confession of that faith."[20]

The intimacy of relationship between the Father and the Son is obscured by introducing less person-centered terms. When Jesus says, "No one knows the Son except the Father, and no one knows the Father except the Son and those to whom the Son chooses to reveal him" (Mt 11:27 NIV), something profound is communicated concerning the relationship between the Father and the Son, as well as the role of the Son as God's self-revelation. Nonfamilial terms such as "God" and "Christ" do not convey this sense of intimate relatedness and unity of purpose—the relational aspects of the Trinity.

Other terms such as "Creator-Redeemer-Sustainer" err by stressing function over identity and personhood. Although these terms certainly communicate true attributes of God, they obscure the distinct personalities and relationships within the Godhead. All three terms could, for example, apply to all three persons of the Trinity. God the Father is Creator, Redeemer and Sustainer, but so is God the Son (Heb 1:2-3). There is a real danger here of falling into the ancient heresy of modalism, where the Father *is* the Son *is* the Spirit—one person who reveals himself in three forms. Humphrey illustrates this by noting an occasion where a person of Jewish faith approved of the titles Creator, Redeemer and Sustainer for God but rejected trinitarian theology.[21]

Some feminist versions seek to retain both personhood and familial identity by replacing the masculine "Son" for Jesus with inclusive terms like "Child," "Only Begotten," "Firstborn" or "God's Own."[22] The NTPI translates Matthew 11:27 as "no one knows the Child except the Father-Mother, and no one knows the Father-Mother except the Child." The INT reads, "No one knows the Only Begotten except Abba God, and no one knows Abba God except the Only Begotten."

Such translations not only misrepresent the meaning of the text but also obscure and confuse rather than clarify. The use of "Child" could carry implications of immaturity that "Son" does not. Jesus is the mighty Son of God in all the glory and magnificence of his exaltation as heir of all things (see Heb 1:3). He is not an immature child. The translation "Child" also risks losing important conceptual links to the Old Testament, where it is prophesied that the Messiah will have a unique Father-Son relationship with God (2 Sam 7:14; Ps 2:7; 89:26). Sonship in these Old Testament contexts carries implications not only of intimacy of relationship but also of heirship to the throne of Israel. In the New Testament, Jesus is identified as God's Son both in his unique relationship with the Father (Mt 11:27; throughout John's Gospel) and in his role as Messiah and representative of Israel (Lk 1:32-33; Mt 2:15; Hos 11:1). The NTPI's "Child" could lose some of these messianic and typological connotations. Nor does the androgynous and obscure "Father-Mother" capture the sense of intimacy represented by the Father-Son metaphor.

The INT's "Only Begotten" and "Abba God" are no better. The introduction of the Aramaic term "Abba" ("father") is a strange "correction" to the text. It is evidently intended to avoid the English word "father," as though the English word itself carried evil connotations. But the Aramaic word means "father" (see Mk 14:36). If the reader is unaware of this meaning, then the phrase "Abba God" carries no sense at all; if the reader knows that "Abba" means "Father," then why not use this translation? The rendering "Only Begotten" is probably also misguided. The term is derived from the Greek word *monogenēs*, which appears in texts like John 1:14, 18; 3:16, 18; 1 John 4:9. It has traditionally been translated "only begotten." Many New Testament scholars have argued, however, that the term means "only" or "unique," with no implications of begetting.[23] Etymologically, it is probably derived from *monos* ("only") and from *genos* ("kind"), not *gennaō* ("beget"). While a word's etymology does not necessarily determine its present meaning (see chap. four), the root *genos* would render unlikely the sense "begotten." *Monogenēs* probably means "unique," "one of a kind." These texts seem to indicate that Jesus is the *unique Son of God,* not that he is eternally generated or begotten by the Father. For the NTPI to choose a disputed term like "Only Begotten" to replace the clear and precise "Son" results in confusion rather than clarity.

Language related to the Holy Spirit has also been feminized in some Bible translations. Justification for this is usually drawn from the fact that the Hebrew word for the Spirit, *rûah,* is feminine. The introduction to the Inclusive New Testament (INT) argues that "*ruach,* the Hebrew word for 'spirit,' is always feminine, as is God's *shekinah,* or presence. Accordingly, in our translation the Holy Spirit is always referred to in the feminine."[24] In other feminist literature, the Spirit is sometimes referred to as the "Sophia" or "Sophia-Spirit," adopting the feminine Greek noun *sophia,* which means "wisdom." Justification for this is claimed from the personification of wisdom as a woman in Proverbs 8 and in the apocryphal book of Sirach (Ecclesiasticus).

While the Hebrew noun *rûaḥ* is grammatically feminine, its Greek counterpart, *pneuma,* is neuter. Both nouns can mean "breath," "wind," "spirit" or God's "Spirit." It is strange that the INT uses the feminine gender of an Old Testament Hebrew term to justify its New Testament translation of a Greek neuter noun. The gender of *rûaḥ* and *pneuma* is obviously a grammatical issue, not a biological one. To determine how best to translate references to the Spirit, therefore, we must examine the nature of God's self-revelation.

It should first be noted that the doctrine of the Trinity appears only vaguely in the Old Testament. Though there are occasions where the Spirit's distinct personhood is implied (Gen 1:2; Is 48:16), it is not clearly set out, and the designation "the Spirit of God" represents especially God's active power and vitality (compare Is 40:13). Only in the New Testament is the Holy Spirit clearly revealed as a person distinct from the Father and the Son. It is to the New Testament revelation, therefore, that we must turn to determine how best to translate pronouns related to the Holy Spirit. While neuter pronouns are often used in agreement with the grammatical gender of *pneuma,* in the Gospel of John masculine pronouns also appear.[25] John 16:13 reads, "But when *he* [*ekeinos,* masculine singular], the Spirit of truth, comes" (compare 15:26). This, of course, does not mean that the Spirit is male but that he is a person, not merely a force. Yet to express this personhood, the New Testament writers never used feminine pronouns, even though they were certainly aware of the feminine gender of the Hebrew *rûaḥ*. Perhaps they felt to use a feminine pronoun would have inappropriately introduced the idea of biological gender into the Godhead (two males, Father and Son, and one female consort, the Spirit). The New Testament writers chose either to use neuter pronouns (following the grammatical gender of *pneuma*) or to introduce masculine pronouns (stressing the personality of the Spirit). Since English nouns do not carry grammatical gender and since the pronoun "it" suggests something impersonal, following the pattern of the biblical writers and using masculine pronouns is accurate and appropriate in Bible translation.

Language Related to Jesus Christ

Jesus was certainly a man (that is, a male human being), and any attempts to alter or downplay this fact should be rejected in Bible translation. Moderate gender-inclusive translations retain masculine references for Jesus, whereas some feminist versions attempt to eliminate or downplay them. The introduction to the INT, for example, reads:

> The significance of the Incarnation, for us, is not that God became a man, but that God—all-powerful, all-knowing and seeing, absolute Divinity—became flesh, took on human life and suffering and weakness. To that end, we have kept (though de-emphasized) male pronouns in passages describing Jesus' earthly ministry, but have removed them following the Resurrection.[26]

One wonders why it was necessary to "deemphasize" Jesus' maleness during his earthly life. Surely objections would be raised if a Bible translation chose to deemphasize the femaleness of Mary or Priscilla or Deborah, or any other woman in Scripture for that matter. The elimination of masculine pronouns in gender-specific contexts does nothing to clarify the meaning of the text, and it smacks of misandry,[27] the "hatred of males." It seems to me that the noble (and biblical) goal of correcting the historical oppression of woman has gotten off track when the gender-specific use of "man" and "he" is treated as inherently evil.

Passages stressing the humanity of Jesus Christ. The elimination of masculine pronouns for Jesus in gender-specific contexts should be rejected. In some passages, however, the stress is on Jesus' humanity and not his maleness. In these passages the Greek term *anthrōpos* carries the sense "human being" rather than "man" ("male"). Andreas Köstenberger, on the contrary, repeatedly criticizes the NIVI for inclusive renderings in such passages, claiming that they downplay Jesus' maleness.[28] In John 10:33, for example, the NIV reads, "'We are not stoning you for any of these,' replied the Jews, 'but for blasphemy, because you, a mere man *[anthrōpos]*, claim to be God.'" The NIVI reads, "'Because you, a mere human being, claim to be God.'" Köstenberger asserts that "the change . . . has the effect of downplaying Jesus' maleness during his earthly incarnate state."[29] Yet in this context *anthrōpos* clearly carries the sense "human being" rather than "male." Jesus' opponents are contrasting humanity and deity, not maleness and deity. In passages such as this one, the NIVI rendering "human being" (like the translation "a mortal") brings out more precisely the sense intended by the inspired author (see chap. five). Its rendering is, therefore, better than the NIV's.

A similar case appears in 1 Timothy 2:5, where the NIV reads, "For there is one God and one mediator between God and men *[anthrōpoi]*, the *man [anthrōpos]* Christ Jesus." The NIVI has "between God and human beings, Christ Jesus, himself human." Again Köstenberger argues that "this rendering dilutes the maleness of Jesus during his incarnate state."[30] Wayne Grudem also criticizes the NIVI for translating "human" instead of "man" in 1 Timothy 2:5.[31] Yet the primary point Paul is making is that Jesus is the mediator between God and human beings, not that Jesus is the mediator between God and men (males). To argue otherwise is to deny the inclusivity of the redemptive work of Christ.

Since *anthrōpoi* is more accurately and precisely translated as "human beings" in this case, it seems appropriate to follow the verbal connection in the Greek between *anthrōpoi* and *anthrōpos* (which relates Jesus' humanity to that of all human beings). Paul's point is that Jesus is able to be our mediator because he himself is human. In what sense does this "downplay" the maleness of Jesus? Would any reader suddenly become confused about Jesus' gender because he is referred to as a human being instead of a man? On the contrary, the pronoun "himself" in the NIVI phrase, "himself human" confirms (if there was any doubt) that Jesus was a male, whereas the use of the term "human" makes clear the sense of *anthrōpos* in context. Thus the NIVI's translation is more accurate and more precise than the NIV's.

Köstenberger recognizes that Jesus' humanity is at issue here but still argues for the translation "man":

> The translators are correct in observing that part of Paul's point here is the *humanness* of Jesus: he is able to mediate between God and man because he himself was a man, that is, a human being. But Paul is also clearly thinking of Jesus' earthly life and sacrifice on the cross which he made as a man, a male. Thus *both* truths are emphasized here by Paul, that Jesus was a *human being* and that Jesus, in his incarnate state, was a *man*.[32]

He goes on to add that "the NIVI unduly focuses merely on *one* aspect of Paul's statement, Jesus' *humanity*, while deleting any reference to his earthly identity as a *man*." Two comments are in order in response. First, Köstenberger is wrong in his claim that the NIVI "deletes any reference to his earthly identity as a *man*." As just noted, the NIVI confirms that Jesus was a man with the masculine pronoun "himself." Furthermore, Köstenberger is surely wrong in the importance given to Jesus' maleness in this context. Is it really accurate to say that Paul intends to emphasize Jesus' maleness, as though maleness and humanity were of equal importance here? Surely Jesus' humanity is not just a "part of Paul's point" but is his primary point.

The same criticism can be leveled at Köstenberger's handling of Philippians 2:8. He argues that Jesus suffered "not merely as an undifferentiated human being, but specifically and concretely as a *man*, as the current NIV rightly notes."[33] This again seems to be special pleading. The masculine pronoun "he" (together with the entire context of the New Testament) confirms that Jesus was a man, not an "undifferentiated human being." But what is Paul's primary point? Is it not that at the *kenosis* Jesus took on our humanity? The original NIV recognized this by translating verse 7 as "being made in *human* likeness [*homoiōmati anthrōpōn*]." The NIVI captures the verbal connection in the Greek more clearly by translating *anthrōpos* in the next verse as "human being." I was surprised to find support for this translation in an unlikely place. In his excellent systematic theology textbook, Wayne Grudem himself follows the RSV in translating Philippians 2:8 as "being found in human form he humbled himself and became obedient unto death, even death on a cross."[34]

In these passages Paul is stressing first and foremost the humanity of Jesus, not his maleness. Accusations that the NIVI "de-genderizes" or "neuters" males are both inflammatory and inaccurate. Would any reader become confused in these passages over whether Jesus was a man or woman? Of course not. All masculine pronouns are retained. Yet when Paul is speaking about the Incarnation—the taking on of true human flesh—an inclusive term captures this theological truth more clearly. This is what *anthrōpos* means in these contexts. I have surveyed various works of systematic theology written by evangelicals and have yet to find any significant section devoted to the maleness of Jesus. Even Wayne Grudem's text devotes fifteen pages to the humanity of Christ, but I could find nothing about his maleness.[35] (He deals with 1 Timothy 2:5—where both he and Köstenberger criticize the NIVI translation "human"—in his section on the humanity of Christ![36]) If Christ's maleness were a doctrine of such crucial importance, it would merit at least a footnote in a 1,261-page work on systematic theology. Grudem actually moves in the opposite direction by repeatedly drawing a feminine analogy with reference to Jesus. He draws a connection between the authoritative role of the husband over the wife in marriage to that of the Father over the Son in the Trinity. He writes that "the husband's role is parallel to that of God the Father and the wife's role is parallel to that of God the Son."[37] Grudem, of course, is drawing an analogy and so should not be criticized for "de-genderizing" or "feminizing" Jesus. Yet neither should the NIVI be criticized for stressing the humanity of Christ over his maleness, when the former is obviously the author's point in context (*and* masculine pronouns are retained).

A more difficult decision must be made in regard to John 11:50, where the high priest Caiaphas says of Jesus that "it is better for you that one man *[anthrōpos]* die for the people than that the whole nation perish" (NIV). The NIVI reads "one *person*." Köstenberger writes that "the context seems to suggest that the reference is to one *man*, Jesus." This is a difficult call. It is certainly true that the referent here is a male, and most other inclusive versions retain the word "man" (NRSV, NLT, TEV, NAB, NJB, REB). Yet Caiaphas is stressing Jesus' singularity, not his maleness. It is better that *the one* suffer, not *the many*. Since the many ("the whole nation") is an inclusive reference, referring to men and women, the contrast may best be expressed with an inclusive term: *one person* should suffer rather than *many persons*.

The Adam-Christ analogy. Of greatest difficulty, perhaps, are passages that draw a direct link between Adam and Christ. Köstenberger criticizes the NIVI translation of 1 Corinthians 15:21: "For since death came through a human being, the resurrection of the dead comes also through a human being."[38] The NIV reads "man" in both cases. It should first be noted that the various gender-inclusive versions are divided on this passage. While the NRSV, NIVI, NAB and CEV use an inclusive term, the NLT, TEV, NJB, NCV, GW and REB retain "man." Similarly, in the parallel passage in Romans 5, where Paul develops in detail this Adam-Christ analogy, most inclusive versions retain the term "man" (so NIVI, NRSV, NJB, NLT, TEV, REB, NCV). The NIVI reads in Romans 5:19: "For just as through the disobedience of the one man *[anthrōpos]* the many were made sinners, so also through the obedience of the one man [*tou henos*, literally 'of the one'] the many will be made righteous" (compare vv. 12, 15, 18, 19). Only NAB, CEV and GW use more inclusive language. The NAB and GW refer to "one person," whereas the CEV rewords the text to refer to "Adam's sin." Of course neither of these translations creates theological confusion because the "one person" is identified in context as "Adam" (v. 14), who obviously was a male.

These passages raise complex theological questions. What is Paul's primary point in 1 Corinthians 15:21? Is it that because human beings sinned, a human being must be the agent of redemption? Or is it that Adam as the first male serves as representative head of the human race in the Fall? Or is it both? Furthermore, does Paul mean to imply that it was essential for our redemption that Jesus was a male? Complementarians would probably say yes because of the issue of male headship. Egalitarians would probably say no except for the historical need to fulfill messianic promises (which are male oriented). We might also ask whether it was specifically Adam's sin or the sin of Adam and Eve (*'ādām* as male and female, Gen 1:27) that resulted in the Fall. Most theologians would probably say the latter, but many would also affirm Adam's unique representative role as head of the human race. Because of the singularity stressed in Paul's comparison between Adam and Christ, I would prefer to err on the side of caution by retaining the singular "man" in both 1 Corinthians 15 and Romans 5. But I will leave it to greater theological minds than my own to provide a definitive answer on this one. This is not a matter of "political correctness" but an effort to understand precisely what Paul meant in these contexts.

Jesus as the Son of Man. The Hebrew and Aramaic phrases *ben 'ādām* and *bar 'ᵉnosh* ("son of man") are Semitic idioms that carry the sense "human being" (for discussion, see chap. six). Seldom do they mean exclusively "a male human being." It is usually appropriate, therefore, to translate these passages with inclusive renderings like "mortal" or "human being." Difficulty arises from the fact that the Greek phrase *ho huios tou anthrōpou* ("the Son of Man") functions in the New Testament as a messianic title for Jesus. Because of the traditional rendering "the Son of Man," all of the moderate inclusive versions, including the NRSV and the CEV, retain the traditional Son of Man title in the New Testament. Feminist versions, on the other hand, adopt phrases like "the Human One."[39]

The problem with retaining the Son of Man title in the New Testament but not in the Old Testament is that Jesus' use of the title is drawn from the Old Testament. In Daniel 7:13-14, for example, the RSV renders, "And behold, with the clouds of heaven there came one like a son of man." The NRSV uses more inclusive (and less archaic) language with the phrase "one like a human being." On the face of it, this translation is perfectly acceptable. Even the most conservative commentators admit that the Aramaic phrase means that this exalted messianic figure had the appearance of a human being (compare Dan 10:16).[40] The problem comes when Jesus refers back to this passage at his trial. He says to the high priest, "You will see the Son of Man . . . coming with the clouds of heaven" (Mk 14:62 NRSV). The Old Testament allusion may be lost to the reader when the NRSV translates Daniel 7:13 as "a human being" but retains the title "Son of Man" throughout the New Testament.

Translators have several options here. Perhaps the most radical is to translate the passage in Daniel inclusively as "like a human" and then translate the Greek phrase similarly as something like "the Human One." This is what the NTPI does. This rendering is not inaccurate because the title probably stresses Jesus' humanity *and* points to the exalted figure of Daniel 7. But this seems to be an unnecessary change.

Although the title "the Son of Man" is an unusual English phrase, it is also unusual Greek. I. Howard Marshall writes, "The phrase *ho huios tou anthrōpou,* literally 'the son of the man,' is something of an oddity in Greek, and we can be certain that it owes its origin to a Semitic phrase."[41] The very strangeness of the idiom to English ears accurately captures the sense of the original, since the phrase also sounded strange and stilted to first-century Greek ears. This allowed the phrase *ho huios tou anthrōpou* to take on a titular and technical sense very quickly among the early Christians, just as "the Son of Man" has taken on such a sense among English readers. Thus there seems to be no reason to find an alternative for the traditional "the Son of Man." In order to retain the Old Testament allusion, translators might retain the phrase "like a son of man" in Daniel 7, with a marginal note explaining that this means having the appearance of a human being (compare NIVI, CEV, GW). Alternatively, the Daniel passage might be translated "like a human being," with a marginal note explaining that the Hebrew idiom reads literally "like a son of man" (compare NRSV, REB, NLT). Cross-references to the relevant New Testament passages might also be noted.

The translation of allusions is always a difficult issue in Bible translation, since allusions often involve formal verbal connections. When an English translation seeks to capture the sense of the original, formal, or "literal," allusions can be lost. This is not just a problem for gender-inclusive language but for all Bible translation. While functional equivalent versions tend to capture the sense of the original better, literal versions often better retain formal verbal allusions. This is another good reason for using both kinds of translations in serious Bible study.

Messianic passages. It has sometimes been suggested that inclusive language in the Old Testament obscures messianic prophecies concerning Jesus. An example of this occurs in Psalm 8:4, where the original NIV reads, "What is *man ['îsh]* that you are mindful of him, the son of man *[ben 'ādām]* that you care for him?" The NRSV reads, "What are human beings that you are mindful of them, mortals that you care for them?" The NIVI similarly uses inclusive terms: "What are mere mortals that you are mindful of them, human beings that you care for them?" This translation has been attacked because the psalm is used as a messianic quotation in Hebrews 2:6, not because of the meaning of the psalm itself. Grudem writes that the NIVI rendering has "obscured the connection to Hebrews 2:6"[42] and that "the application to Christ [in Heb 2:6] now looks inaccurate."[43]

To reach a conclusion on this issue we must first determine the meaning of the psalm in its Old Testament context. What do *'îsh* and *ben 'ādām* mean there? It can hardly be denied that the psalmist is speaking inclusively rather than exclusively. He does not mean to ask, "What are males?" but rather, "What are human beings?" It is not men who are "made . . . a little lower than the heavenly beings" (or God[44]) but people. All commentators agree on this. Both "mortals" and "human beings" capture the sense of the original well.

This passage is quoted in Hebrews 2:6-8, which asserts Jesus' superiority to angels: "It is not to angels that he has subjected the world to come" (NIV). This is followed by the quote from Psalm 8:4-6:

> But there is a place where someone has testified: "What is man that you are mindful of him, the son of man that you care for him? You made him a little lower than the angels; you crowned him with glory and honor and put everything under his feet." (Heb 2:6-8 NIV)

Most commentators agree that "man" and "son of man" are here used synonymously and that the latter is not functioning as a christological title.[45] It does not mean *the* Son of Man (a messianic title for Jesus) but "human beings." If this is the case, then the passage does not refer exclusively to Jesus but rather to the destiny of humanity, which has now been fulfilled in Jesus. This is the best interpretation because (1) it agrees with the meaning of the psalm in its Old Testament context and (2) it fits the context of Hebrews 2:8-9:

> In putting everything under him, God left nothing that is not subject to him. Yet at present we do not see everything subject to him. But we see Jesus, who was made a little lower than the angels, now crowned with glory and honor because he suffered death. (NIV)

The reference to "him" here is probably to humanity.[46] Though man's (humanity's) original destiny was to be crowned with glory and honor and for creation to be subject to him (see Gen 1:28), "at present we do not see everything subject to him." In its present fallen state humanity has not achieved its true destiny. Through his suffering and death, however, Jesus has fulfilled the ultimate destiny of humanity by being made for a time "a little lower than the angels" but now "crowned with glory and honor" (vv. 7, 9). William Lane sums this up well: "In Jesus we see exhibited humanity's true vocation. In an extraordinary way he fulfills God's design for all creation and displays what had always been intended for all humankind, according to Ps 8."[47] Psalm 8, both in its Old Testament context and in its context in Hebrews, is about God's destiny for humanity. Jesus fulfills this destiny by acting as the true human representative.

D. A. Carson comes to a similar conclusion when he defends the NRSV's use of inclusive language in this passage: "True, Ps. 8 is there [in Heb 2] *applied* to Jesus, but as the context shows, it is applied to him *qua* human being. It is not a Christological title with univocal reference to Jesus" (italics his).[48] Grudem's criticism of the NIVI reading is valid only if Psalm 8 refers exclusively to Jesus. But this appears not to be the case, either in its Old Testament context or in its citation in Hebrews 2.

Another Old Testament messianic passage in which inclusive language has been criticized for blurring a messianic reference is Psalm 34:20. Compare the RSV with the NRSV:

> RSV: Many are the afflictions of the righteous; but the LORD delivers him out of them all. He keeps all his bones; not one of them is broken.
>
> NRSV: Many are the afflictions of the righteous, but the LORD rescues them from them all. He keeps all their bones; not one of them will be broken.

Grudem argues that this verse is identified in John 19:36 as a messianic prediction and complains that "the specificity of the Messianic prediction, so wonderfully fulfilled in Jesus' death, is lost to the readers of the NRSV."[49] The NIVI, NLT, CEV, NJB and NAB similarly introduce the plural: "He protects all their bones" (Ps 34:20 NIVI).

Several comments are in order. First, it is not at all certain that John 19:36 is referring to Psalm 34:20. Many commentators see instead a Passover lamb allusion drawn primarily from Exodus 12:46 (compare Num 9:12).[50] Even if we assume for the sake of argument that Psalm 34:20 is in view, the context of the psalm suggests that a generic reference is intended. Verse 18 of the psalm reads, "The LORD is close to the brokenhearted, and saves those who are crushed in spirit" (NIV). In the Hebrew text both "brokenhearted" and "those who are crushed" are plurals, suggesting that the singulars in verses 19-20 are also generic, referring to righteous sufferers in general.

It is significant that the Septuagint (LXX) translators understood the reference in the Hebrew text to be general, since they translated using plurals throughout. Psalm 33:20-21 in the Septuagint (= 34:19-20) reads, "Many are the afflictions of the righteous ones and he delivers them from all of them. The Lord guards all their bones, not one of them is broken."

This is not to suggest that the Septuagint necessarily represents the inspired text but only that a natural reading of Psalm 34:19-20 takes the singulars as generic, referring to righteous sufferers in general or to a typical righteous sufferer.[51] This, of course, does not negate a messianic reference, since such psalms are usually viewed as typologically (rather than uniquely) pointing to Christ. Grudem complains that "the specificity of the Messianic prediction" is lost, but the prediction is probably not meant to be specific, but typological. Jesus suffers as the righteous sufferer par excellence.

Conclusion

This chapter has examined inclusive language related to the Godhead—Father, Son and Holy Spirit—and language related to Jesus Christ in his humanity. Masculine terms like "Father," "Lord" and "King" should be retained because they accurately reflect the historical and cultural sense intended by the original author. Language related to Jesus' divine sonship and his lordship should also be retained for the same reason.

On the other hand, in passages where the stress is clearly on Jesus' humanity and not his maleness, the Greek term *anthrōpos* is accurately translated with terms such as "human being" and "human." Likewise, Old Testament messianic prophecies that speak of righteous sufferers in general (Ps 34:20) or humanity as a race (Ps 8) may be accurately translated using inclusive language because these texts point typologically, rather than exclusively, to Jesus Christ.

Eight

SUMMARY & CONCLUSIONS

A CHAPTER-BY-CHAPTER SUMMARY WILL SET THE STAGE HERE FOR A consideration of the implications generated by this study.

Chapter one places the gender-inclusive language debate in the larger context of the history of Bible translation. New Bible translations have always provoked opposition, especially when they have challenged the supremacy of an established version (such as the Vulgate or the KJV) or when they have appeared to be driven by a particular social or theological agenda. The current reaction against gender-inclusive versions has grown out of the perception that these versions are driven by the social agenda of radical feminism. Although it is certainly true that the women's movement has had a significant influence on contemporary English usage, such language changes are neither inherently evil nor necessarily inappropriate. The use of gender-inclusive language in Scripture must be judged first and foremost on whether it accurately reproduces the meaning of the original text. The question this book repeatedly asks is, Do gender-inclusive renderings distort or enhance the message of God's Word?

Chapter two surveys the moderate gender-inclusive (or gender-accurate) versions. These versions seek to use inclusive terms such as "person" and "human being" rather than "man" when the original author was referring to both men and women. These versions include the New Revised Standard Version, the New Jerusalem Bible, the New Century Version, the New American Bible, the Revised English Bible, the Good News Bible, The Message, the Contemporary English Version, God's Word, the New Living Translation, the New International Version (Inclusive Language Edition) and the New International Readers Version. The Contemporary English Version and the New Revised Standard Version are the most inclusive, sometimes introducing inclusive renderings when the original context might suggest an exclusive reference.

Chapter three examines the more radical "feminist" translations. They have a much more sweeping inclusive agenda, often downplaying or obscuring the patriarchal culture of the Bible and even altering masculine imagery related to God. These versions include the *Inclusive Language Lectionary,* The New Testament and Psalms: An Inclusive Version and the Inclusive New Testament.

Chapter four examines the nature of Bible translation in order to establish criteria by which to judge the gender-inclusive versions and argues that a good Bible translation is one that takes a text in the source language and reproduces its meaning, as fully as possible, in the receptor language. Since language by its very nature is idiomatic, accurate Bible translation must focus first and foremost on the *meaning* of the original Hebrew or Greek text rather than on its *form*. When seeking to capture meaning, translators must always keep two distinct contexts in mind: the world of the original author and the world of the contemporary reader. An accurate Bible translation is one that enables the contemporary reader to comprehend the text with the same sense intended by the original author.

Lexical semantics, the study of word meanings, also has importance for Bible translation. Most words in any language do not have a single all-encompassing meaning but a range of potential senses—a "semantic range." The Greek lexeme *anthrōpos,* for example, has a semantic range that includes the various senses "human being," "male human being," "humanity" and so on. It is the context in which the word is used that determines which sense the author intended. It is simplistic and sometimes inaccurate to say that *anthrōpos* means "man" and should be invariably translated as such.

Chapter five turns to masculine generic nouns and pronouns traditionally translated "man" and "he." Greek *anthrōpos* and Hebrew *'ādām* often refer to human beings generally rather than males specifically. In such contexts they may be translated accurately and precisely with inclusive terms such as "human being" and "person." Greek *anēr* and Hebrew *'îsh,* though more commonly used of males, can also refer to human beings. In such cases they may be translated inclusively. If the context confirms that the referents are male, masculine language should be retained. An exception to this occurs when the passage refers specifically to an individual's *humanity,* not his *maleness,* in which case the translation "human being" or "person" is appropriate.

Chapter five also examines a variety of constructions used by inclusive versions to replace masculine singular pronouns, for example, indefinite pronouns, plural constructions, singular "they" and first- or second-person pronouns. Plural constructions work well in proverbial, legal and instructional material because such language, though grammatically singular, is notionally plural, referring to persons or classes of persons. The judicious and cautious use of these techniques can capture accurately the sense intended by the original author. These methods were used not only by ancient Bible translators (the scholars who produced the Septuagint, for example) but also by the New Testament writers themselves.

The excursus following chapter five examines studies related to contemporary English usage. The English language has always been (and continues to be) in a state of flux. Significant usage and perception changes related to the generic use of masculine pronouns and the term "man" are beyond dispute. It is not enough to say, therefore, that if the generic use of "man" was good enough for our parents, it is good enough for our children and our children's children. Empirical studies have demonstrated that masculine generic terms are in significant decline in contemporary English. Many people, especially children, often understand masculine generic terms as referring to males only.

Others may comprehend the generic sense but still feel excluded by its use. In such cases it is propitious to translate according to common usage and so communicate clearly and unambiguously the message of God's Word.

Chapter six examines terms related to "brothers," "fathers" and "sons." The Greek terms *adelphos* and *adelphoi* often carry the sense "brother or sister" and "brothers and sisters" respectively. These translations are not capitulations to a feminist agenda but rather convey exactly what these words meant in their first-century context.

The Greek and Hebrew terms traditionally translated "father(s)" have a much broader semantic range than their English counterparts, and so, in particular contexts, may accurately be translated as "ancestors," "predecessors" or "parents." Since the biblical culture was patriarchal, when male heads of households are the intended referents, terms such as "forefathers" or "fathers" should probably be retained. The Greek and Hebrew terms traditionally translated "son(s)" also have a much broader semantic range than their English counterparts and may accurately be translated as "children" or "descendants" in certain contexts. The Hebrew and Greek "son(s) of . . ." idiom carries a very wide range of senses and may be translated with a variety of English expressions.

Chapters five and six argue that careful case-by-case exegesis must be employed to ensure the accurate use of inclusive language. Traditional versions have sometimes erred by retaining masculine generic terms such as "fathers" without due consideration for the sense intended by the author or for the way these terms are heard and comprehended in contemporary English. Numerous examples are provided showing how the introduction of gender-inclusive language actually enhances the translation, providing more accuracy and precision. On the other side, gender-inclusive versions have sometimes erred by introducing inclusive terms indiscriminately, even in contexts where only males were intended. Both extremes should be avoided, with each passage being judged on its own merit.

It should also be noted in this regard that there is nothing inherently wrong or evil in the use of masculine generics such as "he," "man" or "brother." Both Hebrew and Greek—the primary languages of God's revelation—use masculine generics. The issue is one of contemporary English usage. If, for many readers, the English word "man" no longer conveys the same inclusive sense it once did, other terms should be substituted to capture the sense intended by the author. In this regard it may perhaps be best for the so-called literal versions, which seek to retain the form of the original Greek, to continue to make use of certain masculine generics in their translations. These versions, though often inadequate translations, function well as study tools, enabling the student to see the formal structure of the Greek or Hebrew. When students see "brothers" in a formal-equivalent version and "brothers and sisters" in a functional-equivalent version, they will recognize that although the Greek uses a single masculine generic term, the sense intended by the author is "brothers and sisters." (The latter, of course, is the more accurate translation.)

Finally, chapter seven examines language related to God and Jesus Christ. It argues that masculine titles such as "Father," "Lord" and "King" should be retained with reference to God because they accurately reflect the historical and cultural sense intended by the author. When Jesus called on his disciples to address God as "Father," he was using a masculine metaphor, not an androgynous "Mother-Father" one. To eliminate masculine God language is to distort the divinely inspired metaphors of Scripture. Retaining masculine pronouns for the Father, Son and Spirit also helps to protect the sense of three distinct persons of the Trinity. Introducing feminine pronouns for the Spirit could promote pagan ideas of a male god with a female consort.

With reference to Jesus Christ, traditional titles such as "Son of God" and "Son of Man" should normally be retained, since such titles carry specific historical connotations. Gender-neutral language such as "Child of God" can obscure such connotations. On the other hand, passages that clearly stress Jesus' humanity rather than his maleness (for example, 1 Tim 2:5; Phil 2:8) can appropriately be translated with terms such as "human being" and "person."

Issues for Further Discussion

A number of issues that are discussed in this book merit more detailed examination. In regard to some of these issues I have expressed a particular perspective. Others I have left open-ended. The following are representative:

1. How should the Hebrew *'ādām* be translated with reference to corporate humanity (compare Gen 1:27)? Should "man" be retained in such contexts, or should it be replaced with a term such as "humanity"? I have favored the latter option, but this issue needs to be examined from a theological perspective that is broader than the scope of this book permits.

2. Does Paul's comparing and contrasting Adam and Christ (Rom 5:12-21; 1 Cor 15:21) place the stress on Jesus' humanity or on his maleness? How does the issue of Adam as representative head of the human race relate to this?

3. Should the term "fathers" be retained when male heads of household are the referents? In Genesis 48:21, for example, Jacob tells Joseph, "God will be with you and take you back to the land of your fathers." "Fathers" here means his father Jacob, as well as his grandfather Isaac and great-grandfather Abraham. Neither "ancestors," "fathers" nor "forefathers" captures precisely the sense of the Hebrew term *'ābôt*.

4. How should Old Testament passages relating to the study of Torah (as in Psalm 1) be translated? Those relating to other activities in which only males would normally have participated? Similarly, how much inclusive language should be used in the Proverbs, where father-to-son instruction may be in view?

5. When a general principle is taught with an illustration, should the gender-specific illustration be retained? For example, is it important to retain the masculine gender of the "man" who looks at his face in a mirror in James 1:23?

The Problem of Consistency: How Much Inclusive Language?

Translators must answer another difficult question: How consistently should gender-inclusive language be introduced? Even if we conclude that inclusive language can provide a clear and accurate translation, should it be introduced in every generic context? The problem is that contemporary English usage today is very mixed, with both masculine generics and inclusive terms in common use. Yet translating inclusively only occasionally or haphazardly results in inconsistency. Versions such as the NRSV, which consistently render masculine generics inclusively, are actually *more* inclusive than the general public. A version such as the REB, on the other hand, which has perhaps 60 percent inclusive renderings, is probably closer to general speech; yet it is also inconsistent and haphazard in its use of such language. What is the solution?

I would suggest that the best policy is to adopt the consistent use of gender-inclusive language whenever the original text clearly intends to include both men and women. This rule should not be slavishly followed, however, and masculine generics may be used when poor or awkward English style would otherwise result. Furthermore, when the context makes it uncertain whether both men and women would be included in a particular passage, translations should probably err on the side of caution and either retain masculine references or introduce language that would allow an inclusive reference without specifying it (for example, "How blessed are *those* . . . ").

The Next Step in the Debate

As we have seen, the guidelines established at the Conference on Gender-Related Language in Scripture have already begun to crumble, with significant modifications being introduced. Revised guidelines allow for terms such as "human being" for generic "man" and "brothers and sisters" for *adelphoi*. In addition, an important phrase was added to the end of the guidelines: "Some details may need further refinement." One cannot help but wonder, when all of the guidelines have been critically scrutinized and "refined," how many of the revisions introduced by the NIVI will be viewed as perfectly acceptable. Even with the two "minor" alterations already introduced, hundreds of NIVI renderings may be seen not only as acceptable but actually as *improvements in accuracy* over the NIV.

This raises several important issues. Should the IBS now reverse its decision not to revise the NIV, especially in light of the important "discovery" that *adelphoi* often means "brothers and sisters"? Should not this rendering be introduced into subsequent revisions of all NIVs?

Furthermore, how should *'ābōt* be translated when the sense in context is clearly "ancestors" rather than "fathers"? What about "children" for *huioi* when both males and females are the referents? Whether or not the NIVI issue is revisited, it is time for evangelical scholars to set aside their personal agendas and begin a serious discussion of the issues that remain.

The Real Battle for the Bible: The Relativization of God's Truth

World magazine called the decision regarding whether or not to publish the NIVI in North America the "Battle for the Bible." The real battle for the Bible, however, is not whether inclusive language will appear in contemporary Bible versions. Some such language is inevitable if translators are going to utilize contemporary English to capture the sense intended by the biblical authors. The *real* battle is whether we will relativize biblical truth by translating according to our own social and political agendas or will allow the message of God's Word to set the agenda.

The danger of relativization may be seen in the call for two NIVs, one inclusive and one noninclusive. Aida Spencer, in an otherwise excellent critique of the NIV controversy, suggests that the IBS should have held to its initial response and should have continued to offer both inclusive and noninclusive editions of the NIV.[1] From one perspective Spencer's suggestion is legitimate, since different readers hear masculine terms differently. Some hear them exclusively, others inclusively. It might be argued that two versions would simply cater to the different connotations that these words carry for different readers. But I fear the precedent that this would set. The impression of subjectivity that two editions would give to the average reader would ultimately be counterproductive, affirming the popular misconception that you can make the Bible mean whatever you want. Readers would adopt a "you-can-have-your-Bible-and-I-can-have-mine" attitude. "You can have a Bible that supports your agenda and I can have one that supports mine." Accepting the legitimacy of two (or more!) NIVs risks relativizing biblical truth.

As evangelicals affirming the authority and inspiration of God's

Word, we must reach common ground on this issue, establishing translation principles that will affirm both faithfulness to the original text and sensitivity to the perceptions of contemporary readers.

The Need for Unity in the Church

Another danger in the present debate is the disunity and division that it is provoking in the evangelical church. Although I agree with my complementarian friends that there is a danger in abolishing all gender role distinctions in the church and the home, I am also convinced that the greatest danger facing the evangelical church is not the increasing role of women but the divisions and schisms that this issue is creating.

In the past the evangelical church has been divided over issues such as the charismatic gifts, Calvinism versus Arminianism, and dispensational theology versus covenant theology. It seems to me that there is much healthy dialogue and mutual respect among evangelicals today on these issues.[2] In the case of the role of women in ministry, however, the schism appears to be widening, with churches, denominations and theological schools polarizing and shutting down constructive dialogue. The same appears to be happening over the inclusive language debate.

If healthy dialogue and debate is to continue, it is essential that all parties acknowledge the necessity for Christian love, unity and mutual respect. Gender-accurate language of the kind advocated in this book becomes a relatively minor issue when it is compared with the fundamentals of the faith: the triune nature of God, the person and work of Christ, the sanctifying work of the Holy Spirit. Both the women-in-ministry issue and the gender-inclusive language debate must be kept in appropriate perspective. Neither issue should be allowed to break believers' fellowship or hinder the more pressing concern of taking the gospel of Jesus Christ across all cultural boundaries to the ends of the earth.

Inclusive Language and the Feminist Agenda

Some will no doubt suggest at this point that I am being naive and that my call for unity ignores the very real social and political agendas at play in the present debate. Language not only reflects culture but creates culture. The feminist push for inclusive language is not intended simply to mirror the current state of the English language but to transform the language and so change the way we think about men and women.

I am well aware of the agendas at work in the present debate. There is no doubt that the push for inclusive language is driven on the one side by feminist concerns, just as the push against it is driven by complementarian concerns. It is precisely because these agendas are present that clarity of expression and hermeneutical sophistication must be brought to the debate. Yet the fact that inclusive language has its roots in the women's movement does not automatically negate its legitimacy. There are two reasons for this.

First, even the most vehement antifeminist must admit that some good has come out of the women's movement. Although many Christians today do not believe that women should serve in leadership roles over men, few would dispute that they should have the right to vote. But it was not so long ago in our nation's history that women were denied this basic right. The social and political oppression of women is a fact of history and, in many places throughout the world, a present reality. We must not forget that the fundamental supposition of the women's movement—that women are equal to men in dignity and value—is a biblical truth (Gen 1:27; Gal 3:28). Although many radical feminist proposals may stand in opposition to biblical standards, to reject everything about the women's movement is to throw the baby out with the bath water. If gender-inclusive language helps to clarify the value and dignity that God bestows on women and men alike, then it serves a very useful purpose.

Second, the undeniable connection between the women's movement and gender-inclusive language is a negative link only if such language actually misrepresents God's Word. Yet as we have seen throughout this book, this is not necessarily the case. The kind of inclusive language advocated here seeks first and foremost to attain precision and accuracy in translation. If (and only if) a gender-inclusive rendering more accurately reflects the author's intended meaning, then that translation should be adopted. If a large percentage of contemporary readers have the impression of being excluded by generic masculine terms, then those terms are inaccurate and should be revised in ways that convey more precisely the author's intention of inclusion. This is not "rewriting the Bible," as some have suggested; it is more accurately translating the sense intended by the Holy Spirit. Fears of creeping feminism remain unfounded if evangelicals remain steadfast and uncompromising in their goal of *representing the author's intended meaning* in a contemporary English idiom that is appropriate and accurate. It is here, rather than with a sweeping condemnation of gender-inclusive language, that evangelicals must draw their line in the sand.

Conclusion: Inclusive Language for an Inclusive Gospel

Throughout this book I have dealt almost exclusively with hermeneutical and linguistic issues rather than social or theological ones. Yet in closing I must add that perhaps the most important reason for using inclusive language is the nature of the gospel itself. In Galatians 3:28 Paul writes that in Christ there is neither "Jew nor Greek, slave nor free, *male nor female*." While complementarians and egalitarians may disagree over whether this verse is intended to eliminate distinct roles for men or women in the church and the home, there is one point on which we can all certainly agree: Paul is here stressing the *full inclusion* of men and women in the gift of salvation provided through Jesus Christ. If we ask which translation, "a *man* is justified by faith" (Rom 3:28 NIV) or "a *person* is justified by faith" (NIVI), brings out *better* the inclusive sense so central to this apostolic gospel, the answer appears to me to be obvious.

Appendix 1
Guidelines Established at the Conference on Gender-Related Language in Scripture

Focus on the Family Headquarters; Colorado Springs, Colorado
May 27, 1997

A. Gender-related renderings of Biblical language which we affirm:

1. The generic use of "he, him, his, himself" should be employed to translate generic 3rd person masculine singular pronouns in Hebrew, Aramaic and Greek. However, substantival participles such as *ho pisteuōn* can often be rendered in inclusive ways, such as "the one who believes" rather than "he who believes."

2. Person and number should be retained in translation so that singulars are not changed to plurals and third-person statements are not changed to second-person or first-person statements, with only rare exceptions required in unusual cases.

3. "Man" should ordinarily be used to designate the human race or human beings in general, for example in Genesis 1:26-27; 5:2; Ezekiel 29:11; and John 2:25.

4. Hebrew *'ish* should ordinarily be translated "man" and "men" and Greek *anēr* should almost always be so translated.

5. In many cases, *anthrōpoi* refers to people in general, and can be translated "people" rather than "men." The singular *anthrōpos* should ordinarily be translated "man" when it refers to a male human being.

6. Indefinite pronouns such as *tis* can be translated "anyone" rather than "any man."

7. In many cases, pronouns such as *oudeis* can be translated "no one" rather than "no man."

8. When *pas* is used as a substantive, it can be translated with terms such as "all people" or "everyone."

9. The phrase "son of man" should ordinarily be preserved to retain intracanonical connections.

10. Masculine references to God should be retained.

B. Gender-related renderings which we will generally avoid, though there may be unusual exceptions in certain contexts:

1. "Brother" *(adelphos)* and brothers *(adelphoi)* should not be changed to "brother(s) and sister(s)."

2. "Son" *(huios, bēn)* should not be changed to "child," or "sons" *("huioi")* to "children" or "sons and daughters." (However, Hebrew *bānîm* often means "children.")

3. "Father" *(patēr, 'ab)* should not be changed to "parent," or "fathers" to "parents," or "ancestors."

C. We understand these guidelines to be representative and not exhaustive.

Revisions Subsequently Introduced

1. The phrase "or human beings in general" was dropped from guideline A.3. It now reads: *"Man" should ordinarily be used to designate the human race, for example in Genesis 1:26-27; 5:2; Ezekiel 29:11; and John 2:25.*

2. The phrase "and brothers" was dropped from guideline B.1 and the following sentence was added: *However, the plural* adelphoi *can be translated "brothers and sisters" where the context makes clear that the author is referring to both men and women.*

3. Added to guideline C is the clause: *and that some details may need further refinement*

Appendix 2
Comparing the Gender-Inclusive Versions

Section 1: The Use of Generic "Man" and Resumptive Masculine Pronouns

The following chart compares the use of generic "man" in eleven gender-inclusive versions and four noninclusive, or traditional, versions. I have chosen one hundred verses in which generic "man" is used, either the Hebrew terms *'ādām, 'îsh* or *'ᵉnôsh,* or the Greek terms *anthrōpos* or *anēr.* The verses are drawn mostly from examples found throughout this book. Most examples are clearly generic, that is, they are clearly intended to refer to persons, both male and female. In some others, the text makes it uncertain whether only males or both males and females are intended (for example Jn 18:14; Acts 4:4). In a few cases, the context would seem to indicate that males only are intended (for example, 1 Sam 4:10). I have included a few of these latter passages so that readers can identify the most inclusive versions, sometimes introducing inclusive terms in questionable or even doubtful passages. By listing the specific verses, the chart enables readers to examine these passages themselves to determine whether the passage is indeed an inclusive reference.

It should be noted that the table does not reflect a scientific study, since these verses have not been chosen completely at random. The primary purpose of the table is to provide an opportunity for comparative and representative analysis.

Key to Symbols

A check mark (√) indicates that "man" is rendered inclusively (with a term like "person," with a plural construction and so on). A minus sign (-) indicates that the term "man" (or occasionally, "mankind") is retained, thus producing a noninclusive rendering. An asterisk next to the check (√*) indicates that an inclusive term is followed by a masculine resumptive pronoun. For example,

Galatians 6:1 NIV reads, "If someone *[anthrōpos]* is caught in a sin, you who are spiritual should restore him." "Someone" is an inclusive rendering for *anthrōpos*, but the resumptive pronoun "him" is masculine.

Abbreviations of Bible Versions

Inclusive versions

NRSV New Revised Standard Version
REB Revised English Bible
NJB New Jerusalem Bible
NAB New American Bible (inclusive only in the NT and Psalms)
GNB Good News Bible
CEV Contemporary English Version
GW God's Word
NIVI New International Version (Inclusive Language Edition)
NLT New Living Translation
NCV New Century Version
NIrV New International Reader's Version

Traditional versions

KJV King James Version
NKJV New King James Version
NASB New American Standard Bible
NIV New International Version
RSV Revised Standard Version

Key to Hebrew and Greek Terms

Hebrew

a = *'ādām*
b = *'îsh*
c = *'enôsh*

Greek

d = *anthrōpos*
e = *anēr*

Verses	Traditional Versions					Inclusive Versions										
	KJV	NKJV	NASB	NIV	RSV	NRSV	REB	NJB	NAB	GNB	CEV	NLT	NIVI	GW	NCV	NIrV
Gen 1:27 (a)	–	–	–	–	–	√	√	–	–	√	√	√	√	√	√	√
Gen 3:22 (a)	–	–	–	–	–	–	–	–	–	√	√	√	–	–	–	–
Gen 5:2 (a)	N/A	–	–	–	–	√	–	–	–	√	√	√	√	√	√	√
Gen 6:5 (a)	–	–	–	–	–	√	√	√	–	√	√	√	√	√	√	√
Gen 6:7 (a)	–	–	–	–	–	√	√	√	–	√	√	√	√	√	√	√
Gen 9:6 (a)	–	–	–	–	–	√	√	–	–	√	√	√	√	√	√	√
Ex 9:19 (a)	–	–	–	–	–	√	–	–	–	√	√	√	√	√	√	√
Ex. 10:7b (b)	–	–	–	√	–	√	–	√	–	–	√	√	√	–	√	√
Ex 12:4 (b)	–	–	–	√	√	√	√	√	√	√	√	√	√	√	√	√
Ex 21:12 (b)	–	–	–	–	–	√	–	√	–	√*	√	√	√	√*	√*	√
Ex 21:22 (b)	–	–	–	–	–	√	–	√	–	–	√	√	√	–	–	–
Ex 32:28 (b)	–	–	–	√	–	√	√	–	√	–	–	√	√	√	√	√
Ex 33:8 (b)	–	–	√*	√	–	√	√*	–	√	√	√	√	√	√	√	√
Lev 18:5 (a)	–	–	–	–	–	√	√	√	–	√	√	√	√	√	√	√
Lev 24:17a (b)	–	√	–	√	–	√	√*	√*	√	√	√	√	√	√	√	√
Num 8:17 (a)	–	–	–	–	–	√	√	√	–	–	–	√	√	√	√	–
Deut 1:35 (b)	–	–	–	–	–	√	–	√	–	√	√	√	√	√	√	√
Deut 4:32 (a)	–	–	–	–	–	√	–	√	–	√	√	√	√	√	√	√
Deut 19:15 (b)	–	–	–	–	–	√	√*	√	–	√	√	√	√	√*	√	√

	KJV	NKJV	NASB	NIV	RSV	NRSV	REB	NJB	NAB	GNB	CEV	NLT	NIVI	GW	NCV	NIrV
Judg 17:6 (b)	–	√*	–	√*	–	√	√*	√*	√*	√	√	√	√	√*	√	√
1 Sam 2:25 (b)	–	–	–	–	–	√	√*	√*	–	√	√	√	√	√*	√	√
1 Sam 4:10 (b)	–	–	–	–	–	√*	√	–	–	√	√	–	–	√*	√*	–
1 Sam 5:9 (b)	–	–	–	√	–	√	√	√	√	√	√	√	√	√	√	√
1 Sam 15:29 (a)	–	–	–	–	–	√	√	√	–	√	√	√	√	√*	√	√
1 Sam 26:23 (b)	–	–	–	–	–	√*	–	√	–	√	√	√	√	√	√	√
1 Kings 9:5 (b)	–	–	–	–	–	√	–	–	√	√	√	√	√	√	√	–
2 Chron 19:6 (a)	–	–	–	–	–	√	–	√	–	√	√	√	√	√	√	√
Job 2:4 (b)	–	–	–	–	–	√	–	√*	–	√	√	–	√	–	–	√
Job 5:17 (c)	–	–	–	–	–	√	√	√	–	√	√	√	√	√	√	√
Job 7:17 (c)	–	–	–	–	–	√	–	√	–	√	√	√	√	√*	√	√
Job 9:32 (b)	–	–	–	–	–	√	√	√	–	√	√	√	√	√	–	–
Psalm 1:1 (b)	–	–	–	–	–	√	√*	√	√	√	√	√	√	√*	√	√
Psalm 22:6 (b)	–	–	–	–	–	√	–	√	√	√	√	–	√	–	–	√
Psalm 32:2 (a)	–	–	–	–	–	√	–	√	√	√	√	√	√	√	√	√
Psalm 39:6 (b)	–	–	–	–	–	√	√*	√	√	√	√	√	√	√	√	√
Psalm 43:1 (b)	–	–	–	–	–	√	–	√	√	√	√	√	√	√	√	√
Psalm 62:12 (b)	–	√*	–	√*	–	√	√*	√	√	√	√	√	√	√*	√	√
Psalm 92:6 (b)	–	–	–	–	–	√	√	√	√	√	√	√	√	√	√	√
Psalm 103:15 (c)	–	–	–	–	–	√	√*	√*	√	√	√	√	√	√	√	√
Psalm 104:23 (a)	–	–	–	–	–	√	–	–	√	√	√	√	√	√	√	√

	KJV	NKJV	NASB	NIV	RSV	NRSV	REB	NJB	NAB	GNB	CEV	NLT	NIVI	GW	NCV	NIrV
Psalm 112:1 (b)	–	–	–	–	–	√	–	√*	√	√	√	√	√	√*	√	√
Prov 3:13 (a)	–	–	–	–	–	√	–	√	–	√	√	√	√	√	√	√
Prov 6:27 (b)	–	–	–	–	–	√	–	–	–	√	√	–	–	–	√	√
Prov 11:17 (b)	–	–	–	–	–	√	√	√	–	√	√	√	√	√*	√	√
Prov 16:1 (a)	–	–	–	–	–	√	√*	√	–	√	√	√	√	√	√	√
Prov 16:2 (b)	–	–	–	–	–	√	√*	√	–	√	√	√	√	–	√	√
Prov 20:24b (a)	–	–	–	–	–	√	√*	√	–	√*	√	√	√	√*	√*	√
Prov 21:16 (a)	–	–	–	–	–	√	√*	√	–	√	√	√	√	√	√	√
Prov 29:20 (b)	–	–	–	–	–	√	√*	√	–	√	√	√	√	√*	√	√
Eccles 1:3 (a)	–	–	–	–	–	√	√*	√	–	√	√	√	√	√	√	√
Eccles 3:13 (a)	–	–	–	√*	–	√	√*	√	–	√	√	√	√	√	√	√
Isaiah 2:22 (a)	–	–	–	–	–	√	√	√	–	√	√	√	√	√	√	√
Isaiah 17:7 (a)	-	–	–	–	–	√	√	–	–	√	√	√	√	√	√	√
Jer 5:26b (b)	–	–	–	–	–	√	√	√	–	√	√	√	√	√	√	√
Hosea 6:9a (b)	–	–	–	–	–	√	√	√	–	√	√	√	√	–	√	√
Jonah 3:7 (a)	–	–	–	–	–	√	–	√	–	√	√	√	√	–	√	√
Mt 4:4 (d)	–	–	–	–	–	√	–	√	√	√	√	√	√	√	√	√
Mt 6:5b (d)	–	–	–	–	–	√	√	√	√	√	√	√	√	√	√	√
Mt 7:9 (d)	–	–	–	√*	–	√	√*	√*	√*	√	√	√	√	√	√	√
Mt 7:24b (e)	–	–	–	–	–	–	–	–	–	–	√	√	–	√	–	–
Mt 12:12 (d)	–	–	–	–	–	√	–	–	√	√	√	√	√	√	√	√

	KJV	NKJV	NASB	NIV	RSV	NRSV	REB	RJB	NAB	GNB	CEV	NLT	NIVI	GW	NCV	NIrV
Mt 12:41 (e)	–	–	–	–	–	√	–	–	–	√	√	√	√	–	√	√
Mt 14:35 (e)	–	–	–		–	√	√	√	–	√	√	√	√	√	√	√
Mt 15:11 (d))	–	–	–	–	–	√	√*	√	√	√	√	√	√	√*	√	√
Mark 2:27 (d)	–	–	–	–	–	√	–	–	–	√	√	√	√	√	√	√
Mark 7:21 (d)	–	–	–	–	–	√	√	√	√	√	√	√	√	√*	√	√
Mark 10:9 (d)	–	–	–	–	–	√	–	√	√	√	√	√	√	√	√	√
Mark 10:27 (d)	–	–	–	–	–	√	–	√	√	√	√	√	√	√	√	√
Luke 2:52 (d)	–	–	–	–	–	√	–	√	–	√	√	√	√	√	√	√
Luke 11:24 (d)	–	–	–	–	–	√	√	√	√	√	√	√	√	√	√	√
Luke 15:4 (d)	–	–	–	√*	–	√*	√*	√*	–	√	√	√	√*	–	√*	√*
John 2:25b (d)	–	–	–	–	–	√	√	√	√	√	√	√	√	√	√	√
John 3:4 (d)	–	–	–	–	–	√	√*	√	√*	–	–	–	√	–	√	√
John 4:28b (d)	–	–	–	√	√	√	√	√	√	√	√	√	√	√	√	√
John 6:10a (d)	–	√	√	√	√	√	√	√	√	√	√	√	√	√	√	√
John 18:14	–	–	–	–	–	√	–	–	–	–	√	√	√	–	–	√
Acts 4:4 (e)	–	–	–	–	–	√	–	–	–	√	√	–	√	–	√	√
Acts 5:29 (d)	–	–	–	–	–	√	–	–	–	–	√	√	√	√	√	√
Acts 10:26 (d)	–	–	–	–	–	√	–	–	√	–	√	√	√	–	√	–
Rom 1:23 (d)	–	–	–	–	–	√	–	√	–	√	√	√	√	√	√	√
Rom 3:4 (d)	–	–	–	–	–	√	–	√	√	√	√	√	√	√	√	√
Rom 3:28 (d)	–	–	–	–	–	√	√	√	√	√	√	√	√	√*	√	√

	KJV	NKJV	NASB	NIV	RSV	NRSV	REB	RJB	NAB	GNB	CEV	NLT	NIVI	GW	NCV	NIrV
Rom 4:8 (e)	–	–	–	–	–	√	–	√	–		√	√	√	√	√	√
Rom 5:12 (d)	–	–	–	–	–	–	–	–	√	–	√	√	–	√	–	–
Rom 10:5 (d)	–	–	–	–	–	√	√	√	√	√	√	√	√	√*	√	√
1 Cor 1:25 (d)	–	–	–	–	–	√	√	√	√	√	√	√	√	√	√	√
1 Cor 2:9 (d)	–	–	–	√	–	√	√	–	√	√	√	√	√	√	√	√
1 Cor 3:21 (d)	–	–	–	–	–	√	√	√	√	√	√	√	√	√	√	√
1 Cor 11:28 (d)	–	–	–	–	–	√	√*	√*	√*	√	√	√	√	√	√	√
1 Cor 13:1 (d)	–	–	–	–	–	√	–	√	√	√	√	√	√	√	√	√
2 Cor 5:11 (d)	–	–	–	–	–	√	√	√	√	√	√	√	√	√	√	√
Gal 6:1 (d)	–	–	–	√*	–	√	√*	√	√	√	√	√	√	√	√*	√
1 Thess 4:8 (d)	–	–	–	–	–	√	–	√	√	√	√	√	–	√	√	√
Titus 3:10 (d)	–	–	–	√*	–	√	√*	√*	√	√	√	√	√	√	√	√
Heb 2:6 (d)	–	–	–	–	–	√	–	√*	–	√	√	–	√*	√*	√	√*
James 1:12 (e)	–	–	–	–	–	√	–	√	–	√	√	√	√	√	√	√
James 1:19 (d)	–	–	√	√	–	√	√	√	√	√	√	√	√	√	√	√
James 1:20 (e)	–	–	–	–	–	√	√	√	–	√	√	√	√	√	√	√
James 1:23b (e)	–	–	–	–	–	√	√*	√*	–	√	√	√	√	√*	√	√
Rev 21:3 (d)	–	–	–	–	–	√	√	√	√	√	√	√	√	√	√	√
Total Inclusive Verses	0	4	3	17	3	97	59	78	NT & Ps: 39	90	97	93	94	87	92	91
RMP†	N/A	2	1	7	0	3	24	12	NT & Ps: 4	2	0	0	2	19	5	2

†Resumptive Masculine Pronouns

Comment

The table reveals that of the traditional versions, the NIV is by far the most inclusive, with seventeen of the hundred verses already translated in an inclusive manner. This, as noted in chapters one and two, is a result of its dynamic, or functional-equivalent, methodology, which translates more according to sense than form. Seven of these inclusive renderings are followed by a masculine resumptive pronoun. Changes in the English language are evident from the fact that the KJV, though not the most literal of the versions, nevertheless uses generic "man" in every case (the only exception is Gen 5:2, where the KJV transliterates *'ādām* as "Adam"). In the sixteenth century "man" still carried a very strong inclusive sense.

Of the modern versions that specifically identify themselves as gender inclusive, the REB is by far the least consistent in its inclusive policy, with only fifty-nine of one hundred verses rendered in an inclusive manner. Of these fifty-nine, twenty-four are also followed by a masculine resumptive pronoun. The GW, while quite consistent in its inclusive policy (87 of 100 verses), also frequently retains the masculine resumptive pronoun (19 times), as stated in its preface. The NJB is also less inclusive than the others (78 of 100 verses) and retains masculine resumptive pronouns twelve times.

The rest of the versions fall roughly in the same sphere, though the NRSV and the CEV are clearly the most inclusive (97 of 100 verses). In my opinion, these two versions err more frequently than the others in rendering verses that have masculine referents in a gender-inclusive manner. The most gender-accurate versions are the NIVI, the NLT, the GNB, the NCV, GW and the NIrV. While all of these err at individual points, they are generally consistent in their sensitivity to the historical context of individual passages.

Section 2: A Sampling of Other Inclusive Terms in Various Versions

Brothers and Sisters

Romans 12:1 (NIV): Therefore, I urge you, brothers *[adelphoi]*, in view of God's mercy, to offer your bodies as living sacrifices.

KJV "brethren"	NKJV "brethren"	NASB "brethren"	RSV "brethren"	NRSV "brothers and sisters"	REB "my friends"	NJB "brothers"	NAB "brothers"
GNB "my friends"	CEV "dear friends"	NLT "dear Christian friends"	NIVI "brothers and sisters"	GW "brothers and sisters"	NCV "brothers and sisters"	NIrV "brothers and sisters"	

Romans 14:10 (NIV): You, then, why do you judge your brother *[adelphos]*?

KJV "brother"	NKJV "brother"	NASB "brother"	RSV "brother"	NRSV "brother or sister"	REB "fellow Christian"	NJB "brother"	NAB "brother"
GNB "others"	CEV "followers of the Lord"	NLT "another Christian"	NIVI "brother or sister"	GW "other Christians"	NCV "brothers or sisters"	NIrV "brothers and sisters"	

1 Corinthians 14:39 (NIV): Therefore, my brothers *[adelphoi]*, be eager to prophesy, and do not forbid speaking in tongues.

KJV "brethren"	NKJV "brethren"	NASB "brethren"	RSV "brethren"	NRSV "friends"	REB "friends"	NJB "brothers"	NAB "brothers"
GNB "friends"	CEV "friends"	NLT "brothers and sisters"	NIVI "brothers and sisters"	GW "brothers and sisters"	NCV "brothers and sisters"	NIrV "brothers and sisters"	

"Father(s)" with Reference to Prior Generations

Exodus 13:5 (NIV): When the LORD brings you into the land . . . which he swore to your ancestors *['ābôt]*.

KJV "fathers"	NKJV "fathers"	NASB "fathers"	RSV "fathers"	NRSV "ancestors"	REB "forefathers"	NJB "ancestors"	NAB "fathers"
GNB "ancestors"	CEV "ancestors"	NLT "ancestors"	NIVI "ancestors"	GW "ancestors"	NCV "ancestors"	NIrV "your people long ago"	

Genesis 17:4 (NIV): As for me, this is my covenant with you: You will be the father *['āb]* of many nations.

KJV "father"	NKJV "father"	NASB "father"	RSV "father"	NRSV "ancestor"	REB "father"	NJB "father"	NAB "father"
GNB "ancestor"	CEV "father"	NLT "father"	NIVI "father"	GW "father"	NCV "father"	NIrV "father"	

"Father(s)" or "Parent(s)"?

Proverbs 15:5 (NIV): A fool spurns his father's *['āb]* discipline, but whoever heeds correction shows prudence.

KJV "father's"	NKJV "father's"	NASB "father's"	RSV "father's"	NRSV "parent's"	REB "father's"	NJB "father's"	NAB "father's"
GNB "parents"	CEV "parents"	NLT "parent's"	NIVI "parent's"	GW "father's"	NCV "parent's"	NIrV "parents"	

Hebrews 12:9 (NIV): Moreover, we have all had human fathers *[pateres]* who disciplined us.

KJV "fathers"	NKJV "fathers"	NASB "fathers"	RSV "fathers"	NRSV "fathers"	REB "fathers"	NJB "fathers"	NAB "fathers"
GNB "fathers"	CEV "fathers"	NLT "fathers"	NIVI "parents"	GW "fathers"	NCV "fathers"	NIrV "parents"	

"Son" or "Child"?

Exodus 13:14 (NIV): In days to come, when your son *[bēn]* asks you, "What does this mean?" say to him, "With a mighty hand the LORD brought us out of Egypt."

KJV "son"	NKJV "son"	NASB "son"	RSV "son"	NRSV "child"	REB "son"	NJB "son"	NAB "son"
GNB "son"	CEV "children"	NLT "children"	NIVI "children"	GW "children"	NCV "son"	NIrV "children"	

"Sons" or "Children"?

Job 42:16 (NIV): After this, Job lived a hundred and forty years; he saw his children *[bānîm]* and their children to the fourth generation.

KJV "sons"	NKJV "children"	NASB "sons"	RSV "sons"	NRSV "children"	REB "children"	NJB "children"	NAB "children"
GNB "grand-children"	CEV "children"	NLT "children"	NIVI "children"	GW "children"	NCV "children"	NIrV "children"	

Isaiah 30:9 (NIV): These are rebellious people, deceitful children *[bānîm]*.

KJV "children"	NKJV "children"	NASB "sons"	RSV "sons"	NRSV "children"	REB "children"	NJB "children"	NAB "children"
GNB —	CEV —	NLT —	NIVI "children"	GW "children"	NCV "children"	NIrV "children"	

"Sons/Children" in Proverbial Material

Proverbs 15:20 (NIV): A wise son *[bēn]* brings joy to his father, but a foolish man despises his mother.

KJV	NKJV	NASB	RSV	NRSV	REB	NJB	NAB
"son"	"son"	"son"	"son"	"child"	"son"	"child"	"son"
GNB	CEV	NLT	NIVI	GW	NCV	NIrV	
"children"	"children"	"children"	"children"	"son"	"son"	"children"	

Proverbs 20:7 (NIV): The righteous man leads a blameless life; blessed are his children *[bānîm]* after him.

KJV	NKJV	NASB	RSV	NRSV	REB	NJB	NAB
"children"	"children"	"sons"	"sons"	"children"	"children"	"children"	"children"
GNB	CEV	NLT	NIVI	GW	NCV	NIrV	
"children"	"children"	"children"	"children"	"children"	"children"	"children"	

Proverbs 5:1 (NIV): My son *[bēn],* pay attention to my wisdom, listen well to my words of insight.

KJV	NKJV	NASB	RSV	NRSV	REB	NJB	NAB
"son"	"son"	"son"	"son"	"child"	"son"	"son"	"son"
GNB	CEV	NLT	NIVI	GW	NCV	NIrV	
"child"	"son"	"son"	"son"	"son"	"son"	"son"	

Proverbs 4:10 (NIV): Listen, my son *[bēn],* accept what I say, and the years of your life will be many.

KJV	NKJV	NASB	RSV	NRSV	REB	NJB	NAB
"son"	"son"	"son"	"son"	"child"	"son"	"child"	"son"
GNB	CEV	NLT	NIVI	GW	NCV	NIrV	
"child"	"child"	"child"	"son"	"son"	"child"	"son"	

"Sons" or "Descendants"?

Numbers 13:33 (NIV): We saw the Nephilim there (the descendants *[bānîm]* of Anak come from the Nephilim).

KJV	NKJV	NASB	RSV	NRSV	REB	NJB	NAB
"sons"	"descendants"	"sons"	"sons"	"descendants"	"sons"	"Anakim"	"Anakim"
GNB	CEV	NLT	NIVI	GW	NCV	NIrV	
"descendants"	"Anakim"	"descendants"	"descendants"	"descendants"	"Anakim"	"children"	

"Sons/Children of God"

Galatians 3:26 (NIV): You are all sons *[huioi]* of God through faith in Christ Jesus.

KJV "children"	NKJV "sons"	NASB "sons"	RSV "sons"	NRSV "children"	REB "sons"	NJB "children"	NAB "children"
GNB "children"	CEV "children"	NLT "children"	NIVI "children"	GW "children"	NCV "children"	NIrV "children"	

"Son of Man" in the Old Testament

Psalm 8:4 (NIV): What is man that you are mindful of him, the son of man *[ben 'ādām]* that you care for him?

KJV "son of man"	NKJV "son of man"	NASB "son of man"	RSV "son of man"	NRSV "mortals"	REB "a human being"	NJB "child of Adam"	NAB "mortals"
GNB "mere mortals"	CEV "us weaklings"	NLT "mere humans"	NIVI "human beings"	GW "the Son of Man"	NCV "human-beings"	NIrV "a son of man"	

"Son of Man" in Ezekiel

Ezekiel 2:1 (NIV): And he said to me, "Son of man *[ben 'ādām]*, stand upon your feet, and I will speak with you."

KJV "son of man"	NKJV "son of man"	NASB "son of man"	RSV "son of man"	NRSV "O mortal"	REB "O man"	NJB "son of man"	NAB "son of man"
GNB "mortal man"	CEV "son of man"	NLT "son of man"	NIVI "son of man"	GW "son of man"	NCV "Human"	NIrV "son of man"	

"Son of Man" in Daniel 7:13

Daniel 7:13 (NIV): In my vision at night I looked, and there before me was one like a son of man *[bar 'ᵉnosh]*, coming with the clouds of heaven.

KJV "the Son of man"	NKJV "the Son of Man"	NASB "a Son of Man"	RSV "a son of man"	NRSV "a human being"	REB "a human being"	NJB "a son of man"	NAB "a son of man"
GNB "a human being"	CEV "a son of man"	NLT "who looked like a man"	NIVI "a son of man"	GW "the Son of Man"	NCV "a human being"	NIrV "a son of man"	

Jesus Christ in His Humanity

Philippians 2:8 (NIV): And being found in appearance as a man *[anthrōpos],* he humbled himself.

KJV	NKJV	NASB	RSV	NRSV	REB	NJB	NAB
"a man"	"a man"	"a man"	"in human form"	"in human form"	"sharing the human lot"	"like a human being"	"human in appearance"
GNB	CEV	NLT	NIVI	GW	NCV	NIrV	
"a human being"	"like one of us"	"in human form"	"a human being"	"a human appearance"	"living as a man"	"as a human being"	

1 Timothy 2:5 (NIV): For there is one God and one mediator between God and men *[anthrōpoi],* the man *[anthrōpos]* Christ Jesus.

KJV	NKJV	NASB	RSV	NRSV	REB	NJB	NAB
"the man"	"the Man"	"the man"	"the man"	"himself human"	"himself human"	"himself a human being"	"himself human"
GNB	CEV	NLT	NIVI	GW	NCV	NIrV	
"the man"	"truly human"	"the man"	"himself human"	"a human"	"himself human"	"man"	

The Adam/Christ Analogy

1 Corinthians 15:21 (NIV): For since death came through a man *[anthrōpos],* the resurrection of the dead comes also through a man *[anthrōpos].*

KJV	NKJV	NASB	RSV	NRSV	REB	NJB	NAB
"a man"	"a man"	"a man"	"a man"	"a human being"	"a man"	"one man"	"a human being"
GNB	CEV	NLT	NIVI	GW	NCV	NIrV	
"a man"	"Adam"	"a man"	"a human being"	"a man"	"one man"	"a man"	

Notes

A Note on the Hebrew and Greek Used in This Book

[1]These standard transliterations may be found in the *Journal of Biblical Literature*'s "Instructions for Contributors," in the *Society of Biblical Literature Membership Directory and Handbook,* 1994, and in other sources.

Chapter 1: Introduction

[1]F. C. Grant, *Translating the Bible* (Greenwich, Conn.: Seabury, 1961), pp. 36, 38. I have updated Grant's translation of Jerome's letter.

[2]F. F. Bruce, *History of the English Bible,* 3rd ed. (New York: Oxford University Press, 1978), pp. 22-23. In 1428, forty-three years after Wycliffe died, his remains were dug up and burned by order of the church.

[3]Ibid., pp. 24-53.

[4]J. Isaacs writes: "Tindale's honesty, sincerity, and scrupulous integrity, his simple directness, his magical simplicity of phrase, his modest music, have given an authority to his wording that has imposed itself on all later versions. With all the tinkering to which the New Testament has been subject, Tindale's version is still the basis in phrasing, rendering, vocabulary, rhythm, and often in music as well. Nine-tenths of the Authorized New Testament is still Tindale, and the best is still his" ("The Sixteenth-Century English Versions," in *The Bible in Its Ancient and English Versions,* ed. H. W. Robinson [Oxford: Clarendon, 1940], p. 160).

[5]Bruce, *History of the English Bible,* pp. 96-112.

[6]Eugene H. Glassman, *The Translation Debate* (Downers Grove, Ill.: InterVarsity Press, 1981), p. 15.

[7]Cited by Bruce, *History of the English Bible,* p. 107.

[8]"'The Translators to the Reader,' Preface to the King James Version." Reproduced in appendix C of *God's Word into English,* by Dewey M. Beegle (New York: Harper & Brothers, 1960). For this quote, see p. 146.

[9]Ibid., p. 142.

[10]Preface to the Revised Standard Version (sponsored by the Division of Christian Education of the National Council of Churches of Christ in the United States of America, 1952), p. iii.

[11]John William Burgon, *The Revision Revised* (London: John Murray, 1883; reprint, Paradise, Penn.: Conservative Classics, n.d.), pp. vi, vii.

[12]For descriptions and reviews of many of the Bible translations available today, see Jack P. Lewis, *The English Bible: From KJV to NIV,* 2nd ed. (Grand Rapids,

Mich.: Baker Book House, 1991); Lloyd R. Bailey, ed., *The Word of God: A Guide to English Versions of the Bible* (Atlanta: John Knox, 1982); Philip W. Comfort, *The Complete Guide to Bible Versions* (Wheaton, Ill.: Tyndale House, 1991); David Otis Fuller, ed., *Which Bible?* 5th ed. (Grand Rapids, Mich.: Grand Rapids International Publications, 1975); Sakae Kubo and Walter Specht, *So Many Versions? Twentieth Century English Versions of the Bible,* rev. ed. (Grand Rapids, Mich.: Zondervan, 1983).

[13]Glassman, *Translation Debate,* p. 15.

[14]For a sane and sober assessment of this "KJV only" controversy, see James R. White, *The King James Only Controversy: Can You Trust the Modern Translations?* (Minneapolis: Bethany House, 1995), and the earlier work by D. A. Carson, *The King James Version Debate: A Plea for Realism* (Grand Rapids, Mich.: Baker Book House, 1979).

[15]James Jasper Ray, *God Wrote Only One Bible* (Eugene, Ore.: Eye Opener Publishers, 1983); Gene Nowlin, *The Paraphrased Perversion of the Bible* (Collingswood, N.J.: The Bible for Today, 1974); James Kevin, *The Corruption of the Word* (Williamsburg, N.M.: Micro-Load Press, 1990); Gail Riplinger, *New Age Bible Versions* (Munroe Falls, Ohio: A. V. Publications, 1993); Riplinger, *Which Bible Is God's Word?* (Oklahoma City, Okla.: Hearthstone Publishing, 1994); Peter Ruckman, *The Bible "Babel"* (Pensacola, Fla.: Bible Baptist Bookstore, 1964).

[16]Whether or not masculine generics are really in decline is discussed in detail in the excursus between chapters five and six.

[17]Adding to the confusion is the fact that the term is sometimes used in this sense (see the "feminist" versions surveyed in chap. 3). Other designations such as "gender-neutral" might also be misleading if taken to mean that gender distinctions between men and women are being "neutralized" or eliminated. As we shall see, in these "gender-inclusive" versions they are not.

[18]Wayne Grudem, "What's Wrong with 'Gender Neutral' Bible Translations?" (paper delivered at the national convention of the Evangelical Theological Society in Jackson, Miss., November 1996), p. 1. This work was later significantly revised and published by the Council on Biblical Manhood and Womanhood (1997). I will identify these two versions as "What's Wrong" (1996) and "What's Wrong" (rev. 1997). An abbreviated version of the paper was also published in the *CBMW News* 1, no. 3 (1996).

[19]Grudem, "What's Wrong" (1996), p. 8.

[20]Grudem writes in the conclusion to this paper: "The NRSV has made some improvements over the RSV in a number of verses where inclusive language can be used in ways that do not distort the sense of the original text" ("What's Wrong" [1996], p. 17).

[21]Grant Osborne rightly notes this connection between inclusive language and a dynamic or functional equivalent methodology ("Do Inclusive-Language Bibles Distort Scripture? 'No,'" *Christianity Today,* October 27, 1997, p. 33). Wayne Grudem, in a parallel article, disputes this, noting that the very

idiomatic Living Bible was for the most part not gender inclusive ("Do Inclusive-Language Bibles Distort Scripture? 'Yes,'" *Christianity Today,* October 27, 1997, p. 39; compare Grudem, "What's Wrong" (rev. 1997), p. 13. Yet the Living Bible was produced thirty years earlier, before many of these language changes had taken place.

[22]For more examples of gender-inclusive renderings in "traditional" translations, see chapter two.

[23]Only the New Testament and Psalms in the NAB have received gender-inclusive revisions thus far. Grudem, "What's Wrong" (rev. 1997), p. 23, incorrectly claims that the NAB is not gender inclusive.

[24]Walter Wink, "The New RSV: The Best Translation, Halfway There," in *The Christian Century,* September 19-26, 1990, p. 829. Negative evaluations of the NRSV came from some feminists who claimed that the translation did not go far enough in its use of inclusive language and should have introduced inclusive language for God.

[25]D. A. Carson, "A Review of the New Revised Standard Version," *The Reformed Theological Review* 50, no. 1 (1991): 8.

[26]John Stek, "A Review of the New Revised Theological Standard Version," *The Reformed Theological Review* 50, no. 1 (1991): 8-10.

[27]Robert L. Thomas, review of the NRSV in *The Master's Seminary Journal,* Spring 1991, pp. 111-15.

[28]Grudem, "What's Wrong" (1996), p. 17.

[29]Doug LeBlanc, "Hands Off My NIV!" *Christianity Today,* June 16, 1997, p. 53.

[30]The title is an allusion to Harold Lindsell's 1976 book. In the 1970s and 1980s it became a rallying cry for evangelicals who were concerned that Christian colleges and seminaries were abandoning the doctrine of inerrancy.

[31]Susan Olasky, "The Battle for the Bible," *World,* April 19, 1997, pp. 14-15, 18.

[32]Wayne Grudem, "Comparing the Two NIVs," *World,* April 19, 1997, p. 18. An expanded version of this article, "Comparison of Current NIV with Inclusive Language NIV and New International Reader's Version," adds the NIrV to the comparison. This expanded version appeared on the CBMW Web site.

[33]Doug LeBlanc, "Bible Translators Deny Gender Agenda," *Christianity Today,* July 14, 1997, p. 62.

[34]By some estimates the NIV has captured approximately 45 percent of the market.

[35]LeBlanc, "Hands Off My NIV!" pp. 52-55.

[36]Susan Olasky, "Bailing Out of the Stealth Bible," *World,* June 14/21, 1997, p. 16.

[37]Joel Belz, "Getting Trust Back," *World,* June 14/21, 1997, p. 5.

[38]*American Heritage Electronic Dictionary,* 3rd ed. (Boston: Houghton Mifflin, 1992).

[39]Olasky incorrectly defines egalitarianism as "the denial of any distinctions between men and women." The issue is actually one of distinctions of roles, not distinctions per se.

[40]In a letter to *World* dated March 28, 1997, Ken Barker, secretary of the CBT, pointed out the correct definition of the term "unisex" and informed the magazine that no one on the CBT believed in the elimination of gender distinctions. Olasky continued to use the term in subsequent articles: "The Battle for the Bible," *World*, April 19, 1997 (6 times); "Bailing Out of the Stealth Bible," *World*, June 14-21, 1997 (4 times).
[41]Joel Belz, "The Ultimate Journalistic Sin," *World*, April 19, 1997.
[42]Grudem, "Comparing the Two NIVs," p. 18.
[43]Even in this case textual variants would make it necessary to make scholarly decisions about these "exact quotes."
[44]A similar conclusion, that *World*'s reporting was unfair and slanted, was reached by a three-member Evangelical Press Association ad hoc panel. In a July 1, 1997, report, the panel concluded that *World* had engaged in a one-sided "set-up job" in its reporting, using "inflammatory language" and "slanted, first-person editorializing" to suggest that translators were distorting biblical texts. This "falls seriously short of upholding the EPA code" because accuracy is "gravely incomplete." This committee's report was unofficial until the EPA board considered its findings. (Reported in *Christianity Today*, August 11, 1997, p. 58.)
[45]Ken Barker is cited in *Christianity Today*, July 14, 1997, p. 62, as saying, "The majority [of CBT members] would probably understand 1 Timothy 2:12 as prohibiting women from serving as pastors—and that's where I stand." Wayne Grudem similarly reported that "the majority of NIV translators were complementarian, not egalitarian" ("NIV Controversy: Participants Sign Landmark Agreement," *CBMW News* 2, no. 3 [1997]: 1).
[46]This should also answer the accusation that the NIrV had secretly adopted inclusive language without warning parents of the fact (see Olasky, "Stealth Bible," p. 14; "Battle for the Bible," p. 16). The translators of the NIrV considered the adoption of such language a natural part of the simplification and contemporization of the NIV.
[47]Olasky, "The Stealth Bible," pp. 14, 15.
[48]Doug Koop, "Battle for the Bible, or Battle for the Bugle? A Populist Crusade Won't Solve the Problem," *Christian Week* 11, no. 7, July 4, 1997.

Chapter 2: The Gender-Inclusive Versions

[1]There are many hundreds of examples of this in the Old Testament. It is interesting that the *New Scofield Reference Bible* (New York: Oxford University Press, 1967) often changes the KJV translation "children" back to "sons."
[2]For other examples, see Matthew 8:12; 13:38; 17:25-26; 27:56; Mark 2:19; Luke 5:34; 6:35; 16:8; 20:34; John 4:12; 12:36; Acts 3:25; 7:23; Romans 9:26; 2 Corinthians 3:7, 13; Galatians 3:26; Ephesians 2:2; Colossians 3:6; 1 Thessalonians 5:5.
[3]It is striking that the KJV translators rendered *huios* with the inclusive term "child" only in the expressions "son of the devil" and "son of hell." Does this reflect a gender bias?

[4]The difficulty related to using gender-inclusive resumptive pronouns for singular constructions is a complex and divisive issue. For more on resumptive pronouns, see the discussion of the NAB and the REB in this chapter, as well as the full discussion in chapter five.

[5]See also Exodus 36:1-2; Leviticus 24:17; Esther 1:8; Ecclesiastes 2:26; Isaiah 29:21; Daniel 10:16.

[6]Note again that while the NKJV uses an inclusive term for *'îsh* ("a person"), the resumptive masculine pronoun "his" is retained.

[7]See also Numbers 31:28; Micah 2:12; Numbers 19:18; 1 Samuel 9:2; 9:22; 16:18; 2 Samuel 4:11.

[8]See the discussion of literal and dynamic equivalent translations in chapter three.

[9]For complete listings, consult these terms in the Hebrew and Greek indexes to the *NIV Exhaustive Concordance,* ed. Edward W. Goodrick and John R. Kohlenberger III (Grand Rapids, Mich.: Zondervan, 1990).

[10]See also Genesis 29:22; Exodus 30:33; 34:31; Leviticus 18:27; Deuteronomy 27:14; Judges 21:9; 1 Samuel 10:25; 1 Chronicles 16:43; Jeremiah 4:25; 18:11; 27:5; Proverbs 28:28.

[11]See, for example, Matthew 13:25; 23:28; Luke 1:25; 7:31; 11:46; John 2:10; 4:28; 5:34; 6:14; Acts 5:38; 17:30; 18:13; Romans 12:17-18; Philippians 2:7; Colossians 1:28; 2:22; Titus 3:8, 10; 1 Timothy 2:12; 2 Timothy 3:2; James 1:19; Revelation 8:11; 9:4, 7, 10; 11:13; 16:2, 8.

[12]Andreas Köstenberger, "A Comparison of the NIV and the NIVI," *CBMW News,* June 1997, p. 13.

[13]For a discussion of translation philosophy, see chapter four. On contemporary English usage, see the excursus. On consistency in translation, see conclusions in chapter eight.

[14]As explained in chapter one, the KJV was a revision of earlier versions. See F. F. Bruce, *History of the Bible in English,* 3rd ed. (New York: Oxford University Press, 1978), pp. 37-110. Much of the material that follows is taken from Robert C. Dentan, "The Story of the NRSV," in *The Making of the New Revised Standard Version* (Grand Rapids, Mich.: Eerdmans, 1991), pp. 1-21, and Bruce M. Metzger, "To the Reader," in *The Holy Bible,* New Revised Standard Version (New York: Oxford University Press, 1989).

[15]Walter Harrelson, "Inclusive Language in the NRSV," in *The Making of the New Revised Standard Version* (Grand Rapids, Mich.: Eerdmans, 1991), p. 73.

[16]Ibid., p. 76.

[17]The reference is to the Division of Education and Ministry of the National Council of Churches of Christ.

[18]Metzger, "To the Reader."

[19]In a few instances, perhaps through oversight, "brothers" was retained in the NRSV: Luke 14:12; 18:29; 21:16; John 20:17; Acts 15:1. In a few others, *adelphos* is rendered as "neighbor" (Lk 6:42; Mt 7:4), "friend" (Lk 6:42), "disciple" (Lk 7:13), "the community" (Jn 21:23), "members of your family"

(1 Cor 8:12) or "members of the church" (1 Tim 6:2).
[20]Metzger, "To the Reader."
[21]Harrelson, "Inclusive Language," p. 75.
[22]Ibid., pp. 78-79.
[23]Ibid., p. 76.
[24]Dentan, "Story of the NRSV," p. 15.
[25]The potential confusion between adult "sons" and younger children also appears in Proverbs 10:5, Malachi 3:17 and elsewhere.
[26]Harrelson, "Inclusive Language," pp. 81-82.
[27]Ibid., p. 83.
[28]See the discussion of sonship language in chapters six and seven.
[29]*The New Jerusalem Bible* (New York: Doubleday, 1985).
[30]Compare Job 17:10; Psalm 104:23; Proverbs 6:27; Isaiah 65:20; Matthew 7:26; Mark 2:27; 1 Corinthians 2:9.
[31]Review in *The Princeton Seminary Bulletin* 7, no. 2 (1986): 188.
[32]Note the use of the gender-exclusive "himself" in the NCV's own preface.
[33]From the preface to *The Holy Bible,* New Century Version (Dallas: Word, 1987, 1988, 1991). Preliminary research and development for the NCV was done by the World Translation Center in Fort Worth, Texas.
[34]Preface to the New Century Version.
[35]*The New American Bible with Revised Psalms and Revised New Testament* (Washington, D.C.: Confraternity of Christian Doctrine, 1986, 1991).
[36]In *Eternity* magazine (October 1987, p. 48), Russell Hitt reviews the revised edition and praises the translation for its balanced and accurate approach in passages that normally divide Catholics and Protestants
[37]Preface to the revised NAB, pp. xv-xvi.
[38]Preface to the revised NAB, p. xvi.
[39]Compare Mark 2:27; Luke 2:52; Romans 1:23; 4:8; Hebrews 2:6; James 1:12, 20, 23; 3:2.
[40]Preface to the revised NAB, p. xvi.
[41]*The Revised English Bible* (Oxford University Press and Cambridge University Press, 1989).
[42]Compare Romans 3:4; 5:7; James 1:12.
[43]Robert Bratcher, "The Revised English Bible," *The Bible Translator* 43, no. 3 (1992): 347.
[44]Preface to the *Good News Bible* (New York: Bible Societies/HarperCollins, 1994).
[45]C. S. Rodd, "Talking Points from Books," *The Expository Times,* August 1994, pp. 321-22.
[46]In addition to Peterson, five exegetical consultants are named: William Klein, Darrell Bock, Donald Hagner, Moisés Silva and Rodney Whitacre.
[47]Introduction to *The Message: The New Testament in Contemporary English* (Colorado Springs, Colo.: NavPress, 1993).
[48]From "The Contemporary English Version," in *The Holy Bible,* Contemporary

English Version (New York: American Bible Society, 1995).
[49]*God's Word* (Grand Rapids, Mich.: World Publishing, 1995).
[50]From the slipcover of *God's Word.*
[51]Preface to *God's Word,* pp. xi-xii.
[52]What the editors identify as the distinguishing characteristic of this version is that it reproduces the *style* of the original Hebrew, Aramaic or Greek, as well as capturing the author's meaning in contemporary idiom. But any good functional or dynamic equivalent translation seeks to accomplish this.
[53]Preface to *The Holy Bible,* New International Version: Inclusive Language Edition (London: Hodder & Stoughton, 1995, 1996), p. vi.
[54]Preface to the NIVI, p. vi.
[55]Susan Olasky referred to this passage from the NIVI preface in her article "The Battle for the Bible," *World,* April 19, 1997, p. 18. It is perhaps significant that the quote given in the statement stopped short of the final qualifying phrase that appears in the NIVI preface, "when this could be done without compromising the message of the Spirit."
[56]Some of these will be discussed in chapters five and six.
[57]"Introduction to the New Living Translation," in *Holy Bible,* New Living Translation (Wheaton, Ill.: Tyndale House, 1996), p. xliv.
[58]"A Word About the New International Reader's Version," in *Holy Bible,* New International Reader's Version (Grand Rapids, Mich.: Zondervan, 1995, 1996), p. vi.

Chapter 3: The Feminist Versions

[1]The "feminist" versions, for example, generally identify themselves as "gender inclusive." On the other hand, many feminists, especially evangelicals, reject the kind of rewriting of Scripture that is found in what I am calling the "feminist" translations.
[2]Division of Education and Ministry, National Council of the Churches of Christ in the U.S.A. (Atlanta: John Knox; New York: Pilgrim Press; Philadelphia: Westminster Press, 1983).
[3]Introduction to *An Inclusive Language Lectionary* (ILL). The text contains no page numbers, so none are cited here.
[4]Preface to ILL.
[5]Ibid.
[6]Introduction to ILL.
[7]"Other Exclusive Imagery," in appendix to ILL.
[8]Introduction to ILL.
[9]Elizabeth Achtemeier, "The Translator's Dilemma: Inclusive Language," *Interpretation* 38, no. 1 (1984): 66.
[10]Peter McGrath and David Gates, "Scrubbing the Scriptures," *Newsweek,* October 24, 1983, p. 112.
[11]Richard N. Ostling, "O God Our [Mother and] Father," *Time,* October 24, 1983, p. 57.

[12]*The New Testament and Psalms: An Inclusive Version* (New York: Oxford University Press, 1995).
[13]These editors included Victor Roland Gold, Thomas L. Hoyt Jr., Sharon H. Ringe, Susan Brooks Thistlethwaite, Burton H. Throckmorton Jr. and Barbara A. Withers.
[14]General introduction to *The New Testament and Psalms: An Inclusive Version,* pp. viii-ix.
[15]Ibid., p. ix.
[16]Ibid., p. xv.
[17]Ibid., pp. viii-ix.
[18]Ibid., pp. xix-xx.
[19]Ibid., p. xi.
[20]Ibid., p. xiv.
[21]Ibid., pp. xii-xiii.
[22]Ibid., pp. xiii, xvii-xviii.
[23]Ibid., p. xi.
[24]Ibid., p. ix.
[25]Introduction to the INT, p. xi.
[26]Ibid., p. xii.
[27]Ibid., p. xiii.
[28]Ibid., p. xiii, citing Elisabeth Schüssler Fiorenza, *In Memory of Her: A Feminist Theological Reconstruction of Christian Origins* (New York: Crossroad, 1983).
[29]Ibid., p. xiii.
[30]Ibid., pp. xvii-xviii.
[31]Later in the introduction (p. xxi) the translators seem to modify this perspective by stating that "while the patriarchy and sexism of the first century clearly oppressed women, it was just as clearly part of the mores of the time, and for that reason it may be considered amoral rather than immoral." Yet how could the oppression of women, if sinful today, be "amoral rather than immoral" in the first century? Surely oppression is sin in God's eyes in any culture.
[32]Introduction to the INT, p. xvi.
[33]Ibid., p. xvi.
[34]Though I would not agree with her perspective, feminist theologian Carole Fontaine is at least more consistent when she writes, "Where language for God is male-exclusive, where the text is explicitly misogynist, we must translate it as it stands—and then repent of it in our study notes by calling attention to other textual evidence that disagrees with the verse under discussion, offering reasons for the view presented and perhaps even suggesting alternative meanings" ("The *NRSV* and the *REB:* A Feminist Critique," *Theology Today,* October 1990, p. 277).

Chapter 4: What Is a Bible Translation?

[1]H. M. Wolf, "When 'Literal' Is Not Accurate," in *The NIV: The Making of a*

Contemporary Translation, ed. Kenneth Barker (New York: International Bible Society, 1991), p. 127.

[2]On the nature and process of Bible translation, see J. Beekman and J. Callow, *Translating the Word of God* (Grand Rapids, Mich.: Zondervan, 1974); Eugene A. Nida, *Toward a Science of Translating* (Leiden: Brill, 1964); Eugene A. Nida and Charles R. Taber, *The Theory and Practice of Translation* (Leiden: Brill, 1982). See also the collection of E. Nida's essays in *Language Structure and Translation: Essays by Eugene A. Nida,* selected and introduced by Anwar S. Dil (Stanford, Calif.: Stanford University Press, 1975). On a more popular level, see Eugene H. Glassman, *The Translation Debate* (Downers Grove, Ill.: InterVarsity Press, 1981); Eugene A. Nida, *God's Word in Man's Language* (New York: Harper & Brothers, 1952).

[3]Beekman and Callow, *Translating the Word of God,* p. 22.

[4]Glassman, *The Translation Debate,* p. 57. I am indebted to Glassman for pointing me to some of the translation resources cited below.

[5]The NIV adds an adjective ("proper"), a verb ("confine") and a gerund ("boasting"), and it repeats the word "field." The NIV also chooses better English equivalents with the words "limits," "field" and so on.

[6]E. Nida, "Translation or Paraphrase," *The Bible Translator,* July 1950, pp. 105-6. The italics are mine.

[7]For this category and the following ones, see Daniel B. Wallace, *Greek Grammar Beyond the Basics* (Grand Rapids, Mich.: Zondervan, 1996), pp. 77-107.

[8]Ibid., pp. 104-6. This suggestion was contributed by my former student Kelley Mata.

[9]For further discussion on the Greek genitive, see Wallace, *Greek Grammar,* pp. 72-136, or the other intermediate and advanced Greek grammars. For more on the failure to discern the meaning of the genitive distinct from "of," see Nida, *Toward a Science of Translating,* pp. 207-8; Nida and Taber, *Theory and Practice,* pp. 35-37; Beekman and Callow, *Translating the Word of God,* chap. 16.

[10]Norman Mundhenk, "What Translation Are You Using?" *The Bible Translator,* October 1974, pp. 419-20.

[11]These examples are from Wolf, "When 'Literal' Is Not Accurate," pp. 127-36.

[12]D. A. Carson, "The Limits of Dynamic Equivalence in Bible Translation," *Notes on Translation,* October 1987, p. 1.

[13]For a discussion of Greek word order, see A. T. Robertson, *A Grammar of the Greek New Testament in Light of Historical Research* (Nashville: Broadman, 1934), pp. 417-25.

[14]Glassman, *Translation Debate,* p. 25.

[15]Wayne Grudem, "Do Inclusive-Language Bibles Distort Scripture?" *Christianity Today,* October 27, 1997, pp. 29, 30; Grudem, "What's Wrong" (rev. 1997), p. 11 (see chapter 1, n. 18).

[16]Other Greek plurals, such as *ta hagia* ("the Holy Place"), also must be

translated with English singulars. For these and many other examples, see Robertson, *A Grammar of the Greek New Testament,* pp. 403-9.

[17]The examples that follow are from Aida Besançon Spencer, "Power Play: Gender Confusion and the NIV," *Christian Century,* July 2-9, 1997, pp. 618-19.

[18]The Holy Spirit, of course, does not have biological gender. The pronoun "he" traditionally used for the Spirit in English indicates *personhood,* not sexual identity.

[19]This search was conducted with *Accordance.* I searched for all of the verses in these versions that contain the words "man" or "men." From this database I searched for verses that did *not* contain the Hebrew words *'îsh, 'ādām, 'enôsh, zākār,* or the Greek terms *anthrōpos, anēr, arsēn.*

[20]In an article opposing dynamic equivalence, Robert Thomas writes that "a certain degree of interpretation is unavoidable, no matter how hard the translator tries to exclude it. Yet a characteristic of formal equivalence is its effort to avoid interpretation as much as possible by transferring directly from the surface structure of the source language to the surface structure of the receptor language" ("Dynamic Equivalence: A Method of Translation or a System of Hermeneutics?" *The Master's Seminary Journal* 1 [Fall 1990]: 149-75; quote, p. 154).

[21]For an excellent discussion of this issue of meaning and significance, see Gordon D. Fee and Douglas Stuart, *How to Read the Bible for All Its Worth* (Grand Rapids, Mich.: Zondervan, 1981, 1993), chap. 4.

[22]*Foxe's Christian Martyrs of the World* (Philadelphia: Charles Foster, n.d.), p. 351.

[23]Henry Knyghton, cited by Glassman, *Translation Debate,* p. 13.

[24]" 'The Translators to the Reader,' Preface to the King James Version." Reproduced in Dewey M. Beegle, *God's Word into English* (New York: Harper & Brothers, 1960), appendix C. The quote appears on p. 134.

[25]This discovery regarding the nature of New Testament Greek is especially associated with the work of Adolf Deissman. See his work *The New Testament in the Light of Modern Research* (London: Hodder & Stoughton, n.d.) and *Light from the Ancient East* (New York: Harper & Brothers, 1922).

[26]See chapter six for a discussion of this term.

[27]See especially J. P. Louw, *The Semantics of New Testament Greek* (Philadelphia: Fortress, 1982); Moisés Silva, *Biblical Words and Their Meanings* (Grand Rapids, Mich.: Baker, 1983); Don Carson, *Exegetical Fallacies,* 2nd ed. (Grand Rapids, Mich.: Zondervan, 1996); D. A. Cruse, *Lexical Semantics* (Cambridge: Cambridge University Press, 1986); Peter Cotterell and Max Turner, *Linguistics and Biblical Interpretation* (Downers Grove, Ill.: InterVarsity Press, 1989).

[28]These definitions are taken from the *American Heritage Electronic Dictionary,* 3rd ed. (Boston: Houghton Mifflin, 1992).

[29]Though a number of these senses of *sarx* do appear as part of the definition of "flesh" in a standard English dictionary, they surely arose from the influence of the KJV on the English language. Just because these senses exist in English (and

so appear in a dictionary) does not mean that they represent common English.

[30]It is interesting to note that in the preface to the original KJV, the translators defend the policy of using a variety of English words for a single Hebrew or Greek term ("'The Translators to the Reader,' Preface to the King James Version," pp. 149-50). In many places this was done for stylistic reasons, not to capture a more accurate sense of the original.

[31]See Cotterell and Turner, *Linguistics and Biblical Interpretation,* pp. 22-23, 63, 84-85.

[32]Wayne Grudem, for example, repeatedly argues that *'ādām* has "male overtones," even when it refers to human beings in general. He claims from this that "man" should be used in translation to capture these male overtones. See Wayne Grudem, "Do Inclusive-Language Bibles Distort Scripture? 'Yes,' " *Christianity Today,* October 27, 1997, p. 28.

[33]For the various senses of *ekklēsia* in the New Testament, see W. Bauer et al., *A Greek-English Lexicon of the New Testament* (Chicago: University of Chicago Press, 1979), pp. 240-41. "Called out ones" is not one of these senses.

[34]This point was emphasized especially by J. Barr, *Semantics of Biblical Language* (Oxford, U.K.: Oxford University Press, 1961). See also Cotterell and Turner, *Linguistics and Biblical Interpretation,* pp. 113-15, 129-33; Carson, *Exegetical Fallacies,* pp. 28-32; Silva, *Biblical Words and Their Meanings,* pp. 44-51.

[35]See Cotterell and Turner, *Linguistics and Biblical Interpretation,* pp. 45-47.

[36]Ibid., p. 46.

[37]C. S. Rodd, "Talking Points from Books," *The Expository Times,* August 1994, p. 321.

Chapter 5: Inclusive Language: Generic "Man" and "He"

[1]Francis Brown, S. R. Driver and Charles A. Briggs, *The New Brown, Driver and Briggs Hebrew and English Lexicon of the Old Testament* (1907; reprint, Lafayette, Ind.: Associated Publishers and Authors, 1981), p. 9.

[2]W. Bauer et al., *A Greek-English Lexicon of the New Testament* (Chicago: University of Chicago Press, 1979), pp. 68-69.

[3]See Exodus 30:33, 38; Leviticus 17:10 (in parallel with "soul"); 18:27; 22:3; Numbers 13:32; 36:8; Deuteronomy 27:14; 1 Samuel 5:9; 11:15; 1 Kings 8:38; 13:25; Ezra 2:1; Nehemiah 4:13; 8:16; Esther 9:2; Jeremiah 5:1; 18:11; 23:14; 23:27; 29:32; 36:31; 51:45; Zechariah 11:6. These passages, like those in the following note, are open to interpretation, and a translation decision must be made on a case-by-case basis. The plural construct of *'îsh* is explicitly inclusive in Judges 9:49, where we learn that all the *people* of the tower of Shechem died, about a thousand men and women.

[4]Some other difficult passages include Exodus 33:4; 36:1-2; Leviticus 22:3; Numbers 5:8; 11:10; 19:20; Deuteronomy 22:26; Joshua 24:28; 1 Samuel 2:13; 6:15; 2 Samuel 15:30; 1 Kings 21:13; 22:17; 2 Kings 23:35; 1 Chronicles 16:43; 2 Chronicles 18:16; Ezra 1:4; Nehemiah 7:6; Ecclesiastes 9:14; Isaiah 13:14;

Jeremiah 11:2, 9; 34:10; Ezekiel 46:18; Micah 2:11; Haggai 2:12; Zechariah 1:21. In all of these examples, the NIV (and in many cases, other noninclusive versions) uses an inclusive term, but it is difficult to determine whether the original author was thinking of men or of persons generally.

[5]Wayne Grudem overstates the case when he says that "the Greek word *anēr* is used when an author wants to specify a man or men in distinction from a woman (or women). The word is a specifically male term that can mean 'man' or 'husband,' depending on the context" ("What's Wrong with 'Gender Neutral' Bible Translations?" paper read at the national convention of the Evangelical Theological Society in Jackson, Miss., November 1996; obtained from the Council on Biblical Manhood and Womanhood, which published a revised version in 1997; see p. 9). In fact, *anēr* can mean "a person."

[6]*Exegetical Dictionary of the New Testament,* ed. Horst Balz and Gerhard Schneider (Grand Rapids, Mich.: Eerdmans, 1990), 1:99.

[7]Compare Luke 5:18; 11:31; Mark 6:44; Luke 9:14; John 6:10; Acts 4:4.

[8]The NIVI notes in the margin the possibility that "men" are intended.

[9]Another possibility is that Jesus simply ignores the women and children, assuming they will follow the actions of the men. This, however, seems very unlike the Jesus of the Gospels, who elsewhere shows such special concern for women and children who are present. In this episode Jesus has just taken the five loaves and two fishes from a young boy (Jn 6:9). Though the disciples dismiss children as irrelevant, Jesus welcomes them (Mk 10:13-16).

[10]See L. Morris, *The Gospel According to John,* New International Commentary on the New Testament (Grand Rapids, Mich.: Eerdmans, 1971), p. 344 n. 21.

[11]As mentioned in the note at the beginning of the book, I present Greek words in their nominative, or "lexical," forms in order to avoid confusing non-Greek students with a multiplicity of case forms. The form in this passage is actually the accusative *auton,* since the word is functioning as a direct object.

[12]Grudem, "What's Wrong" (1996), p. 8.

[13]William Strunk Jr. and E. B. White, *Elements of Style* (New York: Macmillan, 1979), p. 60.

[14]Andrea Lunsford and Robert Connors, *The St. Martin's Handbook* (New York: St. Martin's, 1989).

[15]Strunk and White, *Elements of Style,* p. 60.

[16]H. Ramsey Fowler et al., *The Little, Brown Handbook* (Boston: Little, Brown, 1983), p. 195.

[17]Lunsford and Connors, *St. Martin's Handbook,* p. 223.

[18]See Miriam Meyers, "Current Generic Pronoun Usage: An Empirical Study," *American Speech* 65, no. 3 (1990): 228-37; G. Jochnowitz, "Everybody Likes Pizza, Doesn't He or She?" *American Speech* 57, no. 3 (1982): 198-203; Ann Bodine, "Androcentrism in Prescriptive Grammar: Singular 'They,' Sex-Indefinite 'He' and 'He or She,'" in *The Feminist Critique of Language: A Reader,* ed. D. Cameron (London: Routledge, 1990); Sharon Zuber and Ann M. Reed, "The Politics of Grammar Handbooks: Generic *He* and Singular *They,*" *College*

English 55, no. 5 (1993): 515-30.

[19]The examples are from Bodine, "Androcentrism in Prescriptive Grammar," p. 168.

[20]John C. Hodges and Mary E. Whitten, *Harbrace College Handbook* (New York: Harcourt Brace Jovanovich, 1977), pp. 58-59.

[21]Jochnowitz, "Everybody Likes Pizza," p. 198.

[22]Cited by C. S. Rodd, "Talking Points from Books," *The Expository Times*, April 1994, p. 322.

[23]Zuber and Reed, "Politics of Grammar Handbooks," p. 4.

[24]Bodine, "Androcentrism in Prescriptive Grammar," p. 168.

[25]Meyers, "Current Generic Pronoun Usage," pp. 235-36. Speakers cited include former presidential candidate Gary Hart, Harvard University paleontologist Stephen Jay Gould, U.S. Senator Kent Conrad, Harvard Law School professor Alan Dershowitz, PBS journalist Jim Lehrer and others.

[26]Bodine, "Androcentrism in Prescriptive Grammar," p. 170. She goes on to say that since gender has social implications and number does not, "they" should be preferred.

[27]Meyers, "Current Generic Pronoun Usage," pp. 228-37; V. E. Wheeless, C. Berryman-Fink and D. Serafini, "The Use of Gender-Specific Pronouns in the 1980s," *Encoder* 9 (1982): 35-46. Meyers found that 34 percent chose "he," 32 percent chose "they," and the rest other options. Wheeless et al. found that 42 percent each chose "he" or "they."

[28]Grudem, "What's Wrong" (1996), p. 3; Grudem, "What's Wrong" (rev. 1997), p. 4.

[29]Grudem, "What's Wrong" (1996), p. 3; Grudem, "What's Wrong" (rev. 1997), p. 3.

[30]Even if Grudem's complaint were justified, further clarity could easily be achieved by translating the participle as "*the one who abides* in me" or "*whoever* abides in me."

[31]Grudem, "What's Wrong" (1996), p. 3; compare "What's Wrong" (rev. 1997), p. 3.

[32]Grant Osborne, "Do Inclusive-Language Bibles Distort Scripture?" *Christianity Today*, October 27, 1997, p. 38.

[33]Grudem, "What's Wrong" (rev. 1997), p. 5.

[34]In this case the Greek grammatical change is less than it seems in English, since both forms are actually imperatives (command forms). What is a third-person imperative in Greek ("let him") becomes a second-person imperative in English.

[35]Grudem, "What's Wrong" (1996), p. 6.

[36]Ibid.; Gruden, "What's Wrong" (rev. 1997), p. 5.

[37]*American Heritage Electronic Dictionary*, 3rd ed. (Boston: Houghton Mifflin, 1990).

[38]*Webster's II: New Riverside University Dictionary* (Boston: Riverside, 1984).

[39]This is assuming that the Masoretic text is the original reading and that the

LXX translators altered the Hebrew. It is possible, of course, that the original Hebrew text had a plural and that it is the Masoretes, not the LXX translators, who altered the reading. I am grateful to Danny Hays for pointing out this possibility to me.

[40]D. A. Carson, "A Review of the New Revised Standard Version," *The Reformed Theological Review* 50, no. 1 (1991): 9.

[41]For similar examples in the NIVI, see Judges 15:10; Ruth 2:5; 1 Samuel 17:26; 2 Samuel 2:14; 4:2; 1 Kings 8:25 ("successor" for NIV "man").

[42]See chapter three.

[43]Writing on another passage, Grant Osborne points out that although it is primarily *men* who are being addressed in the original context, *men and women* would be addressed in the modern setting. "In many of those instances, communication is better served by changing the pronouns lest the modern reader mistakenly think only males are being addressed" ("Do Inclusive-Language Bibles Distort Scripture?" p. 34).

[44]Grudem, "What's Wrong" (1996), p. 16.

[45]A. Köstenberger, "The Neutering of 'Man' in the NIVI," *CBMW News* 2, no. 3 (June 1997): 9.

[46]See R. Brown, *The Gospel According to John (I-IX),* Anchor Bible (New York: Doubleday, 1966), 29:129.

[47]Grudem, "What's Wrong" (1996), p. 11; Grudem, "What's Wrong" (rev. 1997), pp. 8-9.

[48]*American Heritage Electronic Dictionary.*

[49]C. S. Rodd, "Talking Points from Books," *The Expository Times,* August 1994, p. 322.

[50]Grudem, "What's Wrong" (1996), p. 11; Grudem, "What's Wrong" (rev. 1997), pp. 7-8.

[51]Jesus, of course, was probably speaking Aramaic, but the inspired text records his words in Greek.

[52]I am grateful to Richard Erickson, who read an earlier draft of this work, for this insight.

[53]Grudem, "What's Wrong" (rev. 1997), p. 7.

[54]I am assuming (because of my own beliefs) the historicity of the creation account as given in Genesis 1-2. I recognize that some readers will have a view of these events that is more symbolic and less historical.

[55]This example also points to another common confusion, that between the *sense* of a word and its *referent.* A word may carry the sense "human being" yet have as its referent a male (Adam). Just because the referent in one case is male does not mean that his word carries male connotations in other contexts.

Excursus: Contemporary English Usage

[1]"Man," in *Oxford English Dictionary,* 2nd ed. (Oxford: Clarendon, 1989), 9:284.

[2]"Man," in *Webster's II. New Riverside University Dictionary* (Boston: Riverside,

1984), p. 721.

[3]J. W. Schneider and S. L. Hacker, "Sex Role Imagery and Use of the Generic 'Man' in Introductory Texts: A Case in the Sociology of Sociology," *American Sociologist* 8 (1973): 12-18.

[4]L. C. Wilson, "Teachers' Inclusion of Males and Females in Generic Nouns," *Research in the Teaching of English* 12 (1978): 155-61.

[5]J. A. Sniezek and C. H. Jazwinski, "Gender Bias in English: In Search of Fair Language," *Journal of Applied Social Psychology* 16 (1986): 642-62.

[6]Cited in Dale Spender, *Man Made Language* (London: Routledge and Kegan Paul, 1980), p. 152.

[7]L. Harrison, "Cro-Magnon Woman—In Eclipse," *The Science Teacher* 42, no. 4 (1975): 8-11.

[8]L. Harrison and R. N. Passero, "Sexism in the Language of Elementary School Textbooks," *Science and Children* 12 (1975): 22-25.

[9]W. Martyna, "Beyond the He/Man Approach: The Case for Nonsexist Language," in *Language, Gender and Society,* ed. B. Thorne, C. Kramarae and N. Henley (Rowley, Mass.: Newbury House, 1983), pp. 25-37.

[10]W. Martyna, "Comprehension of the Generic Masculine: Inferring 'She' from 'He,'" paper presented at the American Psychological Association, 85th Annual Convention, San Francisco, August, 1977, p. 9. Cf. her paper "What Does 'He' Mean? Use of the Generic Masculine," *Journal of Communication* 28 (1978): 131-38; and her dissertation, "Using and Understanding the Generic Masculine: A Social-Psychological Approach to Language" (Ph.D. diss., Stanford, 1979).

[11]W. Martyna, "The Psychology of the Generic Masculine," in *Women and Language in Literature and Society,* ed. Sally McConnell-Ginet, Ruth Borker and Nelly Furman (New York: Praeger, 1980), pp. 69-78.

[12]Donald G. MacKay and D. Fulkerson, "On the Comprehension and Production of Pronouns," *Journal of Verbal Learning and Verbal Behavior* 18 (1979): 661-73. Reported by Philip M. Smith, *Language, the Sexes and Society* (Oxford: Basil Blackwell, 1985), p. 52. See also the studies of D. G. MacKay, "Psychology, Prescriptive Grammar and the Pronoun Problem," *American Psychologist* 35, no. 5 (1980): 444-49.

[13]Virginia Kidd, "A Study of the Images Produced Through the Use of the Male Pronoun as the Generic," *Moments in Contemporary Rhetoric* 1 (1971): 25-30.

[14]See the review of literature in William R. Todd-Mancillas, "Masculine Generics = Sexist Language: A Review of Literature and Implications for Speech Communication Professionals," *Communication Quarterly* 27 (1981): 107-15. Thirteen of fourteen studies surveyed by Todd-Mancillas showed that masculine generics are understood as masculine specifics, while true generics and inclusive constructions are better understood to include women. Fourteen studies are also surveyed by Jeanette Silveira, "Generic Masculine Words and Thinking," in *The Voices and Words of Women and Men,* ed. Cheris Kramarae (Oxford: Pergamon, 1980), p. 167. In each study, generic masculine

terms led to male perception more often than did neutral words.

[15]Martyna, "Comprehension of Generic Masculine," 9.

[16]Martyna, "Beyond He/Man Approach," 32-33.

[17]J. Moulton, "The Myth of the Neutral 'Man,' " in *Sexist Language: A Modern Philosophical Analysis,* ed. M. Vetterling-Braggin (Totowa, N.J.: Littlefield, Adams, 1981), p. 108.

[18]Ibid., pp. 109-10.

[19]Ibid., 111.

[20]Grudem, "What's Wrong with 'Gender Neutral' Bible Translations?" (1996), p 7; Grudem, "What's Wrong," (rev. 1997), pp. 18-22. See chapter 1, n. 18.

[21]Grudem, "What's Wrong" (1996), 12.

[22]Grudem, "What's Wrong" (rev. 1997), 18-22.

[23]Anyone who has ever watched a national spelling context can attest to the fact that the number of words and senses in a dictionary far surpasses that of common usage and perception. The recent success of the board game Balderdash—where players attempt to fool others by creating meanings for obscure words in the dictionary—demonstrates the same phenomenon.

24Wayne Grudem, "NIV Controversy: Participants Sign Landmark Agreement," *CBMW News* 2, no. 3 (1997): 4; cf. "What's Wrong" (rev. 1997), 22-23.

[25]For the absurd results of such an approach see *The Concordant Version of the Sacred Scriptures,* rev. ed. (Saugus, Calif.: Concordant Publishing Concern, 1955) and *Concordant Literal New Testament* (1926; reprint, Canyon Country, Calif.: Concordant Publishing Concern, 1976).

Chapter 6: Inclusive Language: Other Generic Terms

[1]See W. Bauer et al., *A Greek-English Lexicon of the New Testament* (Chicago. University of Chicago Press, 1979), p. 16.

[2]E. Nida, "Translation or Paraphrase," *The Bible Translator,* July 1950, pp 105-6.

[3]*American Heritage Electronic Dictionary,* 3rd ed. (Boston: Houghton Mifflin, 1992).

[4]See Wayne Grudem, "NIV Controversy: Participants Sign Landmark Agreement," *CBMW News,* June 1997, p. 5.

[5]Strangely, while the NCV uses "brothers and sisters," its children's edition (ICB) retains "brothers."

[6]After writing a review of the New Living Translation for the *Journal of the Evangelical Theological Society,* I received a letter from Tyndale House president Mark Taylor indicating that in the revision of the NLT presently being prepared, *adelphoi* is more consistently rendered as "brothers and sisters," not "Christians" or "dear friends." This is a positive development for this excellent translation.

[7]The material in this letter was passed on to me by my colleague Ron Youngblood, who was one of the participants at the Conference on Gender-Related Language in Scripture.

[8]Grudem, "What's Wrong" (rev. 1997), p. 17 (see chap. 1, n. 18).
[9]These statistics are from the Hebrew to English index of the *NIV Exhaustive Concordance,* ed. E. W. Goodrick and J. R. Kohlenberger III (Grand Rapids, Mich.: Zondervan, 1990).
[10]"Ancestor" is the first definition of "forefather" given in the *American Heritage Dictionary* and is listed in *Roget's International Thesaurus* as a synonym.
[11]Francis Brown, S. R. Driver and Charles A. Briggs, eds., *The New Brown, Driver and Briggs Hebrew and English Lexicon of the Old Testament* (1907; reprint, Lafayette, Ind.: Associated Publishers and Authors, 1981), p. 450, point out, however, that in no case is it clear that both parents are dead.
[12]The *American Heritage Electronic Dictionary* defines the verb "to orphan" as losing one or both parents. But Grudem's point is well taken, since this is not how most people would understand the term.
[13]The CEV, like the NRSV, uses the term "orphans."
[14]For other examples, see 1 Kings 2:4; 1 Chronicles 9:23; 15:4; 2 Chronicles 6:16; 21:7; Psalm 22:23; 77:15; Malachi 3:6.
[15]See also 2 Chronicles 29:21; 31:19; 35:14; Leviticus 6:22; 24:9; Numbers 3:9 and so on.
[16]Leviticus 10:15; Ezekiel 5:10; 18:20; Hosea 9:13; 11:10.
[17]An interesting case occurs in 2 Kings 4:4, where the widow's two children are called *yᵉlāday* ("children") in 2 Kings 4:1 and *bānîm* in verses 4 and 5. Is this two boys? Or a boy and a girl? In verse 6 the Hebrew text has "she said to her son" (not "one of her sons" or "her older son," for example). While most translations assume there were two sons (NIV, RSV, NLT, KJV, NKJV, NASB), this may be a son and a daughter, in which case the NRSV's "children" would be the more accurate. I am reluctant to make such a suggestion, however, since I am not a Hebrew scholar and I have not found a commentary that even suggests this possibility!
[18]See also Deuteronomy 1:31; 6:2.
[19]See the similar examples in relation to "man" in chapter five.
[20]2 Kings 2:3; 4:38; 5:22.
[21]Genesis 6:2(?); Job 1:6; 2:1; 38:7. The issue here is idiomatic English, not gender inclusion. Contemporary translations often use the terms "angels" (NIV, NLT, CEV) or "heavenly beings" (NRSV, TEV).
[22]See 2 Samuel 7:14; Psalm 2:7; 89:26.
[23]KJV, NKJV, NIV, NRSV, NLT, CEV, REB, NJB, NAB, NCV, GW. TEV uses "people."
[24]The singular *huios* in Revelation 21:7 may be an exception ("He who overcomes will inherit all this, and I will be his God and he will be my son") because of the probable allusion to 2 Samuel 7:14, which speaks of the Davidic king (the Messiah) as God's son.
[25]Grudem, "NIV Controversy," p. 5.
[26]Ibid. Grudem also notes that it "obscures the connection with Christ as *son*

in the very context." This issue is addressed in the next chapter.

[27]See, for example, Mark 2:5; Matthew 21:28; Luke 2:48; 15:31; 16:25; 1 Timothy 1:2, 18; 2 Timothy 1:2; Titus 1:4; Philemon 1:10.

[28]Among the inclusive versions, only REB and NJB retain "son[s]." The NIVI is unique in alternating between "sons" and "children." "Children" appears for *huioi* in verses 5 and 7, whereas "sons" is used in verse 6.

[29]Grudem, "NIV Controversy," p. 5.

[30]The messianic significance of this passage is dealt with in chapter seven.

[31]R. Laird Harris, Gleason L. Archer Jr. and Bruce K. Waltke, *Theological Wordbook of the Old Testament* (Chicago: Moody Press, 1980), 1:114.

[32]Genesis 11:5; Psalms 12:1, 8; 31:19; 45:2; 58:1; 89:47; 107:8, 15, 21, 31; 145:12; Ecclesiastes 1:13; 2:3; 3:10, 18, 19; 8:11; 9:12; Jeremiah 50:40; Mark 3:28; Ephesians 3:5. "Son of man" is retained in Psalm 53:2.

[33]Psalms 21:10; 33:13; Proverbs 8:31; Daniel 2:38; Joel 1:12. "Children of men" appears in Lamentations 3:33. The NIV retains "son of man" when it occurs in poetic parallelism with other terms for "man": Job 25:6; 35:8; Psalms 8:4; 144:3; Isaiah 51:12 (but see Isaiah 56:2 and Jeremiah 51:43, where "man" is used in parallelism).

[34]In Daniel too, many otherwise inclusive versions retain "son of man" for the prophet (Dan 8:17; see NLT, NAB, NJB).

[35]But see the NJB and the REB, which retain "son."

[36]See Proverbs 1:8, 10, 15; 2:1; 3:1, 11, 21; 4:1, 10, 20; 5:1, 7; 6:1, 3, 20; 7:1, 24; 8:32; 19:27; 23:15, 19, 26; 24:13, 21; 27:11. In 27:11, "my son" (NIV) becomes "my child" (NIVI), but this may have been a slip.

[37]Some inconsistency is exhibited, however. When Proverbs 3:11-12 is cited in Hebrews 12:5-6, the term "child" is used instead of "son."

[38]See also Proverbs 13:24; 15:20; 17:2, 21, 25; 19:13, 18, 26; 28:7; 29:17. NIVI retains "a wise son" in 10:5, but this may have been a slip.

[39]See also Matthew 16:27, where the RSV translates the substantival adjective "each one" as "each man."

[40]Grudem, "What's Wrong" (1996), p. 1.

[41]In these kinds of constructions, *oudeis* may be viewed either as an indefinite pronoun or as a substantival adjective. See Bauer, *Greek-English Lexicon,* p. 591; F. Blass and A. Debrunner, *A Greek Grammar of the New Testament,* trans. and ed. R. W. Funk (Chicago: University of Chicago Press, 1961), sec. 302.

[42]Grudem, "What's Wrong" (1996), p. 1. In his conclusion Grudem also writes, "The NRSV has made some improvements over the RSV in a number of verses where inclusive language can be used in ways that do not distort the sense of the original text" (p. 17).

Chapter 7: Language Related to God & to Jesus Christ

[1]More generally, God is identified as the father of all humans as their creator in Acts 17:28.

[2]See Francis Brown, S. R. Driver and Charles A. Briggs, eds., *The New Brown,*

Driver and Briggs Hebrew and English Lexicon of the Old Testament (1907; reprint, Lafayette, Ind.: Associated Publishers and Authors, 1981), p. 297. In Isaiah 42:14 God's sudden redemption after apparent passivity is analogous to the pains of a woman in childbirth: "For a long time I have kept silent, I have been quiet and held myself back. But now, like a woman in childbirth, I cry out, I gasp and pant" (NIV).

[3]Donald Bloesch, *The Battle for the Trinity* (Ann Arbor, Mich.: Servant Books, 1985), p. 34. Compare Sirach 4:11; 6:22; 24:1 and so on.

[4]Bloesch, *Battle for the Trinity,* p. 21. As the notes below indicate, I am indebted to the works of Donald Bloesch and Edith Humphrey for the material in this section.

[5]Ibid., p. 35; compare pp. 24-25.

[6]I am indebted to my colleague Glen Scorgie for this insight.

[7]Edith M. Humphrey, "Why We Worship God as Father, Son and Holy Spirit," *Crux,* June 1996, pp. 2-12; quote from p. 5.

[8]Bloesch, *Battle for the Trinity,* p. 26.

[9]Elisabeth Schüssler Fiorenza, "Toward a Feminist Biblical Hermeneutics," in *Readings in Moral Theology, No. 4,* ed. Charles E. Curran and Richard A. McCormick (New York: Paulist, 1984), p. 376; cited by Bloesch, *Battle for the Trinity,* p. 59.

[10]Garrett Green, "The Gender of God and the Theology of Metaphor," in *Speaking the Christian God: The Holy Trinity and the Challenge of Feminism,* ed. Alvin F. Kimel Jr. (Grand Rapids, Mich.: Eerdmans, 1992), pp. 44-64; quote from p. 60; cited by Humphrey, "Why We Worship God," pp. 6-7.

[11]Humphrey, "Why We Worship God," p. 7.

[12]Ibid., p. 10.

[13]Elizabeth Achtemeier, "Female Language for God: Should the Church Adopt It?" in *The Hermeneutical Quest* (Allison Park, Penn.: Pickwick, 1986), p. 100; cited by Humphrey, "Why We Worship God," p. 8.

[14]These various names are cited by Bloesch, *Battle for the Trinity,* p. 44, and Humphrey, "Why We Worship God," p. 8.

[15]Rosemary Ruether, *Sexism and God-Talk* (Boston: Beacon, 1983), p. 12; cited by Bloesch, *Battle for the Trinity,* p. 44.

[16]Bloesch, *Battle for the Trinity,* p. 39.

[17]Virginia Ramey Mollenkott, *The Divine Feminine* (New York: Crossroad, 1983); cited by Bloesch, *Battle for the Trinity,* p. 53.

[18]Bloesch, *Battle for the Trinity,* p. 53.

[19]Some others mentioned by Humphrey are "Creator, Liberator, Comforter," "Source, Word and Spirit," "Mother, Brother, Holy Partner" and "Mother, Lover, Friend." Bloesch also notes "Shepherd, Helper, Refuge."

[20]Martha E. Stortz, "The Mother, the Son and the Bullrushes: The Church and Feminist Theology," *Dialog,* Winter 1984, pp. 21-26; cited by Bloesch, *Battle for the Trinity,* p. 52.

[21]Humphrey, "Why We Worship God," p. 7. Humphrey draws this anecdote

from Paul Minear, "The Bible and the Book of Worship," *Prism* 3 (1988): 52-53.

[22]The ILL and the NTPI use "Child of God," whereas the INT uses a variety of terms. See chapter three.

[23]See L. Morris, *The Gospel According to John* (Grand Rapids, Mich.: Eerdmans, 1971), p. 105; R. Brown, *The Gospel According to John I-XII,* Anchor Bible (New York: Doubleday, 1966), 29: 13-14; D. Moody, "'God's Only Son': The Translation of John iii 16 in the RSV," *Journal of Biblical Literature* 72 (1953): 213-19. Brown points out that the term is used of Isaac in Hebrews 11:17. Isaac was Abraham's "one of a kind" son, but he was not his "only begotten," since Abraham also fathered Ishmael.

[24]Introduction to the Inclusive New Testament, p. xvii.

[25]See John 15:26. One reason for using masculine pronouns here is that the Greek word *paraklētos,* "Comforter" or "Advocate," is masculine. In some of the verses, however, masculine pronouns are retained where *paraklētos* does not appear.

[26]Introduction to the Inclusive New Testament, p. xix.

[27]*Misandry* (from *miscō* + *andros*) is parallel to *misogyny* ("the hatred of women").

[28]Andreas J. Köstenberger, "The Neutering of 'Man' in the NIVI," *CBMW News,* June 1997, pp. 8-13.

[29]Ibid., p. 9.

[30]Ibid., p. 10.

[31]Wayne Grudem, "Do Inclusive-Language Bibles Distort Scripture?" *Christianity Today,* October 27, 1997, p. 29.

[32]Köstenberger, "The Neutering of 'Man,'" p. 10.

[33]Ibid., p. 9.

[34]Wayne Grudem, *Systematic Theology* (Grand Rapids, Mich.: Zondervan, 1994), p. 550.

[35]Ibid., pp. 529-43.

[36]Ibid., p. 541.

[37]Ibid., p. 257; compare pp. 460-61.

[38]Köstenberger, "The Neutering of 'Man,'" p. 9.

[39]See chapter three.

[40]E. J. Young, *The Prophecy of Daniel* (Grand Rapids, Mich.: Eerdmans, 1953), p. 154; C. F. Keil, *The Book of Daniel* (Grand Rapids, Mich.: Eerdmans, 1955), p. 234; J. F. Walvoord, *Daniel: The Key to Prophetic Revelation* (Chicago: Moody Press, 1971), p. 168.

[41]I. H. Marshall, *The Origins of New Testament Christology* (Downers Grove, Ill.: InterVarsity Press, 1976), pp. 63-64.

[42]Wayne Grudem, "NIVI Controversy: Participants Sign Landmark Agreement," *CBMW News,* June 1997, p. 5; Grudem, "What's Wrong" (rev. 1997), pp. 12-13.

[43]Wayne Grudem, "Comparing the Two NIVs," *World,* April 19, 1997, p. 15.

[44]The meaning of *'elōhîm* here is disputed. See the commentaries.

[45]See William Lane, *Hebrews 1-8,* Word Biblical Commentary 47A (Dallas: Word, 1991), p. 47; John MacArthur Jr., *Hebrews,* MacArthur New Testament Commentary (Chicago: Moody Press, 1983), p. 45.

[46]See F. F. Bruce, *The Epistle to the Hebrews,* New International Commentary on the New Testament (Grand Rapids, Mich.: Eerdmans, 1990), p. 75 n. 35; MacArthur, *Hebrews,* pp. 47-48. For a contrary view, see P. E. Hughes, *A Commentary on the Epistle to the Hebrews* (Grand Rapids, Mich.: Eerdmans, 1977), pp. 86-87.

[47]Lane, *Hebrews 1-8,* p. 48.

[48]D. A. Carson, "A Review of the New Revised Standard Version," *The Reformed Theological Review* 50, no. 1 (1991): 9.

[49]Wayne Grudem, "What's Wrong with 'Gender Neutral' Bible Translations?" (paper read at the national convention of the Evangelical Theological Society in Jackson, Miss., November 1996), p. 4; Grudem, "What's Wrong" (rev. 1997), p. 3.

[50]See Morris, *Gospel According to John,* p. 823. C. K. Barrett considers this to be the Evangelist's understanding, though his source may have drawn from Psalm 34:20 (*The Gospel According to St. John* [London, 1955], p. 558). Brown (*The Gospel According to John I-XII,* 2:953) and others suggest that both allusions are present, though priority is usually given to the Passover imagery.

[51]Grudem's comment that the psalm is attributed to David is irrelevant, since David is speaking in the third person of the afflictions of the righteous ("What's Wrong" [1996], p. 4).

Chapter 8: Summary & Conclusions

[1]Aida Besançon Spencer, "Power Play, Gender Confusion and the NIV," *Christian Century,* July 2-9, 1997, p. 619.

[2]See, for example, the irenic tone of the four views presented in the recent work *Are Miraculous Gifts for Today?* ed. Wayne Grudem (Grand Rapids, Mich.: Zondervan, 1996). Another manifestation of this is the dialogue created by the Dispensational Study Group at the Evangelical Theological Society's annual meetings.